Mr. McGuire: I just want to say one word to you – just one word.
Ben: Yes, sir.
Mr. McGuire: Are you listening?
Ben: Yes, I am.
Mr. McGuire: "Plastics."
Ben: Exactly how do you mean?
Mr. McGuire: There's a great future in plastics. Think about it. Will you think about it?
Ben: Yes, I will.

The Graduate (1967)

Plastic Dreams

Charlotte & Peter Fiell

Plastic Dreams

Synthetic Visions in Design

Fiell Publishing Limited

Published by Fiell Publishing Limited
www.fiell.com

A catalogue record for this book is available from
the British Library

ISBN 978-1-906863-08-1

Project Concept: Charlotte & Peter Fiell
Editorial: Charlotte & Peter Fiell
Texts: Charlotte & Peter Fiell
Picture Sourcing: Charlotte Fiell & Jennifer Tilston
Proofing & Copy Editing: Quintin Colville, Rosanna Negrotti
Design: Mark Thomson
Production: Judy Rasmussen

Printed in Italy

FSC

Mixed Sources

Product group from well-managed
forests and other controlled sources

Cert no. CQ-COC-000015
www.fsc.org
© 1996 Forest Stewardship Council

Contents

Charles and Ray Eames, *DAR*
chair from the *Plastic Shell Group*
for Zenith Plastics and Herman
Miller, 1948–1950

Plastic Dreams – Synthetic Visions in Design

Over the last 150 years, the role of plastics within the field of design has been fundamental to the development of our man-made environment. Synthetic polymers have quite literally moulded the modern world, transforming utopian dreams into three-dimensional realities. Indeed, the impact of plastics has been felt in every area of human life, from healthcare and food distribution to communications, transportation and financial transactions. This book tells the fascinating story of these truly wondrous materials within the context of industrial design. It charts their evolution from the early phenolic resins developed in the mid-nineteenth century to the most advanced technopolymers emerging from today's rapidly moving world of materials science. Moreover, unravelling the history of plastics in design also reveals their extraordinary influence on how we make the things we use, from handcraftsmanship to high-volume automated production systems. Through unceasing technological progress and refinement, synthetic polymers, above all other materials, have been central to this remarkable manufacturing transition, and to the immense social, cultural and economic changes that have flowed from it.

Plastic Dreams also brings this absorbing story into sharp relief by showcasing more than 120 landmark objects. These icons of 'plastic design' range from Isamu Noguchi's *Radio Nurse* monitor and the *Ekco AD 65* radio by Wells Coates, to Ross Lovegrove's *Ty Nant* water bottle and Konstantin Grcic's *MYTO* chair. These selected designs range from the functionally utilitarian to the aesthetically poetic, demonstrating the extraordinary versatility of plastics and the limitless scope their inherent malleability gives to designers in creating objects of cultural significance and everyday usefulness. In addition, through these carefully chosen and wide-ranging exemplars of design excellence this book hopes to demonstrate that plastics can truly be noble and precious, rather than the valueless flotsam and jetsam of mass culture. In the light of pressing environmental challenges they can also be used sustainably, though for this to become a widespread reality our perceptions concerning the role of synthetic polymers will need to alter radically. Finally, this publication is also a celebration of invention: invention of materials, invention of manufacturing processes, invention of new forms and functions. By their very nature, plastics have always been and will long remain the ultimate vehicles of invention – materials that inspire design visions and enable them to become life-enhancing, real-world products.

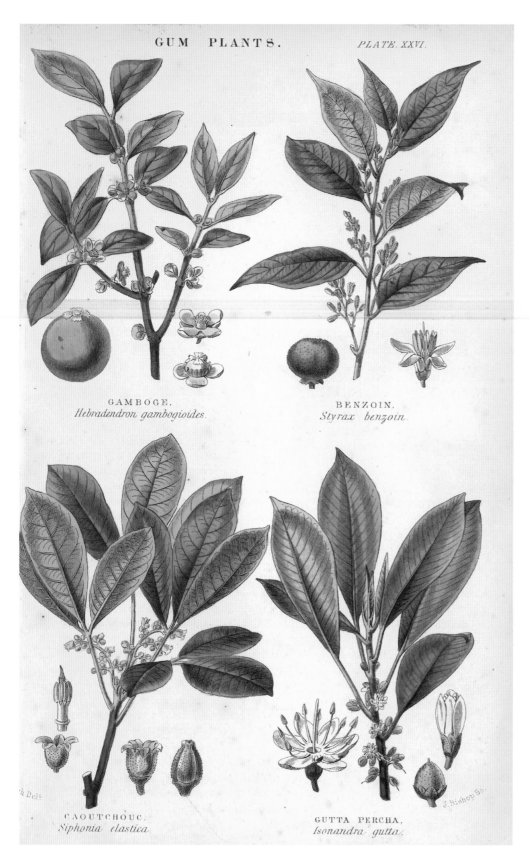

Gum Plants engraving from William Rhind's *Vegetable Kingdom*, c.1860 – showing various rubber plants (Gamboge, Benzoin, Caoutchouc and Gutta Percha)

The Family of Plastics: Origins and Uses

Although plastics, which are also known as polymers, play a crucial role in the design and manufacture of a startling array of products that we all encounter every day, most of us have little understanding of the chemistry that lies behind this remarkable group of materials. Essentially, plastics are materials made of long-chained hydrocarbon molecules, with the exact combination of hydrogen and carbon atoms determining the specific properties of different polymers. Although some plastics can be made from animal and plant by-products, such as casein which is derived from milk, the vast majority of plastic compounds are synthesised from fossil fuels, and as such owe their existence to the coal, oil and gas industries.

Plastics can be divided into three groups: thermoplastics, which can be repeatedly heated and then remoulded (such as polypropylene or polyethylene); thermosets, which undergo permanent chemical changes when heated so cannot be reheated and then remoulded (such as melamine and Bakelite); and lastly elastomers, which are either thermosetting or thermoplastic polymers that possess a high degree of elasticity and which, after being subjected to distortion under pressure, will spring back to their original shape (such as natural and silicone rubbers). The different properties of these three groups of plastics are attributable to their different molecular structures and the way those molecules are connected: either rigidly, like a dry stone wall, or more loosely, like a tangle of cooked spaghetti or a handful of springs.

Despite their different molecular structures, however, all plastics share some common attributes: they are excellent electrical and thermal insulators, they have good strength-to-weight ratios, and they are usually relatively durable and highly adaptable to mass production – an extremely useful and versatile set of characteristics. As a booklet produced in 1956 by the Bakelite Company, entitled *The ABCs of Modern Plastics*, pointed out, 'The key to plastics' growth is not that they are miracle materials with *all* desirable properties and *no* limitations. Rather, it is that plastics can be devised and controlled to give the balance or combination of qualities needed for each end product.'[1] Perhaps the best way of thinking about plastics, therefore, is to see them as members of a large and extended family – each sharing similar familial attributes yet being distinctive individuals in their own right. And these different personalities ensure that some members of the family are better suited to particular tasks than others.

The extraordinary form-giving potential of plastics has also ensured that, more than any other medium, plastics have been *the* material of choice for numerous designers over the last century. Notwithstanding the enormous financial commitment that production in plastics often requires, manufacturers have also been persuaded by the economies of scale offered by plastics moulding technologies, whether the process is injection moulding, blow moulding, rotational moulding, thermoforming, vacuum forming, extrusion or calendering. The startling array of options for materials and manufacturing processes has inexorably extended the parameters of product design. In fact, designers now find themselves in an apparently enviable position where almost any of their dreams can be given physical form by combining advanced polymers with state-of-the-art computer-modelling software and rapid-prototyping technology. Only time will tell whether this ease of making is actually a good thing. In the meantime it will clearly be the designers who push the physical and technical limits of these almost magical polymers and their allied moulding processes, creating iconic and progressive designs, just as their predecessors have done since the advent of plastics more than 150 years ago.

Natural Plastics and Early Plastics

The term 'plastic' derives from the Greek word *plastikos*, meaning to mould or shape – a fitting description for the intrinsic qualities that such materials possess. In English, the word 'plastic' was used as an adjective from the sixteenth century onwards to describe materials that were easy to mould; however, it was not until the 1930s that the term began to be widely used to refer to synthetic polymeric materials. Of course, people had used natural plastics such as shellac lacquer, horn and tortoiseshell for centuries, moulding them under heat and pressure into a myriad of forms, including beakers, combs and boxes.

It was Charles Goodyear who really started the plastics industry as we know it today, with the process for vulcanising rubber that he developed in 1839. Before this, rubber had been imported into America from the East Indies and Brazil, but objects made from the raw gum were unstable becoming bone-hard and brittle in the cold of winter, and sticky and glue-like in the heat of summer. After five long years of seemingly futile research, Goodyear solved the temperature-related instability of natural rubber through a curing process that involved adding sulphur under conditions of extreme heat and pressure. This new material was christened Gum-Elastica, and was patented by Goodyear in 1844. Meanwhile in England, Thomas Hancock had also spent several years attempting to stabilise this material, and had succeeded in obtaining a patent for vulcanising rubber with sulphur one month before Goodyear's claim had been approved. Equally importantly, Hancock had also developed the machinery required to process this semi-synthetic material – which he called Vulcanite, after the god of fire – on an industrial scale.

Another early plastic that came to prominence during the mid-nineteenth century was gutta-percha, which was derived from the milky latex sap of rubber plants growing in South-East Asia. Gutta-percha was actually made from the tapped juice of the *palaquium gutta* tree, and several other varieties of *sapotaceae*, which was then thickened into a mouldable material by heating. An English botanist, Thomas Lobb, was reputedly the first Westerner to 'discover' this natural plastic during a plant-collecting journey through the East Indies in 1842. The following year, Dr. William Montgomerie, a senior surgeon posted to Singapore, also observed the native woodsmen using the hardened gum of the *palaquium gutta* for the handles of their *parangs* (machetes) and *kris* (daggers). According to the *Association Medical Journal* (the precursor of the *British Medical Journal*) Montgomerie 'inferred at once the extensive uses to which gutta-percha might be put in the arts of Europe. He purchased a quantity of the raw material, sending from Singapore part of it to Bengal and part to Europe, and suggesting some of the uses to which he fancied it might be applied. The quantity sent to England secured him at once, as the discoverer, the gold medal of the Society of Arts.'[2]

The samples of this natural plastic sent back to England by Montgomerie were seen by Thomas Hancock, who immediately realised that gutta-percha had the potential to become a useful insulating material. Hancock subsequently showed it to his younger brother Charles, who in 1845 founded (in partnership with the chemist Henry Bewley) the Gutta-Percha Company in London, with the aim of commercially exploiting this useful, gum-derived thermoplastic. Importantly, although gutta-percha had the same chemical composition as natural rubber, it possessed a different molecular structure, which meant that it remained hard at room temperature. Gutta-percha (also known as balata) could also be vulcanised with sulphur, as well as other additives, and because its properties were different from those of vulcanised rubber, it was significantly easier to process. To this end, the Gutta-Percha Company developed an extruding machine to produce rods and tubing made of this material, which were used amongst other things to insulate the first submarine telegraph cables. Although this 'gum plastic' was most commonly used as an insulator, gutta-percha was also

Gutta percha hand mirror, British
c.1850

The British Xylonite Company's works at Highams Park, London, 1890s – the first British company to commercially manufacture any plastic material successfully

employed in a wide variety of objects, from golf balls and chemists's bottles to funerary urns and mourning jewellery – it was even used in the construction of a small skiff carried on board the *Prince Albert* on its voyage in search of Sir John Franklin's ill-fated expedition to discover the North-West Passage. At the 1851 Great Exhibition in London, over one hundred designs made of gutta-percha were exhibited, including ornately decorated Revival Style furnishings manufactured by the Gutta-Percha Company.

During the 1850s, two other early plastics were invented. The first, known as Florence Compound, was a shellac and sawdust-based moulding composite developed by Alfred Critchlow. It was chiefly used to make Union Cases – decorated folding containers used to protect daguerreotypes. Based in Florence, Massachusetts, Critchlow's manufacturing company also used this hard and brittle plastic in the manufacture of hairbrushes and hand mirrors, and was one of the first firms to mass produce plastic objects in significant quantities. The second polymeric material, *Bois Durci*, was developed in the 1850s. Its name translates as 'hardened wood', which is indeed a good description of its look and feel. This plastic substance was patented in 1856 by François Charles Lepage, and was made from a mixture of blood (acquired from Parisian slaughterhouses), egg albumen and very fine sawdust. The resulting solution was then stirred and heated until it reached the correct consistency, before being poured into detailed steel moulds which were subjected to steam and pressure. The Société du Bois Durci of Paris subsequently manufactured various small household and decorative items from this hard, semi-glossy thermosetting plastic, including photograph frames, combs, pipe stems and medallions depicting famous people or classical allegories. At this early stage in their development, plastics were still regarded as substitutes for more expensive materials, rather than as valuable in their own right. However, with each new invention they came a step closer to being fit for the purposes of high-volume industrialised production.

Parkesine and the Celluloid Era

The long-awaited breakthrough in plastics development came when Alexander Parkes, who had already patented methods for the cold vulcanisation of rubber, invented a completely new, cellulose nitrate-based material, which he christened Parkesine. Patented in 1861, this first modern plastic was the result of twelve years of intensive research and substantial financial investment. Parkesine was introduced at the 1862 International Exhibition in London as the first synthetic plastic and, three years later, Parkes presented a paper at the Society of Arts which was probably the earliest detailed projection of the future of plastics in industry. As Parkes noted of his new cellulosic material – which was made from a highly flammable mixture of gun cotton (cellulose nitrate) and wood naphtha (methyl alcohol) – 'The applications of this material to manufacturers appear almost unlimited, for it will be available for spinners' rolls and bosses, for pressing rolls in dyeing and printing works, embossing rolls, knife handles, combs, brush backs, shoe soles, floor-cloths, whips, walking sticks, umbrella and parasol handles, buttons, brooches, buckles, pierced and inlaid work, book-binding, tubes, chemical taps and pipes, photographic baths, battery cells, philosophical instruments, waterproof fabrics, sheets and other articles for surgical purposes, and for works of art in general.'[3] Unfortunately, although it could be easily coloured and appeared an ideal moulding material, Parkesine had two inherent problems: it was flammable and its brittleness meant that it cracked easily. Nor was the situation improved by the determination of its inventor to keep the cost below one shilling for every pound in weight, and his willingness to compromise quality in the process. As a result, the material that had been awarded a bronze medal in 1862 for 'excellence of product' never lived up to its early promise, and was soon superseded by plastics with superior characteristics.

One such material was an improved version of Parkesine developed by Daniel Spill, known as Xylonite (its name deriving from *xylon*, the Greek word for 'wood'). Spill, who had previously been employed as works manager at the Parkesine Company, took over the floundering enterprise and renamed it the Xylonite Company in 1869. His more advanced, cellulose-based plastic was used for a variety of products, most notably boxes and handles for knives and brushes, and was also employed as an insulating material for electric cabling. At the same time, the American billiard ball makers Phelan & Collander of Albany, New York, had offered a princely reward of $10,000 to the first person who invented a satisfactory substitute material for ivory, the shortage of which was threatening to harm their business. Inspired by this prize, John Wesley Hyatt experimented with various plastic compounds. Although he did not ultimately find a replacement for ivory, he did invent another thermoplastic material – a composite of shellac and wood pulp – that was successfully used for the manufacture of dominos and checkers. Having patented this new material in 1869 under the trade name Celluloid, Hyatt and his older brother, Isaiah Smith Hyatt, went on to establish their own company a year later. Named the Albany Dental Plate Company, it manufactured dentures that boasted, for the very first time, realistic pink-coloured gums. Unfortunately, though, the dentures tended to soften when exposed to heat, and the camphor used in their composition had an unpleasant taste that was difficult to disguise. Notwithstanding these drawbacks, Celluloid did not dry to a brittle hardness as was the case with earlier cellulosic resins (such as Parkesine and the first Xylonite resin), because the Hyatts used more heat and pressure in its processing. This had the effect of melting the camphor that was used as a plasticiser for the cellulose nitrate, meaning that fewer additional solvents were needed in the production of this useful polymeric compound.

In 1871, the Hyatts' company was renamed the Celluloid Manufacturing Company, and over the next few years it filed more than 250 patents for different types of cellulose-based plastics. Soon other companies began to manufacture very similar thermoplastic cellulose nitrate compounds under a plethora of different trade names. Both branded Celluloid and generic celluloid resins were used for a host of products, from washable collars, brush backs and cutlery handles, to billiard balls, piano keys and toys. Between 1877 and 1884, the Hyatt brothers and Daniel Spill wrangled through successive court cases over their patent claims for the invention of celluloid. It was eventually ruled, however, that Alexander Parkes was its original creator, thanks to his patented use of camphor as a plasticiser for the processing of cellulose nitrate in 1855. Crucially, the presiding judge ruled that all manufacturing of celluloid could continue, which meant that the Hyatts could still make their branded Celluloid resin, while Spill could also produce his variously improved Xylonites.

The commercial success of Celluloid was also considerably accelerated by the Hyatt brothers' pioneering development of early plastics processing machinery. In 1868, J.W. Hyatt was the first to inject molten Celluloid into a mould, and four years later the brothers patented a 'stuffing machine' – an early injection-moulding device that used a ram-like, hydraulically operated plunger and a steam-heated chamber. Using heat and pressure, this apparatus produced extrusions of Celluloid that could be formed into continuous rods, sheets or tubes. In 1878, J.W. Hyatt and the mechanical engineer, Charles F. Burroughs, co-patented an improved version of this celluloid extrusion machine; and Burroughs, who ran his own engineering company from 1870 to 1898, went on to develop other plastic moulding machinery for the Hyatts' Celluloid Manufacturing Company based in Newark. Cellulose nitrate was also used from the 1880s as a coating for photographic plates and, of course, it was subsequently processed as a thin film thereby transforming photography and also heralding the advent of movie making.

The only disadvantage with Celluloid was that it was highly flammable, and much research was dedicated to finding a safer alternative. Although a French chemist, Paul Schützenberger, had invented cellulose acetate as early as 1865, it was not until 1894 that the British inventors, Charles Frederick Cross and Edward John Bevan, patented an improved technique for its production, which acetylised cellulose in order to produce a chloroform-soluble triacetate resin. This new and improved material was used in numerous products, from hair combs and spectacle frames to tool handles and babies's rattles. At around this time, two more processes were introduced that further extended the manufacturing possibilities for plastics: blow moulding, invented in 1881 by William B. Carpenter (a colleague of the Hyatts); and thermoforming, invented by Charles H. Thurber in 1900. That same year, another new plastic was exhibited at the famous Exposition Universelle in Paris. It possessed the trade name Galalith – an amalgamation of the Greek words *gala* (milk) and *lithos* (stone), and a fitting title because this plastic compound was made from casein, the protein found in cow's milk. Successfully commercialised by a German businessman, Carl Kunth, casein plastic was an extremely fine-grained resin that could be used to imitate horn as well as semi-precious stones such as agate, jade, lapis lazuli and onyx. By the dawn of the twentieth century, plastics such as Celluloid and casein were increasingly employed as substitute materials, displacing the natural substances that had been used for centuries. As such, these early plastics often brought a touch of affordable glamour into the lives of ordinary working men and women, who could never have afforded 'luxury' items made from expensive natural materials.

The inventor of Bakelite, Leo Baekeland, in his laboratory, 1910s

Jaxonite covered pot, British 1920s – Jaxonite was a rare and early phenolic plastic resin

Early flashlight, 1920s – made from an early celluloid resin imitating tortoiseshell

Bakelite: the Material of a Thousand Uses

In 1872, the famous German chemist and Nobel Prize winner, Johann Friedrich Wilhelm Adolf von Baeyer, published a scientific paper which described the formation of a 'cement-like substance' in a reaction between a mixture of aldehydes and phenols. During the same year, he also published another paper recording an experiment that he had conducted with phenol-formaldehyde which produced an entirely new resinous material, and paved the way for a fresh departure in chemical research. In England, the engineer James Swinburne pursued further tests into this new synthetic material, while in the United States the Belgian-born chemist, Leo Baekeland, began simultaneous investigations into the potential of this hard, resinous material. The main problem they faced was that it took several months for the phenol and formaldehyde to generate the new plastic material at room temperature. What was needed was a suitable catalyst to speed up the reaction. Swinburne's experiments determined that caustic soda might meet the requirement; but rather than patenting his discovery immediately, he waited for two or three years in the hope of finding an even better solution. He eventually filed his patent in February 1907, only to learn that Baekeland, who had also spent five years patiently investigating phenol-formaldehydes, had obtained a patent the previous day for a similar process using small amounts of an alkaline catalyst.

In his laboratory in Yonkers, New York, Baekeland had developed a boiler-like machine, which he called 'Old Faithful', that enabled him to produce enough heat and pressure to manufacture his first synthetic resins. This type of apparatus, which became known as a Bakelizer, comprised a metal-jacketed steam chamber that could be pressurised by means of an attached pump. Baekeland filed another patent in July 1907, which detailed his use of intense heat and pressure to create a new material, subsequently christened and trademarked as Bakelite. As T.J. Fielding later noted in his *History of Bakelite Limited*, 'Baekeland's work was astonishingly complete and was a masterpiece of systematic investigation. His complete patent specification was truly the birth certificate of the modern plastics industry.'[4] Unlike earlier experiments with phenol-formaldehyde compounds, the chemical reaction used to produce Bakelite was relatively easy to control and could be successfully replicated, and the resulting resinous material was also free from the bubbles that impaired earlier phenolics.

Significantly, Baekeland's process involved control-ling the chemical reaction through the application of heat in distinct stages that produced three different grades of the material: Bakelite 'A', Bakelite 'B' and Bakelite 'C'. Each of these variants had its own particular properties. 'A' could be either liquid or solid, and was used as a varnish or a moulding material; 'B' was a transitional solid that could be softened with heat, allowing it to be moulded in a hot hydraulic press; while 'C' was the compound's final, solid state which could not be reheated or remoulded. This latter version was sold as rods, slabs or blocks that could then be sawn, carved, turned or polished. Fillers such as wood flour, cotton, mica and clay could also be added to Bakelite, as well as dyes, which enabled the production of compounds specially suited to individual industries or specific purposes. Furthermore, Bakelite could be used as a lacquer or protective enamel for metallic surfaces, and could even be used to impregnate wood to proof it against rot.

In March 1912, the General Bakelite Company of New York issued an information booklet on their new invention – which could be transparent, coloured or opaque – stating that, 'Bakelite is a substance which, in its different forms, offers the advantages of hard rubber, Japanese lacquer, celluloid, and in some respects excels the properties of these products. It is not merely a mixture or a so-called "compound" like so many rubber-, shellac-, or other resinous-compositions, but a well-defined chemical substance of specific properties; it thus adds an important member to the industry of plastics… Henceforth a new material has become available which can be manufactured in practically limitless quantities and at a price which allows a wide range of uses.'[5] Clearly this new synthetic material offered previously undreamt-of possibilities both to designers and manufacturers, and within a very short time innumerable applications had been found for this wondrous yet economical plastic, rapturously marketed as 'the material of a thousand uses'. In terms of product design, Bakelite and other phenolic moulding materials such as Durez or Resinox were excellent electrical insulating materials. As such, they were ideal for moulding appliance housings, for instance Jean Heiberg's landmark *DBH 1001* telephone for L.M. Ericsson (1931) or Fredrik Ljungström's *Ribbonaire* table fan for the Singer Sewing Machine Company (1931). They also had a combination of high impact resistance and good chemical resistance that made them extremely useful and durable materials, well suited for all kinds of consumer items as well as industrial mechanical parts, from buttons and ashtrays to grinding wheels and pump valves.

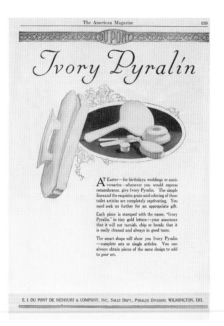

Du Pont De Nemours & Co. advertisement for Ivory Pyralin, 1920 – a celluloid-based resin that imitated ivory

Thermos flask manufactured by Thermos Ltd., c.1925 – moulded in Bakelite

Hairdryer manufactured by
Siemens Ltd. (England), 1930s –
moulded in Bakelite

The 1930s: the First Modern Plastic Age

The 1930s saw the widespread commercial application of various different synthetic polymers, most notably Bakelite, but also urea formaldehyde moulding compounds, cellulose acetate plastics, cellulose nitrate plastics, vinyl resins, casein plastics, acrylic resins and polystyrene. Although most of these compounds had been discovered decades earlier, it was not until the 1930s that they had been sufficiently improved to become viable materials for widespread use within the design and manufacturing industries. This decade also saw the celebration of plastics as truly modern materials, rather than useful substitutes for natural materials. For example, the American Catalin Corporation sold Catalin as 'The Gem of Modern Industry', and emphasised the 'sales appeal' of the resin's 'colour, beauty and texture'. Plastics were now being exploited by designers for their own intrinsic potential, and the results were often startlingly modernistic, as can be seen in the aesthetically progressive and sculptural form of Isamu Noguchi's *Radio Nurse* baby monitor for the Zenith Radio Corporation (1937–1938).

The rapid expansion of plastics usage that occurred during this period was, of course, inextricably linked to the constrained economic climate of the 1930s. These straitened times led embattled manufacturers, especially in America, to seek out the services of professional design consultants – such as Raymond Loewy, Walter Dorwin Teague and Harold van Doren – to differentiate their products from those of their competitors in an increasingly competitive marketplace. This first generation of professional industrial designers was frequently brought in to redesign a company's entire product range, and they often convinced manufacturers to move into plastics for the first time, stressing their modern appeal and pointing out the savings in raw materials and the greater cost efficiencies in mass production that plastics could deliver. The malleability of plastics could also permit the number of elements in a design to be significantly reduced, which facilitated more efficient assembly. Moreover, making the switch from metal to plastic often brought dividends in performance, as with Hoover's streamlined *Model 150* vacuum cleaner (1936), designed by Henry Dreyfuss to use Bakelite for its housing, or Harold van Doren's *Sentinel* scale for the Toledo Scale Company (1935) with its outer casing of white Plaskon, a urea-formaldehyde resin.

Another reason for the increasing use of plastics in the 1930s was that huge progress had also been made in the development of hydraulic presses, including the development of semi-automated models from the late 1920s. As J. Harry DuBois later explained, 'With the introduction of semi-automatic moulds the heating system was in a mould chaise and no longer part of the press; economic conditions suggested dual press operation because the long cure time permitted the operator to change the alternate mould. The depression years fostered "battery" operation with one person running several presses.'[6] Exponential gains in productivity flowed from these revolutionary systems. In addition, presses were also specially created for the compression moulding of thermosetting plastics into specific objects. A pre-eminent example was the enormous press constructed for the General Electric Company in 1934 to mass produce the Plaskon housing of Harold van Doren's prize-winning design for the Toledo Scale Company.

As Van Doren noted in an article from 1936 entitled *Designing for Plastics Production*, 'Not many years ago, six or seven perhaps, the widespread use of plastics was unheard of. The phenomenal increase in their employment for cosmetics, radios, watches, smokers' accessories, even rather large retail store equipment, can be attributed to a number of factors. For one thing, the availability of brilliant colour and pastel shades. Durability of surface, accuracy of dimension, extreme lightness. Perhaps, most of all, the desire for something new, something different. Since the previous use of plastics had been largely industrial and utilitarian rather than decorative, appearance played a comparatively small part. Hence effective and artistic design in the plastic moulding field has a slim background. Personally I believe that the possibilities for beautiful design in plastics have hardly been touched, that the next few years will see the development of designs in the plastic field at the hands of talented and experienced men that will deserve admission to museums along with the best of modern glass, ceramics, and silver.'[7]

Certainly, from the mid-1930s onwards, numerous landmark 'Depression Moderne' designs in plastics were mass produced for the American market, such as Walter Dorwin Teague's miniature *Baby Brownie* camera for Kodak (1934), and *Executive Model No. 115* desk light for Polaroid (1939). Such streamlined products exploited the form-giving malleability of plastics, and demonstrated how synthetic polymers could be used to create functional, affordable and sculpturally refined objects.

Although European designers lagged slightly behind their American counterparts in their adoption

↑↑↑ Xylonite celluloid box manufactured by Halex Ltd., 1930s – this form of Xylonite imitated mother-of-pearl

↑↑ *Bandalasta Ware* bowl manufactured by Brookes & Adams Ltd., c.1930 – moulded in Beetle, a urea-formaldehyde resin produced by Beetle Products Ltd.

↑ *Beetleware* jelly moulds manufactured by Beetle Products Company, 1930s – moulded in mottled urea-formaldehyde resin

Lemon squeezer manufactured
by Dodca, 1930s – moulded in
mottled urea-formaldehyde resin

BT-245 'Tombstone' radio
manufactured by Emerson Radio
& Phonograph Corp., New York,
c.1938 – casing moulded in
onyx-like Catalin

of plastics for high-volume production, some exceptional designs were created within the Bauhaus Modernist idiom, such as the *Ekco AD 65* radio, designed by Wells Coates in 1934. This was the very first circular model to be produced in moulded Bakelite, and it heralded the demise of furniture-like radios that mimicked traditional wooden cabinets. Another product notable for its innovative use of thermosetting plastics was the *Model No. 574* radio (1938–1939), designed by Livio Castiglioni, Pier Giacomo Castiglioni and Luigi Caccia Dominioni for Phonola. It similarly featured a functionally and aesthetically progressive moulded Bakelite housing that was unequivocally Modernist. As *Domus* magazine noted of this radio and another related design, 'the phenolic resins used in moulding [other radios] frequently even reproduce the "veining" of wood or walnut root! These new receivers are no longer anything like furniture. The form of their case is, like that of any machine, generated by guidelines that correspond to the purely scientific requirements and concepts of functionality, the technical requirements of construction and the practical considerations for the devices' use.'[8] In other words, these designs accorded with two of the most fundamental credos of Modernism: 'form follows function' and 'truth to materials'. By these means, they emphasised the unique manufacturing potentialities of plastics by adopting logical design methodologies that exploited these materials for what they were, rather than for what they could pretend to be.

October 1936 saw the opening of the First Modern Plastics Competition, sponsored by *Modern Plastics* journal. The occasion prompted Leo Baekeland to write: 'Twenty-five years ago one could hardly predict the importance that the plastics industry would attain in the world today. There was a mere handful of industries wherein the new materials might be used to advantage. As the months passed, other applications suggested themselves and proved their feasibility. And now there is hardly any field, any branch of industry where plastics are not serving faithfully in one form or another. The structural framework for synthetic plastics is well founded. If past history is any indication of the future, we may expect the industry to grow considerably in the next quarter century.'[9] Little did he realise that this prediction was a serious underestimation of the enormous cultural impact that plastics would have on society in the coming decades. During the 1930s, the term 'plastics' continued to gain common currency, and from the middle of the decade onwards there was general and mounting interest in new synthetic polymers, now seen as a growing and independent family of materials. At the 1935 British

Norman Bel Geddes, *FC-400*
Patriot radio for Emerson Radio
& Phonograph Corp., New York,
1940

Art in Industry exhibition in London, a whole section was devoted to plastics, while at the landmark 1939 New York World's Fair – the theme of which was 'Building the World of Tomorrow' – various plastics companies exhibited futuristic designs made from their latest materials. Rohm and Haas, for instance, displayed transparent Plexiglas furniture designed by Gilbert Rohde, and the Du Pont Corporation introduced the world's first truly synthetic fibre, Nylon (polyamide), and showcased stockings made of this strong, silk-like filament. These utopian glimpses of the future captured the Depression-weary public's imagination, and plastics came to symbolise optimism and forward momentum. However, when war broke out in September 1939 both these visions and the role of synthetic materials were dramatically recast. Instead of being harnessed to the mass production of consumer goods, plastics were identified as essential to the war effort and their further development was prioritised by all sides in the conflict.

The Second World War and Postwar Years: The Moulding of Modern Design

Although frequently overlooked in the annals of design history, the production of military *matériel* has often absorbed a far larger share of a nation's expenditure than any other field of design, especially in time of war. This was never truer than during the Second World War when the American government pumped hundreds of millions of dollars annually into research for military purposes. This colossal injection of funding into the design and development of better-performing military equipment and armaments led to exponential advances in plastic materials and moulding technologies. At the outset of the conflict, both the Allied and Axis powers faced severe shortages of natural materials. The fledgling plastics industry, though, demonstrated its ability to provide efficient substitute materials, and was soon tasked with developing entirely new synthetic polymers with very specific wartime applications.

As the war progressed, these polymers found their way into innumerable military applications, from the domed Plexiglas canopies of fighter planes and the moulded fibreglass-resin fuel tanks of *B-17* bombers, to gas masks and field radio equipment. Moreover, throughout this period, plastics manufacturers used patriotic advertising campaigns not only to emphasise the crucial wartime role of their materials, but to hint at their future peacetime uses. For example, the American Cyanamid Company used the byline: 'Molding the future through chemistry'; while Durez Plastics & Chemicals framed their advertisement for a kitchen mixer designed by Clifford Brooks Stevens in the following terms: 'Here's another design for modern living that's just waiting for America to win the right to enjoy it. We have a tough war on our hands right now. Durez plastics are serving at the fighting fronts. But they'll be back... helping America to enjoy the fruits of victory.' By the early 1940s, a widespread understanding was clearly crystallising in America that plastics would help to serve and define the nation during and beyond the war – a level of popular acceptance and enthusiasm that raised the status of polymeric materials to new heights.

With the end of hostilities and rationing, manufacturers and designers began to look in earnest for peacetime applications for new plastic materials originally developed for military purposes. Charles and Ray Eames, for instance, used a glass-reinforced polyester that had been created for radar housings and crash helmets in their revolutionary *Plastic Shell Group* chairs (1948–1950) for Herman Miller. In 1951, the Society of Industrial Designers' yearbook commented on the increasing role of plastics within industrial design: 'The new materials which appear nearly every day are broadening the palette of the designer... Even the consumer is beginning to learn that the word plastics covers an infinity of different materials, some as unlike as steel and glass. Plastic materials are a special study for the design engineer, and the choice of a material for a particular purpose is a highly technical problem.'[10] The use of plastics, and the new metal alloys also pioneered during the war, ensured that the early 1950s saw industrial equipment – as well as designs for the home, such as vacuum cleaners or radios – becoming ever lighter and more compact. Although initial tooling costs were relatively high for such products, the high-volume manufacturing potential they offered ensured low unit production costs, thereby making them cheaper to produce and less expensive to buy in the stores.

During the 1950s, designs made from synthetic polymers were increasingly used within the domestic environment, from Formica-topped kitchen tables and melamine dinnerware to polyethylene Tupperware food containers and telephones made from glistening plastics in 'designer' hues. In fact, 'Mrs. Homemaker' found the allure of plastic homewares

Durez Plastics & Chemicals Inc.
advertisement for *Supermix*
kitchen mixer designed by
Clifford Brooks Stevens, c.1940

Celanese Celluloid Corporation
advertisement for Lumarith,
1943 – showing wartime uses

far too compelling to resist, thanks to their relatively low cost, apparently hygienic qualities, and tantalising choice of rainbow colours, all of which expressed a compelling and charismatic modernity and dispelled any vestige of the worthy, make-do-and-mend ethos of the Great Depression and the war years. Instead, the 1950s were all about rampant consumerism and endless consumption and, of course, no material was better suited to delivering this enticing cornucopia of new and exciting products than plastics. The decade produced a number of iconic designs in plastics, such as Bernadotte & Bjørn's *Margrethe* mixing bowls (1954) and George Nelson Associates' *Florence* dinnerware range (1952–1955). However, the vast majority of items made from synthetic polymers were of poor quality and questionable taste, and were little more than kitsch novelties trying to turn a profit on the public's overwhelming appetite for the new.

This tidal wave of shoddily made and poorly designed goods comprehensively eroded the status that plastics had struggled so hard to achieve. In fact, they were now commonly seen as tacky, inferior and expendable. As the Italian design entrepreneur Bruno Danese later explained, 'Having the means in hand to accelerate and expand production, manufacturers set their sights on mass consumption. The quality of the object, how long it would last, how it would stand up to use were unimportant; the chief requirement was a swift exchange in the market. Manufacturers backed a policy of low prices, thus instilling in consumers the idea that objects in plastic were commonplace things.'[11] The 1950s witnessed the elevation of mass consumption into a social obligation, and planned obsolescence was promoted as an economic necessity that would maintain jobs and lifestyles. The devastating ecological consequences of this unrestrained consumption were never even contemplated, with products – and especially those made of plastics – seen as ephemeral items that could be discarded without a care when they had become unfashionable or had reached the end of their short usable lives.

↑↑ Group of *Curvalite* surgical retractors made of Perspex, 1943 – this acrylic resin was unharmed by boiling

↑ Radio Corporation of America (RCA) publicity photography demonstrating a record made of 'unbreakable' vinyl, c.1946

René Coulon and Lionel Schein,
Maison tout en plastiques
exhibited at the Salon des Arts
Ménagers, Paris, 1956 – the
world's first all-plastic house

Zanotta stand at *Eurodomus 2*
exhibition, Milan, 1968 – showing
the *Blow* chair designed by De
Pas, D'Urbino and Lomazzi

The Plastic Age of Psychedelic Pop

The 1960s was a decade of unprecedented social change. Characterised by emancipation and permissiveness, these years saw the suburban home-making dream of the 1950s renounced in favour of a utopian vision of alternative, liberated lifestyles. Design acted as a potent barometer of this seismic shift in cultural aspirations, and encapsulated the experimental spirit of a new and younger generation; a generation, moreover, that enthusiastically embraced plastics as inseparable components of an alluring, Space Age future. The rapid expansion of the plastics industry during and after the war meant that by the beginning of the 1960s a vast range of synthetic polymers and moulding processes were available to designers. As the editors of *Modern Plastics: Encyclopedia Issue 1961* noted, 'Changing times in the fast-changing plastics industry are clearly reflected... with more materials available in greater quantities than ever before and with more new and improved processing techniques being developed to convert these materials into a myriad of end-products.'[12] Newer plastics included, among others, polypropylene, polycarbonate and styrene acrylonitrile copolymers, and it was these materials – alongside polyvinyl chloride and polyethylene – that would boldly shape the decade into a glorious kaleidoscopic profusion of bright colours and sculptural forms.

During the early 1960s, technical developments in thermoplastics came thick and fast and, in terms of tonnage, three types of thermoplastics gained significant market prominence: vinyls, polystyrenes and polyolefins (including polypropylene). Not surprisingly, these readily available thermoplastics captured the imagination of designers, and this was especially the case in Italy, which already possessed a well-established plastics manufacturing industry, numerous highly specialised design companies, and immensely talented engineers well versed in turning designers' sketches into three-dimensional realities. During the 1960s, Italian manufacturers such as Artemide, Kartell, Poltronova and Zanotta gave designers unprecedented creative freedom and were happy to finance experimental work. The designs that emerged from these 'ideas factories' were some of the most progressive and aesthetically challenging ever realised, and included Marco Zanuso and Richard Sapper's *Model No. 4999* child's chair and *Grillo* telephone; Joe Colombo's *Boby* trolley and *Acrilica* table light; Achille and Pier Giacomo Castiglioni's *Taraxacum* light; Gatti, Paolini and Teodoro's *Sacco* beanbag; Ettore Sottsass and Perry King's *Valentine* typewriter; and Giancarlo Piretti's *Plia* chair. The

common thread uniting these diverse and striking Italian designs was an imaginative exploitation of plastics that foregrounded their extraordinary formal potential. These influential products were also functionally innovative, and used polymers to create new design typologies seamlessly interwoven with the *zeitgeist* of the Pop era, and with its casual, anything-goes lifestyle of beanbags and light sculptures. Crucially, the use of plastics democratised this flowering of progressive design, making it available to a mass market for the first time in Europe. Instead of being sold in deluxe shops to wealthy clients, high-style design was now being mass produced and then bought off the shelf by young consumers. These designs were often highly futuristic, especially those created by Joe Colombo, and were directly inspired by the period's cultural fixation with space travel and lunar exploration.

The Danish designer, Verner Panton, was also responsible for forward-looking furniture and lighting that embraced similar, utopian themes. His seminal *Panton* chair (1959–1960) was the first single-form, single-material plastic chair to be injection moulded, and his lighting designs were equally noteworthy for their groundbreaking use of new plastics. Furthermore, Panton was commissioned by the German chemical and plastics company, Bayer, to create his famous *Visiona II* installation on board a pleasure boat at the 1970 Cologne Furniture Fair. This hallucinogenic fantasy landscape, with its colour-saturated and cave-like rooms, displayed not only Panton's sculptural furniture and lighting, but also the suitability of Bayer's new synthetic materials for the home furnishings industry. The Finnish designer Eero Aarnio also

Verner Panton, *Panton* chair for Vitra, 1959–1960 – became the world's first single-material, single-piece injection-moulded chair in 1968

made extensive use of plastics to create iconoclastic and futuristic furniture, such as his award-winning *Pastil* chair (1967), and the German designer Luigi Colani employed synthetic polymers for his amazingly fluid and sculpturally organic designs, such as the *Model No. 042984* baby's bath for Sulo (1969), which accentuated the oozing flow of heated plastic. As the design critic Nigel Whiteley later noted, 'What we were witnessing was going beyond the Modernist "truth to materials" principle to a stage at which the associations of plastics became part of the "meaning" of the product: plastic was, in a way, both form and content.'[13]

The early 1960s also saw another new design phenomenon related to the increasing availability of plastics: inflatables made of heat-welded polyvinyl chloride (PVC). In 1963, the French artist and designer Bernard Quentin created an installation entitled *Le Salon d'Avril de l'An 2104*, at the Galerie Iris Clert in Paris, which incorporated the *Cybule*: a blow-up and 'breathing' seating sculpture with a molecular inspiration. He subsequently exhibited an inflatable chair at the 1964 New York World's Fair, and in 1966 his first range of inflatable chairs was put into production by Adamoli of Milan. Around this time, numerous other designers – including Verner Panton and Nguyen Manh Khan'h (Quasar Khan) – also caught what the French news magazine, *Le Nouvel Observateur*, described as 'le virus de la pneumanie' ('the inflatable disease'), and produced an array of designs for inflatable furniture. In *Domus* magazine, Costantino Corsini suggested that, 'pneumatics are now being applied to furnishing and furniture, as designers are attracted to the possibility of ephemeral solutions that satisfy the negation of lasting meanings.'[14] Certainly, the height of the blow-up mania coincided with the student protests of 1968, and suggested a watershed in both society and design. Of all the inflatable plastic designs of the period, however, it was De Pas, D'Urbino and Lomazzi's *Blow* chair (1967) for Zanotta that was the most commercially successful, and which captured the younger generation's desire for transience and impermanence – for playful Pop solutions that were, above all, fun. Already associated with mass rather than elite culture, plastics were seen as the ideal material for such designs, which flagrantly displayed their inherent 'plasticness'.

However, during the 1960s and early 1970s another, more rational approach to the use of plastics in design developed in Scandinavia, and especially in Sweden. Since the early 1950s, Swedish designers had been at the forefront of creating household objects in plastics, and by the late 1950s Swedes were consuming on average five kilograms of plastics per annum, the highest figure in the world at that time. The widespread acceptance of plastics within Swedish society was in large part attributable to the Svenska Plastföreneningen (Swedish Plastics Association), which tirelessly promoted their use through its publication of *Plastvärlden* (Plastic World) magazine, and through events such as the Swedish Plastics Design exhibition held in Stockholm in 1960. There are also several further explanations for the strong foothold gained by plastics in Swedish design during this period: their democratic pricing, their forward-looking modernity, their wipe-clean hygiene, and their colourful hues that dispelled the cheerless grey of short winter days. Unlike their Italian counterparts, who explored the poetic and expressive aspects of synthetic polymers, Swedish designers used plastics more rationally to create high-value yet inexpensive objects that were extremely functional and exceedingly durable – principles that responded to and promoted the Swedish government's social mission to create a high standard of living for all its citizens.

Whereas during the 1960s and early 1970s plastics in Italy and France were considered new materials for experimental invention, their commercial and social potentialities were understood rather differently in Sweden, where companies such as Gustavsberg, Husqvarna and Hammarplast invested considerable resources in the development of 'plastic design'. The resulting products, among them Carl-Arne Breger's *Duett* jug and citrus press (1967), Sven-Eric Juhlin's *Model No. 1099* pitcher and *Model No. 9644* mugs (1969–1970), and Hans Skillius's *Prydan* bowls (1974) were remarkable for harnessing plastics in the pursuit of life-enhancing products for the home. This was the very antithesis of the mindless, throwaway and hedonistic Pop culture celebrated by the glossy magazines and Sunday supplements of the period.

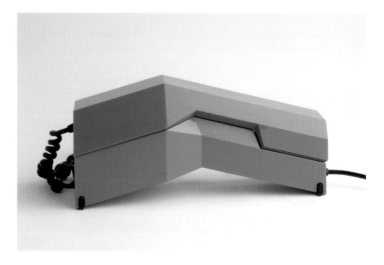

Giorgetto Giugiaro, *Rialto* telephone for SIT (Siemens/Italtel), 1972 – epitomising the hard-edged geometric forms found in plastic product design during the 1970s

By the early 1970s, then, two recognisable approaches to the use of plastics in design had coalesced. The first, the Pop approach, aligned itself with Modernist ideals of 'truth to materials', but vehemently rejected notions of 'good taste'; while the second, Rationalist school was guided by the Modernist principle of 'less is more', and was more closely related to established notions of 'good design'. But what was perhaps most noteworthy was the almost ten-fold increase in plastics consumption during these years, with West Germany boasting the highest per capita figure of nearly fifty kilograms in 1969.[15] However, this golden age of plastics came to a shockingly abrupt end in October 1973, when members of the Organisation of Arab Petroleum Exporting Countries (OAPEC) issued an oil embargo 'in response to the US decision to resupply the Israeli military during the Yom Kippur war'. Oil prices had soon quadrupled, and plastics were no longer the cheap material they once had been.

After the Oil Crisis: Design Rationalism and Post-Modernism

The 1973 Oil Crisis spelt the end of an era for plastics, and the ensuing years saw a necessary reappraisal of synthetic materials within the context of product design. It also prompted a long overdue ecological re-evaluation of the wastefulness and unsustainability of rampant, marketing-fuelled consumerism. The 'plastic fantastic' follies of the 1960s and early 1970s were replaced by a new and sombre rationalism within design, epitomised by Jean-Pierre Vitrac's *Plack* picnic set (1977), and Don Wallance's *Design 10* cutlery (1979). In product and furniture design there was a general move away from the use of plastics, which were now seen as relatively expensive commodities. The global energy crisis of 1979, which occurred in the wake of the Iranian Revolution, further reinforced an awareness of the finite nature of the world's energy resources, and continued to elevate the price of plastics.

This period also saw a return to the craft aesthetic – the very antithesis of the bright and glossy Space Age look that had been so fashionable only a few years before. Although plastics were still used by manufacturers, they were often used (through leatherettes or wood-look laminates) to simulate natural materials, reinforcing the idea that plastics were kitsch substitutes for authentic substances. There were, however, rebellious stirrings within the Italian design community against the safe and conservative blandness of 1970s mainstream design, with its preference for wood, metal, glass and leather over the truthful use of

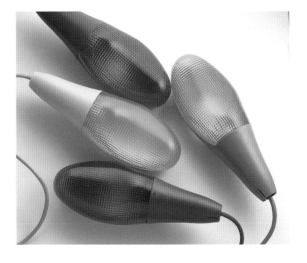

Ross Lovegrove, *Pod Lens* outdoor light for Luceplan, 1998 – employing the same polycarbonate material and moulding technology used to make car taillights

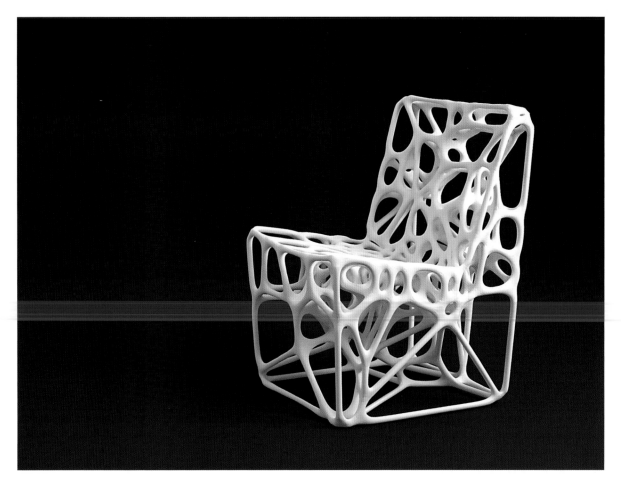

Luka Stepan, *Grown* chair, 2007 –
rapid manufactured in glass-filled
polyamide resin

plastics. There was also an uneasy suspicion that a general malaise in design was eroding the social relevance and political influence of designed objects, and stripping away their cultural value.

In fact, it was the banality of mainstream design that led to the formation of Studio Alchimia in 1976 by Alessandro and Adriana Guerriero, together with Alessandro Mendini – all of whom had been formatively nurtured in the Italian Radical Design Movement of the early 1970s. This new group sought to counter the austere sterility of Bauhaus-style Modernism, and the prevailing and stultifying despotism of 'good taste', through experimental work that would revitalise design practice with dynamic forms and symbolic meanings. Because such work was never destined for industrialised production or mainstream commercialism, injection-moulded thermoplastics and their associated tooling costs were never even

contemplated. Instead, Alchimia's designers, such as Alessandro Mendini, Ettore Sottsass and Michele De Lucchi, were drawn to plastic laminates for three principal reasons: they possessed a wealth of kitsch associations, they could be boldly and colourfully patterned, and they were generally viewed by the design establishment as the essence of bad taste. Alchimia's poetic and intellectually provocative designs drew on an eclectic range of historical sources, and laid the groundwork for the formation of the Memphis design group in 1981, which similarly exploited the decorative potential of patterned laminates in its totemic furniture and lighting designs, but in a less intellectualised and more playful way. The decorative plastic laminates used by both Alchimia and Memphis were produced by the Italian manufacturer Abet Laminati, which had been closely linked with leading designers since the late 1950s, and saw collaborative cultural ventures with the Milanese design community as an important means of promoting its materials. Through Abet's laminates, Alchimia and Memphis were able to produce expensive yet cutting-edge furniture that was sold in stylish galleries, and which not only revitalised Italian design in the late 1970s and early 1980s, but also helped to rehabilitate plastics more generally.

The Chasing of Plastic Dreams

After an unprecedented spike in April 1980, oil prices ebbed and remained relatively low from the mid-1980s to the late 1990s, with the exception of a brief rise in the context of the first Gulf War. This period coincided with a renaissance in plastic design – a second golden age of synthetic polymers in which designers freely exploited the formal, functional and commercial potential of plastics, from the first *Swatch* (1983) to Jasper Morrison's *Air Chair* for Magis (1999). During these years, Kartell reinvented itself commercially and culturally through successful and technologically progressive products made from jewel-like 'technopolymers' designed by, among others, Philippe Starck, Ron Arad and Antonio Citterio. In the meantime, Alessi – an Italian company known for decades for the excellence of its metalware designs – began producing quirky and characterful household objects that epitomised a new Post-Modern direction in plastic design. These included the *Euclid* thermal jug (1992) designed by Michael Graves, and Stefano Giovannoni's numerous brightly coloured and 'cartoonised' products for the home. Other companies such as Magis and Umbra also manufactured designs that exemplified this newfound conviction that plastics were the perfect material for producing eye-catching and inexpensive designs that would be attractive to a global market.

With the rampant, must-have consumerism that accompanied the credit-fuelled boom of the late 1990s and 2000s, there came a further shift within the plastic design industry. Propelled not least by marketing strategies, plastic products were increasingly being sold like seasonal fashion accessories – a profoundly irresponsible use of the world's precious resources, especially given that plastics can take centuries to degrade. During this period of unprecedented consumption, however, some landmark designs were achieved in plastics, including: Jonathan Ive's *iMac* computer (1997), Ross Lovegrove's *Ty Nant* water bottle (1999–2001), and Konstanin Grcic's *MYTO* chair (2007), all of which pushed the formal and technical boundaries of design and manufacturing

Ronan & Erwan Bouroullec, *Vegetal* chair for Vitra, 2008 – produced in injection-moulded polyamide

technology. Today's widespread availability of CAD/CAM software has also made the moulding of complex forms in plastics much easier and more precise. This, in turn, has allowed designers such Zaha Hadid, Karim Rashid and the Campana brothers to create objects – from recyclable shoes and bags to sculptural planters and chess sets – whose subtle and dynamic forms are realised in a wide variety of high-performance polymeric compounds. Moreover, rapid-prototyping technology now allows designers literally to grow their dreams in tanks of epoxy resin – producing Frankenstein-like embryonic designs that may one day make the transition to industrialised mass production.

Yet, in spite of these amazing technological advances, our use of plastics is still too often marked by wastefulness. We can see this everywhere: in food packaging, in gimmicky products whose fascination barely outlasts unwrapping them, in 'free' plastic toys given away by fast food chains. The health issues surrounding plastics should also be taken more seriously, from the carcinogenic toxins found in some PVCs to the hormone-disrupting phthalates used as plasticisers to make plastics flexible. This will necessarily demand a more thoughtful and careful use of plastics than is currently the norm. Given the environmental issues that we face, a philosophy of 'less, but better' – long championed by the industrial designer Dieter Rams – should be our blueprint for the design, manufacture and use of plastic products.

Today, although ambivalence surrounds the use of plastics both in design and in our everyday lives, it would nonetheless be difficult to conceive of a world without them: they are simply some of the most important and useful materials known to man. The statistics surrounding plastics consumption are astounding. Over 200 million tons of plastics are produced globally each year of which, according to Greenpeace, only 3.5 per cent is recycled. Perhaps even more shocking is the fact that fifty per cent of this tonnage is used in disposable items that are discarded within a year, such as the 2.5 million plastic bottles used hourly in America, and the four to five trillion plastic bags produced annually worldwide. However, despite such wanton use of resources, plastics can justly be considered one of mankind's greatest inventions, thanks to their amazing physical adaptability and impressive breadth of performance. These extraordinary characteristics have fitted them for the manufacture of innumerable objects and with an ever-increasing quantitative efficiency that has underwritten vast processes of industrial, economic and cultural activity. They are materials that by their very nature allow exact replication and almost effortless multiplication – properties that have uniquely equipped them for an era of democratic mass culture, and which have improved the living standards of whole populations.

Sadly, though, the relative cheapness that has allowed the benefits of plastics to be shared so widely has also done much to facilitate a heedless consumerist indulgence that threatens our shared natural resources and environment. In future, plastics must be used more sustainably. This means that they should be employed either to make durable objects that have functional and cultural longevity, or to manufacture useful, disposable products that are biodegradable, reusable or recyclable. Bio-plastics with enhanced qualities should also be developed to minimise our environmental impact, while the inexorable dwindling of oil reserves will have its own influence in curtailing excess and emphasising the true worth of synthetic polymers. Mindless quantity must give way to thoughtful quality, and for this to happen we will need talented designers to explore creatively the noble properties of these high-value materials, so that plastics can continue to transform our utopian, but more sustainable dreams into everyday, life-enhancing realities.

Notes

1   *The ABCs of Modern Plastics*, Bakelite Company, p. 1
2   *Association Medical Journal*, March 1856, p. 225
3   Gloag, John, *Plastics and Industrial Design*, p. 14
4   Fielding, T.J., *History of Bakelite Limited*, p. 9
5   *Bakelite, Information No. 2*, General Bakelite Company of New York, p. 5
6   Dubois, J. Harry, *Plastics History USA*, p. 11
7   *Modern Plastics, Catalog Directory*, October 1936, p. 110
8   *Domus*, November 1940, p. 71
9   *Modern Plastics, Catalog Directory*, October 1936, p. 1
10 *US Industrial Design 51*, Society of Industrial Designers, p. 12
11 *Design Since 1945*, Philadelphia Museum of Art, p. 166
12 *Modern Plastics, Encyclopedia Issue for 1961*, September 1960, p. 2
13 *Classic Plastics: A Look at Design 1950–1974*, Fischer Fine Art, p. 8
14 *Domus*, December 1967, p.8
15 Westermann, Andrea, *Plastik und Politische Kultur in Westdeutschland*, p. 387

Fabio Novembre, *Fleur de
Novembre* table for Kartell, 2009
– produced in polycarbonate.

overleaf:
Edson Matsuo, *Melissa Coral*
shoes for Melissa, 2009

Landmark Designs in Plastics: 1925 to Present

Roses
powder box, c.1925

An important early pioneer of plastics in design, Eduard Fornells Marco was born in Barcelona in 1887 to a family originating from Andorra, the small principality nestled in the Pyrenees. He initially trained as a metal engraver and carver in Barcelona, receiving a diploma in 1903. Four years later, he moved to the Spanish port of Santander, where he worked for the Compagnie des Cigares Français, before relocating to Paris in 1909. Soon established in the French capital, he socialised with other Catalan artists and set himself up as a metal engraver and carver. In 1911 he met the master glassmaker René Lalique (1860–1945), and they subsequently worked extensively together. From 1919, by which time he had perfected the engraving of glass, Fornells turned his attention to the production of artistic objects in aluminium, as well as his first designs in plastic. That same year, he opened a workshop specialising in the manufacture of small plastic art objects, and encouraged Etablissements Poulenc Frères (the precursor of Rhône-Poulenc) to develop a moulding press for cellulose acetate – an early thermoplastic made from either wood pulp or cotton linters mixed with acetic acid. In 1925, he exhibited his pioneering work at the Exposition des Arts Décoratifs et Techniques Modernes in Paris, for the most part comprising Art Deco-style boxes made from an early polymer, urea-formaldehyde, such as his elegant *Roses* powder box of c.1925. By 1930, the Fornells workshop in Paris employed several engravers, decorators and technicians to produce packaging for a number of prestigious perfume and cosmetics companies, including Bourjois, Roger & Gallet, Orsay and Worth. Importantly, Fornells used plastic as a noble and precious material, and his distinctive boxes were the result of painstaking experimentation both with colour treatments and stylistic motifs – the latter involving landscape scenes, flowers and birds, alongside more abstract, geometric themes. The *Roses* powder box is a good example of how he used densely decorated moulds in high relief to mass produce designs whose functional value was matched by their aesthetic merit. The substantial and ivory-like feel of the plastic give the box, with its then fashionable pattern of tightly clustered roses, a satisfying and luxurious quality. Apart from his stylish Art Deco powder boxes and perfume packaging, Fornells also developed a new type of billiard ball in 1936. Made of hard and shiny urea-formaldehyde, it had all the attributes of ivory and won official acceptance from the game's various governing bodies. These new billiard balls were also manufactured by Editions E. Fornells of Paris, and were sold under the brand name *For Match*. Fornells was awarded a gold medal for his work at the 1937 Exposition Internationale des Arts et Techniques dans la Vie Moderne, in Paris. The following year, he launched his own line of perfumes sold in exquisitely engraved glass bottles. Fornells, however, never abandoned his fascination with plastics and in the late 1930s and early 1940s, shortly before his death, he travelled to England and Germany to explore the development of new synthetic materials.

Eduard Fornells Marco, Powder box for Editions E. Fornells, 1925 – exhibited at the Exposition des Arts Décoratifs et Techniques Modernes, Paris 1925

Designer: **Eduard Fornells Marco** (Andorran, 1887–1942)
Materials: urea-formaldehyde (UF)
Manufacturer: Editions E. Fornells, Paris, France
Measurements: 10 cm high, 11 cm diameter

Ribbonaire
table fan, 1931

Designer: **Fredrik Ljungström** (Swedish 1875–1964)
Materials: Bakelite/phenol-formaldehyde (PF), ribbon
Manufacturer: Singer Sewing Machine Company, New York (NY),
USA/Diehl Manufacturing Company, Elizabeth (NJ), USA (a division
of Singer)
Measurements: 26 cm high

The Swedish inventor Frederik Ljungström designed
and patented the *Ribbonaire* table fan in 1931, and
then subsequently licensed its manufacture to the
Singer Sewing Company in the United States. Prior to
this, he had also developed an 'improved' bicycle with
his brother, Birger. They put it into mass production
with the help of investment funding from Alfred
Nobel, who wrote of the siblings: 'It is fun to work
with persons of such substantial ability and such
true unpretentiousness.' The brothers also invented
various high-pressure steam boilers as well as a steam
turbine, known as the Ljungström turbine, which was
patented in 1894. Like these earlier inventions, the
two-speed *Ribbonaire* fan was a highly progressive
design. It was considerably safer than other designs
on the market, eliminating the risk of injury with
its use of looped ribbons rather than metal blades.
In addition, the ribbon could be sprayed with pine
essence or perfume to delicately scent a room.
The design's many advantages were marketed in the
following terms: 'Quiet: Will not disturb your sleep
or conversation; Comfortable: Moves a substantial
amount of air without a draft; Economical: Uses no
more current than an ordinary electrical light bulb.'
The fan's shock-proof, dark brown Bakelite housing
was made from five separate mouldings, seamlessly
joined together to provide an elegantly unified Art
Deco-style streamlined form. Although manufactured
by the Singer Sewing Company, its subsidiary, the
Diehl Manufacturing Company, also produced the
Ribbonaire.

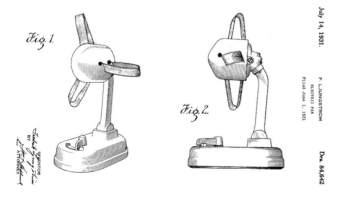

July 14, 1931.

F. LJUNGSTROM
ELECTRIC FAN
Filed June 1, 1931

Des. 84,642

Patent application, 1931

DBH 1001
telephone, 1931

Between 1903 and 1904, Jean Heiberg trained at the Håndverks-og Kunstindustriskole (the National Academy of Craft and Industrial Art) in Oslo, and later studied in Munich under the German painter, Heinrich Knirr (1862–1944). In 1905, Heiberg moved to Paris where he briefly studied with Jules Renard (1864–1910) at the Académie Colarossi, before enrolling in 1908 at the Académie Matisse – recently established by the famous Post-Impressionist artist, Henri Matisse (1869–1954). Heiberg was to remain in the French capital until 1929, becoming a follower of the Fauves and receiving widespread recognition for his own sculptures and paintings, which were reminiscent of the work of Paul Cézanne (1839–1906). After his return to Oslo, Heiberg was commissioned to create a Bakelite casing for a newly developed telephone, which was intended by its manufacturers to replace existing metal designs. The internal layout of this early plastic telephone was devised by a Norwegian engineer, Johan Christian Bjerknes, as part of a joint venture between the Swedish telephone company L.M. Ericsson, and its Oslo-based subsidiary, Elektrisk Bureau – a Norwegian manufacturer of telecommunications equipment. Developed using plaster prototypes, Heiberg's sculptural Art Deco housing for the *DHB 1001* telephone was far more ergonomically

resolved than earlier models. Early thermoset plastics, such as Bakelite, had excellent moulding properties permitting the forming of housings for appliances that were both more complex and more structurally unified. Heiberg fully exploited these potentialities in his visually fluid and rational design. Bakelite, moreover, was a better insulating material for casings than metal, as well as being more hygienic and durable. Although this was not the first time that Bakelite had been used in telephones, the coherent relationship created by Heiberg between the product's handset and the main instrument body established the benchmark for telephone design until the 1950s. The *DHB 1001* was produced from 1932 onwards, and was widely distributed throughout Scandinavia, the UK, Italy, Greece and Turkey. It was manufactured under licence by Siemens in England, and was also produced in France and America. In 1947, L.M. Ericsson introduced the *DBH 15*, an updated version of Heiberg's classic phone whose restyled and softened edges have been attributed to Gerard Kiljan. Importantly, the functional configuration and aesthetic refinement of Heiberg's landmark telephone design also directly inspired Henry Dreyfuss's ubiquitous *Model 302* (1937) for Bell Laboratories.

L.M. Ericsson publicity
photographs showing the
DBH 1001, c.1932

Designer: **Jean Heiberg** (Norwegian, 1884–1976)
Materials: Bakelite/phenol-formaldehyde (PF)
Manufacturers: Elektrisk Bureau (EB), Oslo, Norway/
Telefonaktiebolaget L.M. Ericsson, Stockholm, Sweden
Measurements: 13.7 cm high, 22.5 cm wide, 18 cm deep

Baby Brownie
camera, 1934

One of the greatest pioneers of industrial design, Walter Dorwin Teague studied art and then worked in an advertising agency, before setting up his own industrial design office in 1926. The following year, he began working as a freelance design consultant to the Eastman Kodak Company and, in July 1934, the firm launched Teague's landmark *Baby Brownie* camera – its first model to incorporate a moulded plastic body. Originally retailing for only one dollar, the *Baby Brownie* had a simple yet stylish housing made of black Bakelite. This marked a paradigm shift in the design of Kodak cameras, which had hitherto consisted of pressed cardboard boxes or metal boxes covered in leatherette. With its bold, Art Deco lines, the *Baby Brownie* not only looked more contemporary than earlier *Brownie* models but was also more ergonomically resolved, thanks to a sculptural form that ensured easier handling. This landmark design was also smaller and lighter than previous Kodak cameras, and boasted a range of innovative features including a flip-up metal viewfinder. Between 1934 and 1941, four million units of this small but perfectly formed product were sold, making it one of the first designs in plastic to be manufactured on a truly industrial scale. The *Baby Brownie* used rolls of easy-to-load 127 film which, with its fixed meniscus lens and single shutter speed, made it a straight-forward and accessible 'point and shoot' camera. A truly democratic product, cheap to purchase and cheaper still to manufacture, the *Baby Brownie* fully exploited the potential of Bakelite for the large-scale manufacture of camera housings. Teague subsequently designed other cameras incorporating Bakelite for Kodak, including the more luxurious and streamlined *Bantam Special* (launched in 1936). In 1939, a version of the *Baby Brownie*, with a decorative front plate in enamelled metal, was launched as a functional souvenir of the New York World's Fair.

June 2, 1936.   W. D. TEAGUE ET AL   Des. 99,906
CAMERA
Filed April 16, 1936   2 Sheets—Sheet 1

Fig.1.

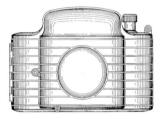

Fig.2.

Walter D. Teague & Chester W. Cruwrine,
INVENTORS:
BY   Newton M. Perrins
Gerald H. Stewart
ATTORNEYS.

Patent application for Kodak *Bantam Special* camera designed by Walter Dorwin Teague, 1936

Designer: **Walter Dorwin Teague** (American, 1883–1960)
Materials: Bakelite/phenol-formaldehyde (PF), aluminium
Manufacturer: Eastman Kodak Company, Rochester (NY), USA
(1934–1941); also manufactured in the UK (1948–1952)
Measurements: 7.8 cm wide

Ekco AD 65
radio, 1934

J.K. White, *Ekco M 25* radio for
E.K. Cole Ltd., 1931 – cabinet-like
housing made of Bakelike

Eric Kirkham Cole established his own company, E.K. Cole Ltd., in 1926 to manufacture an 'eliminator' radio that could be powered directly from AC current rather than from batteries. By 1931, the factory was employing 1,000 workers to mass produce radios bearing the EKCO trade name. That same year, the firm acquired compression-moulding presses, used to introduce its first Bakelite radio, and one year later it held a competition to design a radio cabinet incorporating moulded plastic. Entries were submitted by some of the leading British architects and designers of the day, notably Serge Chermayeff, Raymond McGrath and Misha Black. It was, however, the innovative, circular design by Wells Coates that was named the overall winner. Thoroughly exploiting the mass-manufacturing potential of Bakelite – commonly advertised as the 'material of a thousand uses' – it also revealed Coates's in-depth knowledge of the internal workings of a radio receiver, and the layout of its components. As with his earlier design for a microphone (which served as the BBC's standard model for many years), the eye-catching circular 'wireless' reflected his goal of reducing materials, components and manufacturing costs in order to

facilitate mass production and undercut the competition. Coates described these democratising methods as 'purpose related to purse', and his radio – christened the *AD 65* and launched in 1934 – clearly embodied his mantra. Quickly becoming a bestseller, it was available in two models: the standard version manufactured in warm-toned, walnut Bakelite, and a slightly more expensive variant in stylish, black Bakelite with chromed fittings. Before the radio's launch, Coates wrote of his own role that 'the most fundamental technique is the replacement of natural materials by scientific ones', something he certainly achieved with the *AD 65*'s phenolic plastic casing. Moreover, this landmark design's colour-coded waveband selector and three simple control knobs made it extremely simple to use. Alongside its use of cutting-edge plastics technology, the *AD 65* was one of the first truly Modernist products available to British consumers. Coates went on to design a number of other Bakelite radios for EKCO, including several circular models which together came to symbolise Thirties Modernism in Britain, and consistently conformed to the designer's belief that 'the social characteristics of the age determine its art'.

←← Wells Coates, *Ekco AD 36*
radio for E.K. Cole Ltd., 1935

← Wells Coates, *Ekco AD 75* radio
for E.K. Cole Ltd., 1946

Designer: **Wells Coates** (Canadian/British, 1895–1958)
Materials: Bakelite/phenol-formaldehyde (PF)
Manufacturer: E.K. Cole Ltd., Southend-on-Sea, UK
Measurements: 45.5 cm high, 38 cm wide, 26.5 cm deep

Sentinel
weighing scale, 1935

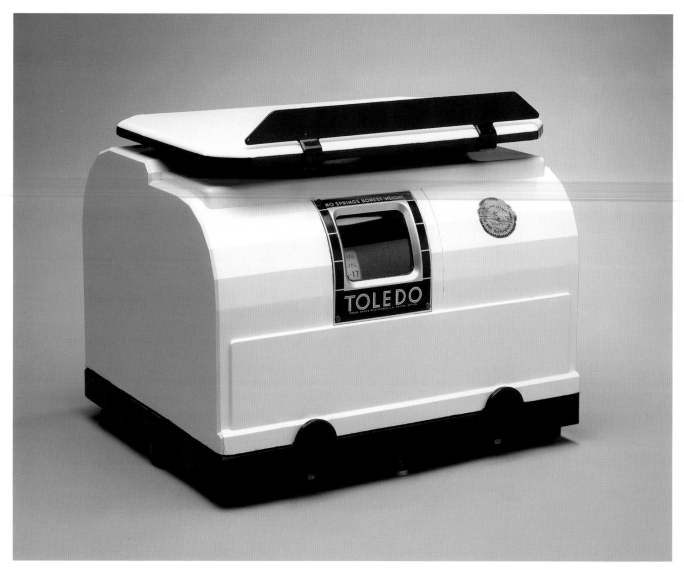

Contemporary photograph
of *Sentinel* scales – showing
rear view

Designer: **Harold van Doren** (American, 1895–1957) and
John Gordon Rideout (American, 1889–1951)
Materials: Plaskon/cellulose-filled urea-formaldehyde (UF)
Manufacturer: Toledo Scale Company, Toledo (OH), USA
Measurements: 40.3 cm high, 45.4 cm wide, 40 cm deep

General Electric advertisement
featuring the *Sentinel* scales
(*Modern Plastics*, 1936)

By the mid-1920s manufacturers had begun to comprehend the phenomenal value of plastics in their pursuit of high-volume mass production, and were now casting around for new synthetic materials that would perform even better. The invention of novel plastic compounds followed swiftly, seen most notably in the formulation of Plaskon, unveiled in 1931. The development of this substance was initiated by the president of the Toledo Scale Company, Hubert D. Bennett, who decided that the company should find an alternative material to heavy cast iron for its scale housings. He initially worked with the designer Norman Bel Geddes, who suggested using sheet metal. At Bennett's instigation, the Mellon Institute also began to synthesise a durable plastic coating that could be used instead of enamel on these proposed sheet metal housings. When, in 1929, preliminary research indicated that urea-formaldehyde might be a suitable material, Bennett funded a fellowship that enabled Arthur M. Howard (1923–2006) to devote himself to further research. Yet, despite this progress, Bennett was captivated by the idea of a wholly plastic housing. The only available synthetic polymer that was sufficiently strong for this type of application was Bakelite, which came in either black or brown. To test its commercial viability, Bennett conducted market research with metal scales enamelled in either white or black. He found that consumers preferred the sanitary appearance of the former, and in some cases refused to buy goods weighed on the latter altogether. Howard responded to this setback by suggesting that urea-formaldehyde could be used as a moulding material rather than just as a coating – an important consideration given that it could potentially be produced in any colour, including white. By 1930, Howard had formulated a promising material: Plaskon – a cellulose-filled, urea-formaldehyde compound. The following year, Harold van Doren and John Gordon Rideout were hired by the Toledo Synthetic Products Company (founded by Bennett) to create a range of products aimed at promoting the use of this new plastic. The duo also designed a radically new grocery scale, known as the *Sentinel*, which was launched in 1935 and possessed an innovative Plaskon housing moulded for the Toledo Scale Company by the plastics division of the General Electric Company. At the inaugural Modern Plastics Competition, held the following year, the *Sentinel* won first prize in the Industrial Group. As Bennett enthusiastically explained, 'The primary purpose of redesigning and actually remaking the Toledo scale was to lessen its weight for great convenience in making selling demonstrations and for improved appearance and service… Through the use of the Plaskon housing the weight of the scale was reduced from 165 pounds to 55 pounds. Large savings in shipping costs are secured. Its finish is permanent. It is infinitely smarter in appearance. And a number of manufacturing economies were accomplished through the use of this new plastic material. And best of all, the new scale has enjoyed an exceptional increase in sales.'

Radio Nurse
baby monitor, 1937–1938

Designer: **Isamu Noguchi** (American, 1904–1988)
Materials: Bakelite/phenol-formaldehyde (PF)
Manufacturer: Zenith Radio Corporation, Chicago (IL), USA
Measurements: 20.3 cm high, 16.5 cm wide, 15.2 cm deep

Japanese-American sculptor, Isamu Noguchi, brought an expressive sculptural sensibility to product and furniture design that became hugely influential in post-war America. Commissioned by the Zenith Radio Corporation, the *Radio Nurse* baby monitor was Noguchi's first commercial design and, as such, displayed a remarkably refined synthesis of form and function. This wireless intercom system was developed by Zenith specifically in response to the parental concern, and even hysteria, that had been whipped up by the media circus surrounding the notorious kidnapping and murder of the aviator Charles Lindbergh's baby son in 1932. This early monitoring system comprised two separate units. The first of these was the *Guardian Ear* microphone, made of enamelled metal, which picked up any sound made by the baby or child. The second, the *Radio Nurse* speaker, housed in moulded Bakelite, emitted any noise from the nursery or bedroom allowing parents to listen into their hopefully sleeping infant. Noguchi's biomorphic design took the form of an abstracted head that, with its horizontal, bar-like incisions was highly reminiscent of the protective mask used in the Japanese sword-fighting martial art of Kendo. The highly stylised form of the receiver, moulded in rich, walnut-coloured Bakelite, was also closely related to Noguchi's rather surrealistic sculptures from this period. As this begins to reveal, Noguchi's driving interest lay in creating everyday objects that were not only useful but also beautiful. Indeed, the year before the *Radio Nurse* was introduced, he wrote an article for *Art Front*, the magazine of the Artists' Union, provokingly entitled, 'What is the Matter with Sculpture?', in which he argued that, 'Sculptors as well as artists should not be forever concerned with pure art or meaningful art, but should inject the knowledge of form and matter in everyday, usable designs of industry and commerce.' His *Radio Nurse* was an accomplished realisation of this manifesto, and also demonstrated that plastic materials, such as Bakelite, could be used to make objects of equally high functional quality and aesthetic integrity. Interestingly, and in an early example of the cachet of a designer's name, the monitor's housing bore the words, 'Design by Noguchi' on its base. Reputedly, however, the resulting Japanese association meant that many *Radio Nurse* monitors were destroyed or thrown away after the bombing of Pearl Harbor – a fate that Noguchi's actual status as an American-born citizen of the United States did not prevent. As a result, very few examples of this beautiful and influential product have survived.

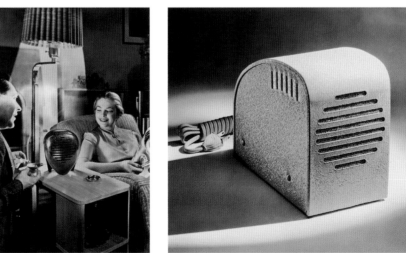

Zenith Radio Corporation publicity photographs showing *Radio Nurse* speaker, c.1938 and (right) *Guardian Ear* microphone made of enamelled metal, c.1938

Model No. 600
adding machine, 1938

In the 1910s, Oliver David Johantgen invented a new type of adding machine, and with the financial backing of a wealthy mid-Western businessman, Carl Buehler, he went on to found the Victor Adding Machine Company in 1918. The company's first machine, the *Model No. 110*, was designed by Johantgen and was launched in 1919. Weighing in at thirty-five pounds, it was the world's first portable calculator and was considerably lighter than its competitors, which often tipped the scales at more than one hundred pounds. By 1925, Victor had sold an astonishing 100,000 calculators; however, sales declined rapidly during the ensuing Great Depression of the 1930s. In 1938 – six years after the death of its inventor and founder – the firm secured the services of Thomas O. Mehan, a chemical engineer who had previously designed a rival calculator for the Brennan Adding Machine Company. Realising that in such a financially difficult climate the company's products had to stand out from those of its competitors, Mehan set to work immediately and developed two new and radically different machines: the streamlined *Model No. 600* and *Model No. 700*. With sixty per cent fewer internal working parts than earlier models, these revolutionary designs were not only more portable, but they also looked better than anything else on the market, thanks to their sculptural Bakelite casings. Indeed, with its gleaming, walnut-brown Bakelite body and stylishly contrasting, two-tone green keys, the *Model No. 600* epitomises the contemporary use of thermosetting plastics to create seductive, streamlined products with sufficient visual allure to capture the public's attention during those lean years. The use of plastic casings also made these designs more structurally unified – with the further benefit that they became easier and cheaper to

Victor Adding Machine Co. advertisement showing electric model, 1947

manufacture. The design's sloping 'full keyboard' was also set at a natural reading angle, which helped to reduce eye strain and operator fatigue. In the 1940s, an electronic version of the *Model No. 600* was launched which, according to the company's advertisements, featured 'a cushioned, feather-touch keyboard' and 'live control keys', making it even faster and easier to use.

Designer: **Thomas O. Mehan** (American, 1900–1955)
Materials: Bakelite/phenol-formaldehyde (PF), metal
Manufacturer: Victor Adding Machine Company, Chicago (IL), USA
Measurements: 19.6 cm high, 23 cm wide, 31.7 cm deep

Model No. 574
radio, 1938–1939

Luigi Caccia Dominioni and Pier Giacomo Castiglioni both studied architecture at the Politecnico di Milano, graduating in 1937. Following this, they both joined forces with the latter's elder brother, Livio Castiglioni, and established a design office in the Piazza Castello, Milan. In 1940, they were commissioned to design an exhibition of radios for the VII Milan Triennale – an event that inspired them to embark on the development of their own highly innovative five-valve radio. The resulting design, the *Model No. 574* radio for Phonola, was extremely progressive for its day and has since entered the annals of Italian design history as the country's first successfully mass-produced product in plastic. It was also the first 'true' Italian radio that was not designed to resemble a piece of furniture. Before its introduction, members of the Italian design cognoscenti, including Gio Ponti, had debated the phenomenon of 'radio furniture', arguing that it was inappropriate to hide new radio technology inside walnut-veneered, pseudo-antique cabinets and the like. Although there had been several earnest attempts in Italy to reform the design and styling of radios, none had been truly successful; that is until the debut

of the radical *Model No. 574*, with its unified, sculptural housing made of Bakelite (in black or brown), or cream urea-formaldehyde. At around the same time, the talented Milanese trio also designed a similarly forward-looking, though not quite so stylish, three-valve radio known as the *Model No. 303*, also manufactured by Phonola. As Ponti noted in the November 1940 edition of *Domus* magazine: 'The architects were responsible not only for the form of their cases but also the rational arrangement of the radio components determined by these cases. This was the only way to achieve the consistency and coherency between container and content that is the basis for a rationally conceived object with a pleasant appearance.' With its straightforward buttons and easy-to-read dial, the *Model No. 574* radio was innovatively conceived to be used either as a tabletop or wall-mounted set. A benchmark for radio design, this seminal Italian product powerfully demonstrated that thermosetting plastics – with their remarkable scope for design integration and visual unity, and their fitting modernity – were the best available materials for radio casings.

Gio Ponti, *Dufono* intercom for Società Radio Brevetti Ducati, 1940 – made of Bakelite

Designers: **Livio Castiglioni** (Italian, 1911–1979),
Pier Giacomo Castiglioni (Italian, 1913–1968)
and **Luigi Caccia Dominioni** (Italian, 1913–)
Materials: Bakelite/phenol-formaldehyde (PF)
Manufacturer: Phonola, Milan, Italy
Measurements: 20 cm high, 25 cm wide, 27 cm deep

Executive Model No. 114
desk light, 1939

Mitchell Polaroid desk light
brochure, early 1940s – showing
Executive Model No. 114 desk light

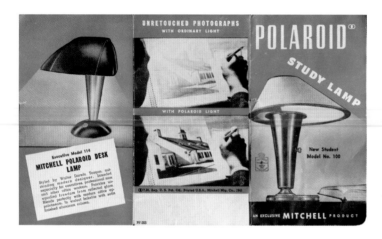

Applying his skills to gasoline pumps, radio cabinets, vacuum cleaners, street lighting, packaging graphics and exhibition stands, Walter Dorwin Teague was one of the most prolific and influential industrial design consultants working in America during the 1930s. It was an era that became known as the 'Design Decade' with hard-pressed manufacturers turning to professional designers to boost the allure of their products in an increasingly competitive marketplace. It comes as no surprise therefore that the founder of the Polaroid Corporation, Edwin Herbert Land, hired Teague to design a stylish lamp incorporating his company's patented, glare-reducing polarising filters. The resulting *Executive Model No. 114* desk light, like so many other consumer items of the time, employed a sleek, streamlined form not for any functional reason but to make the product appear more modern and appealing. The lamp's shell-like shade and half-domed base were moulded in the new wonder material – Bakelite. Known as 'the material of a thousand uses', Bakelite was especially suitable for the manufacture of plastic casings and housings. Interestingly, the Mitchell Manufacturing Company marketed the lamp as: 'Styled by Walter Dorwin Teague, outstanding modern designer' – an early example of designer label cachet. Under licence from Polaroid, the company also produced the *New Student Study Lamp Model No. 100* desk light. Designed by Otto Wolff in 1940, it similarly incorporated polarising filters and the same attractive, walnut-coloured Bakelite in its construction.

Otto Wolff, *New Student Study Lamp Model No. 100* desk light, 1940 – manufactured by Polaroid Corporation, Cambridge (MA), USA and later Mitchell Manufacturing Co., Chicago (IL), USA

Designer: **Walter Dorwin Teague** (American, 1883–1960)
Materials: Bakelite/phenol-formaldehyde (PF), aluminium
Manufacturer: Polaroid Corporation, Cambridge (MA), USA;
later Mitchell Manufacturing Company, Chicago (IL), USA
Measurements: 32.8 cm high

Fada 1000
radio, 1941–1946

Fada Radio & Electric Company
advertisement, 1946 – showing
Fada 1000 series radio

A quintessential American Moderne design, the *Fada* radio was a classic streamliner product. It was originally launched in 1941 by the Fada Radio & Electric Company as the *Model 115*, and was notable for its distinctive two-tone 'Fada-lucent' bullet-shaped cabinet. This was made from a cast, onyx-like phenolic plastic, developed by the American Catalin Corporation of New York in 1927. It was marketed under the brand name Catalin, and was also known as, 'the gemstone of modern plastics'. A transparent and almost colourless phenol-formaldehyde resin, Catalin was formulated without the addition of strengthening fillers such as sawdust or soot. In its syrupy, unset state it could be mixed with brightly coloured dyes, and even pigmented to create striking marbled effects – differentiating it from the blander opacity of other Bakelite-like plastics. Because it was not as structurally strong as normal Bakelite, 'gemloid' radio casings made of Catalin were generally much thicker and this gave them, along with their gleaming surfaces and interesting colouring, a luxurious quality that heightened their appeal. The *Fada* radio was initially offered in a choice of five eye-catching, jewel-like colour combinations, which must have seemed startling to a public used to the dull wooden or dark Bakelite radio cabinets of the period. Indeed, this progressive five-tube design was marketed as 'The Radio of Tomorrow... Today!', and *Fada* advertisements emphasised its 'beauty of appearance' as much as its 'beauty of tone'. A number of variants of this seminal design were manufactured and, in 1946, a redesigned six-tube version was launched as the *Model 1000*. Today, these *Fada* radios are highly prized by collectors, though they do not shine quite as brightly as they once did because the dyes mixed into the liquid Catalin resin have yellowed over time through exposure to ultraviolet light. What was once alabaster white is now a warm and attractive butterscotch, while bright royal blue has turned a bluish olive green.

Designer: unattributed (American)
Materials: Catalin/phenol-formaldehyde (PF), pressed cardboard
Manufacturer: Fada Radio & Electric Company, Long Island (NY), USA
Measurements: 15.2 cm high, 26.3 cm wide

JM-3
record player, 1942

The origins of General Electric can be traced to the inventor Thomas Edison, who established the Edison Electric Light Company in 1878, and a year later invented the first practical electric light bulb. Over the following decades, a continuing culture of pioneering research brought numerous inventions and discoveries, including television broadcasting, and the company also became renowned for its domestic appliances. Its first electric fans were produced in the early 1890s, and were joined by cooking ranges, electric heaters, washing machines, vacuum cleaners and refrigerators. In the process, General Electric transformed the American way of life. Following Edison's development of the phonograph in 1877, the company had also been at the forefront of sound equipment, becoming a trusted name within this burgeoning sector by the 1940s. In 1941 Donald De Tar filed a patent for a new 'record reproducing device' which consisted of an easy-to-use pick-up tone arm that had a bullet-like form. This innovative element was subsequently used in General Electric's *JM-3* record player, which was one of the best examples of how streamlining and Bakelite could be harmoniously combined to create a visually stunning and

functionally superior product. Originally priced at $9.95, General Electric's sales brochure described this portable record player as, 'An excellent example of a water-drop motif executed in plastic styling. Combines elegance of design with extreme usefulness. Small, compact and lightweight... Plays electrically 10-inch or 12-inch records through the speaker of any radio. Crystal pick-up. In beautiful ultra-modern brown plastic.' Unlike the furniture-like record players of the past, this model was a quintessential American Moderne design, with its sweeping and dynamic, tear-shaped form and its distinctive tone arm resembling a miniature, streamlined locomotive. The product's Bakelite casing also enabled a highly unified structure. This, in turn, made it easy to produce, while also ensuring that it was relatively compact and lightweight. These attributes led the manufacturer to suggest that the *JM-3* could 'be placed next to its owner's easy chair so that records may be changed without moving from the chair' – demonstrating irrefutably that plastics, with their plethora of unique properties, could contribute to the ease and pleasure of everyday life.

Contemporary publicity photograph featuring *JM-3* record player, c.1942

Designer: **Donald De Tar** (American, active 1940s)
Materials: Bakelite/phenol-formaldehyde (PF)
Manufacturer: General Electric, Bridgeport (CT), USA
Measurements: 12 cm high, 38 cm wide, 27 cm deep

Retractable desk light
1945

Designer: **André Mounique** (French, active 1940s)
Materials: Bakelite/phenol-formaldehyde (PF) or
urea-formaldehyde (UF), chrome-plated metal, copper
Manufacturer: Société Nouvelle des Etablissements Jumo,
Paris, France
Measurements: 14 cm high (closed)

The design of this light was for a long time attributed to the Budapest-born, Art Deco sculptor Gustave Miklos (1888–1967). However, according to patents filed in France and America in 1945 and 1946 respectively, this 'retractable office lamp' was actually designed by André Mounique, a designer-inventor based in Paris. The patents stated, 'The base and the head are designed so as to be made from a mouldable material which ensures economy of manufacture' and, of course, early synthetic polymers fulfilled these criteria beautifully with their amazing form-giving potential and mouldability. The design featured an innovative retractable arm that allowed the elegant, tear-shaped design to be closed in on itself to create a streamlined, mollusc-like form. The idea behind the design was that a desk light when not in use could be 'arranged into a compact form taking up little space and easily placed in a drawer or employed as a paperweight or as an ornament.' The sweeping form of this unusual lamp is also highly reminiscent of the geometric abstraction and bold massing found in French contemporary sculpture of the time, such as those executed by Constantin Brancusi (1876–1957). The light's shape also powerfully expresses the inherent malleability of the unset thermoset plastics used in its manufacture: black or brown phenol-formaldehyde resin (better known as Bakelite) and white urea-formaldehyde (sold under the Beetle or Beetleware trade names). These revolutionary plastics were the first such materials that could be reliably and successfully moulded into complex sculptural forms. Manufactured by La Société Jumo, this eye-catching light is a quintessential design of the Machine Age thoroughly exploiting the expressive potential of these new synthetic materials.

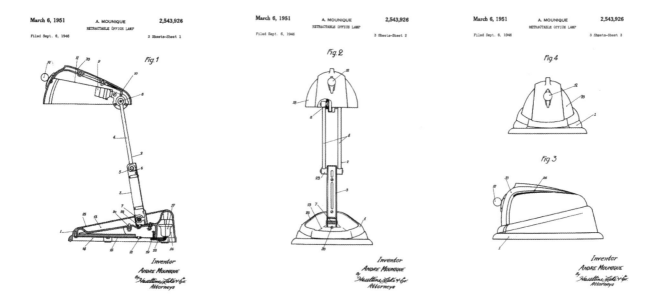

Patent application, filed 1945

Burrite Model No. 123
refrigerator pitcher, 1948

Although designed during the immediate post-war period, Clarence Burroughs' *Model No. 123* pitcher employed a design that harked back to the bold, streamlined Art Deco forms of the 1930s. Paradoxically, despite its retro styling, it was made from the newly available thermoplastic: polystyrene. The nineteenth-century German apothecary Eduard Simon had accidentally discovered this gleaming, state-of-the-art material as early as 1839, but it was not until 1937 that Dow Chemical introduced it to the American market. Even then, it was only when wartime materials restrictions had been lifted that polystyrene became widely available to designers and manufacturers. Created from erethylene and benzene, it was a rigid but quite brittle material with excellent moulding properties, making it perfect for the mass production of inexpensive yet colourful homewares. To this end, Clarence Burroughs used it to create a large number of kitchen and serving items, including this lightweight iced water pitcher, which weighs only 211 g (7.4 oz). Its distinctive design made of three compression-moulded elements, comprises a comfortable handle and a handy cover for the spout that can easily be opened and controlled with a thumb. It was manufactured in a wide range of bright colours, and was part of the extensive Burrite range manufactured by The Burroughs Company, Los Angeles. The company also produced a number of variations of this design, including a slimmer version and an eye-catching two-tone model. 'Burrite' was the trade name for the glossy-surfaced polystyrene produced by The Burroughs Company, a highly influential plastics manufacturing firm founded by Clarence's father, Charles F. Burroughs – whose own father had been an important pioneer of the plastics industry having developed early compression-moulding equipment for the processing of cellulose nitrate.

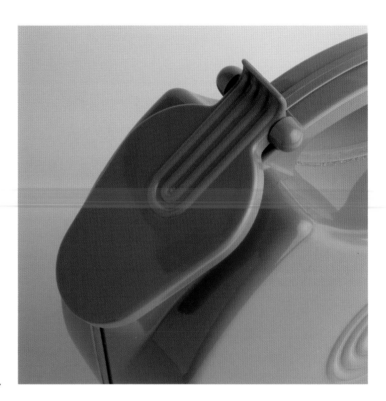

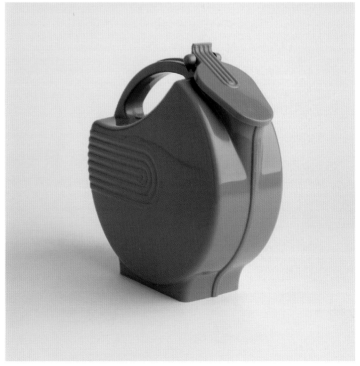

Designer: **Clarence Burroughs** (American, active 1930s–40s)
Materials: polystyrene (PS)
Manufacturer: The Burroughs Company, Los Angeles (CA), USA
Measurements: 21.3 cm high

PAW chair
(Plastic Shell Group), 1948–1950

Developed between 1948 and 1950 in collaboration with Herman Miller, Zenith Plastics, and the engineering department of the University of California, Los Angeles, the *Plastic Shell Group* seating programme was based on the concept of a universal seat shell that could be used with a variety of different types of interchangeable bases. As one of the very first completely integrated seating systems, the *Plastic Shell Group* chairs were also the first to be mass produced in unlined plastic. The July 1951 issue of *Plastics Industry* magazine noted, 'This striking departure in chair design also represents a new direction in plastic production. The Eames chair is the first consumer item to be made by the preform method of reinforced plastic moulding. And it is being produced in the first plant designed and built from the ground up expressly for preform moulding reinforced plastics.' The manufacture of the first 2000 chairs was subcontracted to Zenith, which laid up the initial production models in Zenaloy – a lightweight yet resilient glass-reinforced polyester thermosetting plastic that had previously been used for the manufacture of crash helmets and radar housings. One of the difficulties Zenith's engineering staff encountered was getting a uniform dispersion of the two-inch-long glass fibres over the relatively complex shape of the seat shells. According to *Plastics Industry*, this problem was overcome by using, 'a machine similar to those used in producing felt hats. The dispersed glass fibres, fed into the top of the machine, are deposited on the screen by air currents, which blow through the

screen. As the fibres are deposited on the screen, a dry or liquid resin is mixed in, binding the preform to the proper shape required for the moulded part. In the moulding operation the preform is placed in the female mould, liquid polyester resin is measured and poured in, and the male die descends, closing the mould, dispersing the moulding resin and curing the part.' In fact, it took three years of considerable investment, painstaking research and innovative tool development by Zenith and Herman Miller to perfect this hydraulic press, which was capable of producing the seat shells in sufficient quantities. The earliest examples made using this method had distinctive, corded rope edges around the underside of the seat shells and possessed a unique textural quality, with the individual strands of fibreglass clearly visible. In 1950, the chairs finally went on sale and were initially available in three colours: 'greige', elephant grey or parchment. Later, Herman Miller offered more colour options and also a choice of eleven individual bases. These ranged from a swivelling, wooden dowel-legged base, as featured on the *PAW* chair, to a low rocker base, which was deemed perfect for nursing mothers. For the contract market, Herman Miller also offered beam bases that supported multiple seat shells, which were ideal for hospital waiting areas or airport lounges. Upholstered and side versions were also developed and now, nearly sixty years since its debut, this groundbreaking furniture group is still in production, although today the seat shells are produced in injection-moulded polypropylene.

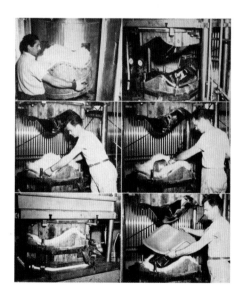 

Series of photographs showing the moulding of the fiberglass seat shell, published in *Plastics Industry* magazine, July 1950

Designers: **Charles Eames** (American, 1907–1978) and
Ray Eames (American, 1912–1988)
Materials: glass-reinforced polyester (GRP), enamelled steel, wood
Manufacturer: Zenith Plastics, Gardena (CA), USA/Herman Miller,
Zeeland (MI), USA
Measurements: 78 cm high, 63 cm wide, 60 cm deep

Model No. 500
telephone, 1949

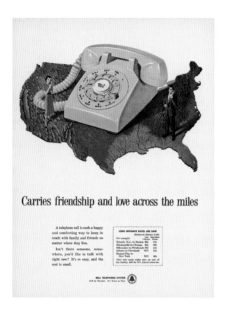

Henry Dreyfuss trained at the Ethical Culture School in New York before apprenticing with the industrial designer Norman Bel Geddes. Employed at the latter's office from 1923 to 1929, Dreyfuss concentrated chiefly on theatrical work, designing costumes, sets and lighting for the Strand in New York and for RKO's vaudeville theatres. Dreyfuss also worked as a consultant to Macy's, before establishing his own design office in New York in 1929. That same year, he won a competition organised by Bell Laboratories to find the 'phone of the future', and in 1930 Dreyfuss was hired as a design consultant to develop telephones for the Bell Telephone Company. These would include his iconic *Model No. 302* of 1937, inspired by an earlier telephone designed by Jean Heiberg for Ericsson, and moulded in Bakelite. It was, however, his attention-grabbing *Model No. 500*, introduced in 1949, that was the most successful and radical telephone of his illustrious design career. While the *Model No. 302* was a classic Art Deco design, with its sweeping edges and bold massing, the *Model No. 500* was a more curvaceous and ergonomically resolved design. This innovative product was the result of several years of intense research and development. AT&T's Bell Laboratories were responsible for its compact internal configuration, while the Henry Dreyfuss office undertook the design of its external casing, which fully exploited the advances in plastic moulding technologies that had occurred during the war. Initially, the *Model No. 500* was produced only in black phenolic plastic, because of the difficulty of getting tonal uniformity in coloured plastic casings. By 1953, however, this obstacle had been overcome and four new colour options were added: ivory, moss green, dark grey and cherry red. Over the succeeding years, more 'designer colours' were added to the range, including: rose pink, lemon yellow, harvest gold, mahogany brown, lime green, dark blue, avocado and pale turquoise. This previously unimagined choice of colours boosted the fashion credentials of the heavy-duty *Model No. 500*, ensuring its commercial success over the next decade, despite the fact that European-styled telephones were often more formally and functionally innovative. In 1959, injection-moulded ABS began to be used for the manufacture of this ubiquitous and sturdy workhorse of a telephone, which dominated telephone design for well over a generation, and whose production only ceased in 1986 – some thirty-seven years after its original debut.

Henry Dreyfuss, *Model No. 302* telephone for Bell Telephone System, introduced 1937

Designer: **Henry Dreyfuss** (American, 1904–1972)
Materials: Bakelite/phenol-formaldehyde (PF)/
from 1959: acrylonitrile-butadiene-styrene (ABS)
Manufacturer: Bell Telephone System, American Telephone &
Telegraph Company (AT&T), Dallas (TX), USA and licensed to
associated companies (including Western Electric)
Measurements: 12.5 cm high, 20 cm wide, 22.5 cm deep

Designer: unattributed (British)
Materials: urea-formaldehyde (UF), mirrored glass, cork
Manufacturer: Thermos, Tottenham, UK
Measurements: 26.5 cm high

Thermos Ltd. advertisement
showing *Model No. 65* flask, 1956

The remarkable looks of this Thermos 'vacuum vessel' (as it was labelled) reflect the bold sculptural confidence found in product design during the postwar period. Unlike earlier flasks and bottles manufactured by Thermos, the *Model No. 65* had an integrated handle, which was made of plastic rather than metal. The design also appears to be the first manufactured by Thermos that offered a stylish, two-tone colour scheme, which must have seemed the very height of fashion when compared with the rather dreary mottled browns and greens used by the company before the war. Apart from the maroon and grey version shown here, the *Model No. 65* also came in a contrasting red and white option, as well as in a number of single-colour variants, including sage green and mid-blue. The four plastic elements of the jug were compression moulded in urea-formaldehyde, and two of them were then glued together to form the main body and handle section. With its arching profile and two finger holes, the handle itself is surprisingly comfortable to use and demonstrated the potential of moulded plastics to create ergonomically refined shapes that conformed to the human body. As with other plastics, the thermosetting polymer used for this design also had the added advantage of being a good insulator of heat, allowing the flask to maintain the temperature of its stored liquid for prolonged periods of time.

Bic Cristal®
ballpoint pen, 1950–1952

In 1938, László József Bíró, a Hungarian journalist, patented the world's first ballpoint pen. The idea emerged while he was working as a magazine editor, when he noticed that printing ink dried rapidly and did not smudge. He subsequently decided that he would develop a pen that could use the same ink. However, because printing ink was more viscous than normal ink it could not be used with a traditional pen nib so, instead, Bíró developed a pen 'point' fitted with a small ball-bearing that rotated as the pen moved over paper, picking up ink from the cartridge and depositing it in a continuous action. In 1943, Bíró's revolutionary writing implement was put into full-scale mass production, and was exclusively used by British and Allied forces not least because, unlike traditional ink pens, Bíró's invention did not leak in unpressurised aircraft cabins. After the war, the 'Biro' went on sale to the general public though, with a price tag of fifty-five shillings in the UK (the equivalent of a secretary's weekly wage) and $12.50 in the USA, it was an expensive purchase. Later, Michel Bich, a pen manufacturer and also an expert in plastics technologies, obtained a royalty licensing agreement to produce Bíró's ballpoint pen. Between 1950 and 1952, Bich and his team developed a considerably improved pen, which fully exploited the potential of newly available plastics. The resulting *Bic Cristal* ballpoint pen wrote more smoothly, and without leaks or jams (annoying problems that had beset Bíró's designs). Moreover, it looked more modern, with its elegant barrel of clear polystyrene and its coloured polypropylene cap. Thanks to the high-volume production made possible by plastic injection-moulding technology, Bich was also able to sell his pens at a fraction of Bíró's earlier prices and, within three years, Société Bic was selling a staggering 42 million units annually. The overwhelming success of the beautifully functional Bic ballpoint pen proved unequivocally that manufacturers could create stylish and democratic plastic products that might achieve previously undreamt of sales figures. To date, Bic has sold well over 100 billion disposable ballpoint pens.

Bic advertisement showing *Bic Orange* ballpoint pen, 1961 – illustration by Raymond Savignac

Designer: **Décolletage Plastique Design Team** (French)
Materials: polystyrene (PS), polypropylene (PP), tungsten carbide
Manufacturer: Société Bic, Clichy, France
Measurements: 14.9 cm long

Schick Model 20
electric shaver, 1950

Launched to celebrate Schick's twentieth anniversary, the *Model 20* electric shaver was a groundbreaking design that employed an ergonomic plastic housing styled by the industrial designer Carl Otto in 1951. Otto had studied engineering at Michigan State University, before working as an automotive stylist for the Duesenberg Motors Company in Auburn, Indiana – renowned for its luxury automobiles. He subsequently joined the offices of Norman Bel Geddes and Raymond Loewy, the latter in order to work on streamlined locomotive designs. In 1951, Otto established his own consultancy on New York City's Fifth Avenue. As *Industrial Design* magazine noted, his design office rapidly 'accumulated an unusually long list of major design projects achieved for companies that run the gamut of consumer product industries'. These included electrical home appliances for General Electric and Electrolux, ranges for Hotpoint and furniture for Heywood-Wakefield. It was, however, his compact *Model 20* electric razor for Schick – developed in collaboration with the company's chief engineer, Norman Gray – that became his most notable and influential design. By rearranging the shaver's internal components, they were able to reduce the design's overall bulk and length, resulting in a wider yet more compact shape that fitted well in the hand. Setting a new ergonomic standard for subsequent shavers, the *Schick Model 20* won an IDI Design Award in 1951. Originally retailing for $26.50, this product was a top-of-the-line model and the specialised moulding of its distinctive dimpled cream-coloured plastic housing was subcontracted to the Shaw Insulator Company of Irvington, New Jersey. Schick also produced the lower-priced *Schick Colonel* electric shaver, which used a similar plastic housing but with its more geometric form was not as comfortable to use. Undoubtedly, the lessons Carl Otto learnt as a young automotive stylist served him well. He transferred them eloquently to the design of mass-produced objects, and also excelled in configuring their functional yet stylish casings from newly available plastics.

Schick advertisement for the
Schick Model 20 shaver, 1951

Carl Otto, *Schick Colonel* electric
shaver for Schick, 1953

Designer: **Carl Otto** (American, d.1986)
Materials: urea-formaldehyde (UF), metal
Manufacturer: Schick, Stamford (CT), USA
Measurements: 9 cm high

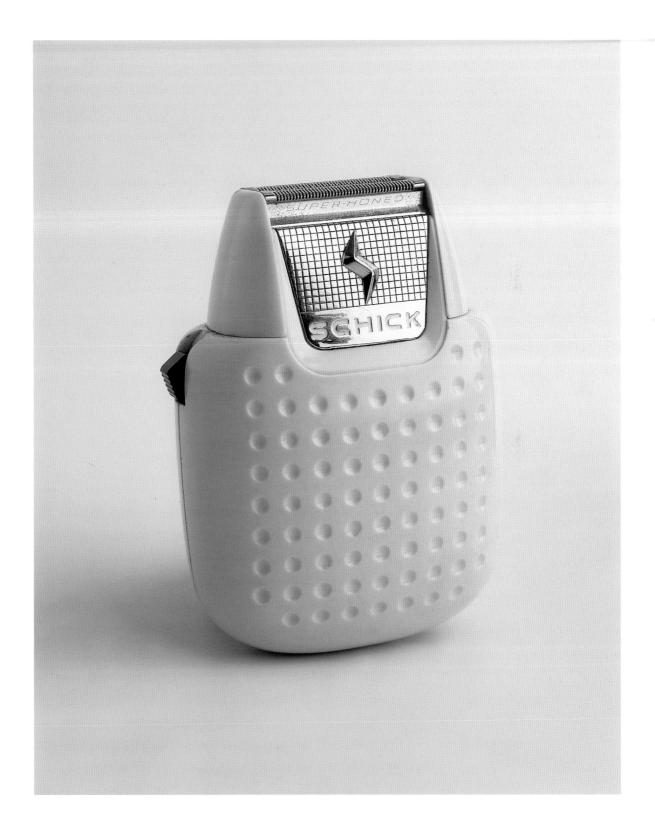

Florence
dinnerware, 1952–1955

Designer: **George Nelson Associates** (American, established 1955)
Materials: melamine-formaldehyde (MF)
Manufacturer: Pro-Phy-Lac-Tic Brush Company, Florence (MA), USA
Measurements: milk jug: 7.5 cm high, 13.5 cm wide, 14 cm deep |
sugar bowl: 10 cm high, 10 cm diameter | divided bowl: 7 cm high,
24 cm wide, 22 cm deep

During the latter half of the nineteenth century, the Florence Manufacturing Company in Massachusetts developed an early plastic known as Florence Compound, made of shellac, resin and wood fibres. This hard yet brittle material was used to manufacture, amongst other things, buttons, revolver cases and, most notably, cases for daguerreotypes (an early type of photograph). The company expanded further to manufacture a wide range of brushes, including revolutionary mass-produced toothbrushes, whose handles were all made of Florence Compound. In 1924, and after a number of improvements had been made to its various types of plastic compounds, the firm changed its name to the Pro-Phy-Lac-Tic Brush Company, in homage to its most successful product. Then, from the mid-1940s onwards, the company sought to diversify its product line with, for instance, the high quality, durable dinnerware lines marketed under the Prolon brand. These were made of melamine-formaldehyde – a resilient thermoset plastic developed during this period by the American Cyanamid Corporation. Designed by Irving Harper of George Nelson Associates, Prolon's stylish *Florence* dinnerware line was inspired by the classic simplicity and graceful elegance of Japanese tableware, whose lustrous lacquer was itself a natural plastic. Unquestionably, the *Florence* range elevated the aesthetics of melamine tableware to a completely new level and, in so doing, confirmed that plastic dinnerware did not have to appear gaudy or cheap. Rather than employing either garishly bright or sickly pastel colours, the *Florence* range came in a dignified and fashionable range of hues: Sunset red, High Noon yellow, Dawn grey and Midnight black. With its sensual, organic forms and gleaming surfaces, the *Florence* range emphasised the noble qualities of this newly available plastic, bringing a welcome touch of stylish glamour to the average mid-century American home.

George Nelson Associates
publicity photograph of
Florence dinnerware, c.1952,
photographed by Jerry
Sarapochiello

Citrus press
1953

One of Sweden's most celebrated designers, Stig Lindberg is best remembered for his whimsical studio ceramics and also for his graceful and practical tableware designs manufactured by Gustavsberg. As a student, he trained at the Konstfackskolan (the University College of Arts, Crafts and Design) and, between 1935 and 1937 at the Kungliga Tekniska Högskolan (the Royal Institute of Technology). After completing his studies, he immediately joined the design studio at the Gustavsberg ceramics factory, where he trained under the expert guidance of Wilhelm Kåge for the next three years. During this period, he also briefly attended the Académie Colarossi in Paris – an experience that would have a significant stylistic impact on his subsequent work. In 1945, and as part of a modernisation programme, Gustavsberg began to manufacture products in the newly available plastics. Four years later, Lindberg succeeded Kåge as the company's artistic director and,

over the next few years, he set about exploring the form-giving potential of various synthetic polymers. His resulting designs were remarkably forward-looking, such as this early citrus press from 1953. With its oval, boat-like form, it was available in either shiny red or bright yellow polystyrene, and was inexpensively priced. Several years after its launch, however, the juicer was demonstrated on a Swedish television programme where, embarrassingly, it broke because the rigid plastic was not resilient enough to withstand too much pressure. As with the other progressive plastic products brought to market during the 1950s, designers and manufacturers were frequently faced with the problem that advanced synthetic materials had not been sufficiently developed and tested for their suitability in a particular design to be a matter of certainty. Only time-consuming, painstaking and costly processes of trial-and-error would accurately gauge a medium's constructional limitations.

Gino Colombini, *KS 1481* citrus press for Kartell, 1957 – made of more durable polyethylene

Designer: **Stig Lindberg** (Swedish, 1916–1982)
Materials: polystyrene (PS)
Manufacturer: Gustavsberg, Gustavsberg, Sweden
Measurements: 10 cm high, 15 cm wide, 11.5 cm deep

KS 1146
covered pail, 1953

Gino Colombini, *KS 1068* long-handled dustpan for Kartell, 1957

Giulio Castelli – whose father had also been an important pioneer of plastic applications – founded Kartell in 1949, shortly after gaining his degree in chemical engineering. He had studied at the Politecnico di Milano under the renowned chemist Giulio Natta who went on to receive a Nobel Prize for his discovery of polypropylene in 1954, and was thus familiar with the very latest developments in plastics technologies. Kartell's first products were motoring accessories such as ski racks and luggage racks. In 1953, however, Castelli's company began to diversify its product line and started producing design-led household goods using newly available injection-moulded plastics. A notable early product was the *KS 1146* covered pail designed by Gino Colombini, which was injection moulded in polyethylene. While the notion of a plastic bucket might not appear impressive to us today, this design was seen as truly groundbreaking in the early 1950s. Not only was it using a state-of-the-art polymer, but it was also aesthetically refined and expressive of postwar stylistic departures. The design incorporated ribs that reinforced the bottom and edges of the bucket, as well as the joints connecting the metal handle. The central strengthening ridge of its cover also doubled up as a handy grip, whose obverse provided storage for a scrubbing brush and soap. Considerably lighter than traditional metal buckets, Colombini's design also had the advantage that it did not rust when placed in contact with water. In 1955, this stylish yet practical design won a Compasso d'Oro – the prestigious design award initiated only the previous year by the famous La Rinascente department store. Colombini went on to design numerous household items in plastic for Kartell, including a colander, a washing tub, a children's lunchbox, a lemon squeezer, dustpans, carpet beaters and several other types of pails. His award-winning products brought plastics to the forefront of design, and their affordability also enabled 'high design' to penetrate into the everyday domestic environment.

Designer: **Gino Colombini** (Italian, 1915–)
Materials: polyethylene (PE), metal
Manufacturer: Kartell, Noviglio, Italy
Measurements: 27.9 cm high, 26.7 cm diameter

Ericofon
telephone, 1954

Designers: **Hugo Blomberg** (Swedish, 1897–1994), **Ralph Lysell** (Swedish, 1907–1987) and **Gösta Thames** (Swedish, 1916–2006)
Materials: acrylonitrile-butadiene-styrene (ABS), polyamide (PA/nylon), rubber
Manufacturer: L.M. Ericsson, Stockholm, Sweden
Measurements: 21 cm high

A truly revolutionary design, the *Ericofon* was the first telephone to integrate earpiece, mouthpiece and dial into a single sculptural unity. In the late 1940s, the Swedish telephone company L.M. Ericsson assembled an in-house design team headed by an engineer, Gösta Thames, with the idea of creating a small, lightweight telephone that would be easier to use than existing models. After working on a number of prototypes, and filing a patent in 1947 for a streamlined single-piece phone, the design team eventually came up with the *Ericofon*'s distinctive, cobra-shaped form. The design of the *Ericofon* incorporated a new lightweight material – shiny ABS plastic – and also benefited from the increasing miniaturisation of technology. Production commenced in 1954. Initially, however, the telephone was marketed for institutional use only. In fact, it seemed to be 'just what the doctor ordered', selling especially well to hospitals, as it was easy for bed-confined patients to use. Two years later, though, the sculptural phone, offered in an array of attractive colours, began to be produced for domestic markets in Europe and Australia, where it became an instant success. The first production models employed a two-piece moulded plastic shell. Around 1960, however, Ericsson made some minor design modifications which, in conjunction with a new manufacturing technique, allowed the casing to be produced as a single moulding. About the same time, the phone also began to be marketed in America, where demand soon exceeded manufacturing capacity by an astonishing 500%. Eventually, production for the US market was transferred to the North Electric Company, which advertised the Ericofon with the by-line: 'Elegance... for eloquence.' Around 1967, a new version with a touch-tone dial was introduced; and, in 1976, Carl-Arne Breger designed the more angular *Ericofon 700* to commemorate Ericsson's centenary.

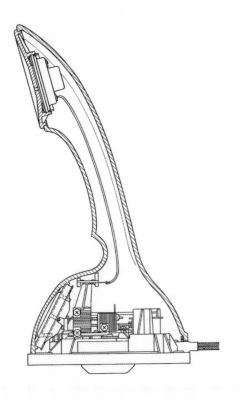

Engineering drawing for the *Ericofon* telephone showing internal layout, c.1954

Wonderlier®
storage containers, c.1954

Designer: **Earl Silas Tupper** (American, 1907–1983)
Materials: polyethylene (PE)
Manufacturer: Tupper Corporation, Leominster (MA), USA
Measurements: 23 cm, 21 cm, 18.5 cm, 17 cm, 14.5 cm diameters

Tupperware Home Party in
Sarasota, Florida, 1958

Earl Silas Tupper inherited his love of invention from his father, who used to construct labour-saving devices on the family farm in Berlin, New Hampshire. In 1936, Tupper met Bernard Doyle, the inventor of a plastic known as Viscoloid – an encounter that influenced his subsequent decision to take a job in the plastics manufacturing division of DuPont. Although only staying on for a year, Tupper would later recall that it was there that 'my education really began'. In 1938, he established his own plastics manufacturing company in Leominster, Massachusetts. The company initially undertook subcontracted work for DuPont, but soon won its own contracts for military products such as gas masks and signalling lamps. During the immediate post-war years, Tupper turned his attention to the design of plastic consumer products – for instance, sandwich picks, bathroom tumblers and cigarette cases – which firms could give away to their customers as promotional sales tools. All the same, plastics in the 1940s still had numerous unpleasant properties, ranging from brittleness and odour to greasiness. To overcome these problems, Tupper developed a technique for purifying black polyethylene slag – a by-product of the oil industry – into a strong, flexible, translucent, non-porous material known as Poly-T® which, moreover, was odourless and non-greasy. At around this time, he also patented his famous airtight and watertight Tupper seal, the design of which was based on the lids used for paint tins. Combining these two innovations, Tupper created a range of airtight plastic containers, only to find that the product line 'fell flat on its face' in stores. His breakthrough was the realisation that his 'burp sealing' system had to be demonstrated before consumers would buy into it. In the late 1940s, the hand tool company, Stanley Works, was successfully selling its household products through a network of local distributors who arranged home demonstration parties. Tupper met with several of these distributors in 1948, including Brownie Wise, who argued that

Tupper's range of food storage containers should only be sold through such demonstrations. Between 1951 and 1958, Wise occupied the position of vice-president of the company – by then known as Tupperware Home Parties. As a skilful saleswoman and motivator, Wise understood the importance of her party hostesses, declaring: 'If we build the people, they'll build the business'. With her large sales force, she transformed the company's fortunes, and Tupperware parties became as famous as Tupperware products. During this period, attractive pastel colours were introduced to make Tupperware even more appealing to home-makers. This is exemplified by the *Wonderlier*® storage bowls shown here, which were advertised with the memorable caption: 'Best thing that's happened to women since they got the vote!' Tupperware containers rapidly became such ubiquitous items in homes across Europe and America that they not only generated a widespread acceptance of plastics in the domestic environment, but came to epitomise the usefulness of synthetic materials in modern everyday life.

Margrethe
mixing bowls, 1954

Rosti Plastic A/S factory in Roskilde, Denmark, 1971 – showing the hand finishing of designs made from Mepal melamine

The second son of King Gustav VI Adolf of Sweden, Count Sigvard Bernadotte was one of the greatest proponents of industrial design in Scandinavia during the postwar period. The seeds of his lifelong dedication to the creation and promotion of good design were sown on a trip to New York in 1950, where he visited the offices of various industrial design consultants and became convinced that, 'Industrial design must be something for Scandinavia and me. Of course, I had worked in all fields of applied and decorative arts, and it seemed that to work for industry, even heavy industry, was an extension of my work so far. To help industry in designing all manner of things used in everyday life, from the smallest to the largest, must be an undertaking that logically fitted well with everything I had been doing.' The year before this formative experience, Bernadotte had met the Danish architect, Acton Bjørn. Together, in 1950, they established a design consultancy that subsequently became the foremost purveyor of Scandinavian modernism. This influential office designed numerous innovative products, many of which incorporated plastics. The *Margrethe* mixing bowls – for which the brief was to design the 'ideal mixing bowl' for those with limited financial means – is, however, the consultancy's best-known product. One of those working in Bernadotte & Bjørn's design team was the young but highly talented Jacob Jensen, who later recalled how the client had quietly and politely accepted their models of the bowls with the words, 'Thank you very much, it looks fine', little realising that they would soon be seen everywhere. The primary reason for the long-standing popularity of these nesting bowls has been their unbelievable durability and functional practicality. Featuring integrated handholds and pouring spouts, they were, with the exception of their non-slip rubber bases, manufactured in melamine-formaldehyde (usually shortened to melamine) – a hard and resilient thermo-setting plastic first synthesised by the German chemist, Justus von Liebig, in 1834. The heyday of melamine came during the 1950s and early 1960s, when it was mainly used to produce fashionable and virtually unbreakable tableware and cookware in bright colours. In fact, the Danish manufacturer, Rosti, was one of the acknowledged leaders in this field of plastic household goods, and produced many stylish designs in their Mepal-Melamine range, from salad servers and eggcups to mixing spoons and jugs. It was, however, the *Margrethe* bowls, named after Bernadotte's niece, Princess Margrethe (now the sovereign of Denmark) that would have the greatest commercial longevity, remaining in continuous production for over fifty years. As Jacob Jensen notes: 'As a plastic bowl it is still unsurpassed. Perhaps we were lucky, but I think nevertheless that its prolonged success is more due to our seriously respecting the fundamental demands which good design must always fulfill.'

Design Group: **Bernadotte & Bjørn** (Sweden/Denmark, est. 1950)
Materials: melamine-formaldehyde (MF), rubber
Manufacturer: Rosti Housewares, Ebeltoft, Denmark
Measurements: 1.5-litre, 2-litre, 3-litre and 4-litre capacity

Designer: **Yki Nummi** (Finnish, 1925–1984)
Materials: polymethyl methacrylate (PMMA)
Manufacturer: Stockmann-Orno, Kerava, Finland;
reissued by Adelta, Dinslaken, Germany
Measurements: 40 cm high

A highly versatile and talented designer, Yki Nummi's work exemplified the innovative nature of Finnish design during the 1950s and 1960s – the so-called Golden Age of Scandinavian design. He initially studied mathematics and physics, before opting to train as a designer at the Taideteollinen Korkeakoulu, Helsinki's university of art and design. After graduating, he worked as a designer for Stockmann-Orno (the manufacturing arm of the famous Helsinki department store) from 1950 to 1975, creating elegant lighting designs notable for their early use of polymethyl methacrylate (acrylic) plastics. His best-known design, the *Modern Art* table light incorporated a section of clear acrylic tubing that functioned as a transparent support for a translucent, milky-white acrylic diffuser. Startlingly progressive for its day, this structurally simple yet aesthetically refined design was selected for the Museum of Modern Art's permanent collection, an honour celebrated in its name. Five years later, Stockmann-Orno's lighting factory produced the *Sky-Flyer* – another sculptural and forward-looking lighting design by Nummi, similarly simple in construction but this time comprising two disc-like diffusers made of moulded white opaque acrylic. Available in two sizes, it was also known as the *Lokki*, meaning 'seagull' in Finnish; and when a number of these lights were hung clustered together they did, indeed, resemble a flock of sea birds riding a breeze. Aside from lighting designs, Nummi also specialised in devising colour schemes for public buildings, most notably Helsinki Cathedral, and also for various localities such as Nokia and Karkkila. As a virtuoso colourist, he headed the design and planning department of the Tikkurila paint factory in Finland from 1958 to 1975, where he helped to develop a paint mixing system. Known as the *Joker* colour chart, it was intended to facilitate and simplify the selection of colours. Nonetheless, it was Nummi's innovative acrylic lighting designs that brought him most recognition, including two gold medals at the Milan Triennale exhibitions in 1954 and 1957, as well as a Pro Finlandia medal in 1971.

Yki Nummi, *Sky-Flyer* hanging lights for Stockmann-Orno, 1960

Table light
1957

This unusual light, designed by Ettore Sottsass in the late 1950s, can be seen as an important antecedent of the Italian Radical Design Movement of the 1960s, and ultimately as a precursor of Post-Modernism in the 1980s. Its sculptural yet functional form was influenced by Sottsass's interest in Constructivist sculpture, as well as his life-long exploration into innovative materials applications. Like other products by Sottsass, this lighting design has a strong totemic presence, evoked by its bold sculptural and elemental simplicity. It is made from just two moulded PMMA shades (one white, the other yellow) held together by four enamelled metal rods, which themselves terminate in eight colourless acrylic feet. In July 1957, this light was featured alongside other functionally innovative and aesthetically progressive lights designed by Sottsass and produced by Arredoluce, in Italy's most influential design magazine, *Domus*. Among them, there was also a hanging model, which incorporated four coloured shades exactly the same as those used for the table light. These simple, moulded acrylic elements, with their gently swelling forms, diffused the light to produce a soft, warm radiance, while at the same time concealing its source. The table light could also be inverted to produce an alternative lighting effect, and the light emitted through its translucent diffusers caused its acrylic feet to glow. Sottsass's early use of plastics for lighting design prefigured the intense experimentation with polymers that occurred in the Italian lighting industry during the 1960s, and which in turn spawned a plethora of eccentric, Space Age designs, fully exploiting the astonishing optical qualities offered by modern plastics.

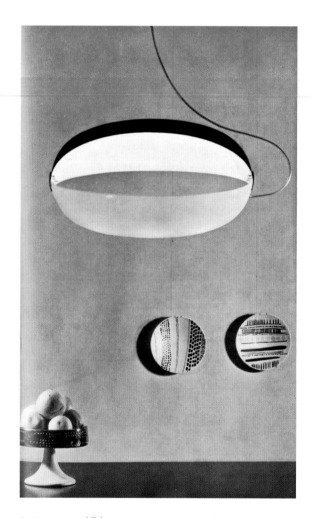

Contemporary publicity photograph showing hanging light designed by Ettore Sottsass for Arredoluce, c.1958 – also incorporating acrylic diffusers

Designer: **Ettore Sottsass** (Austrian/Italian, 1917–2007)
Materials: polymethyl methacrylate (PMMA), enamelled metal
Manufacturer: Arredoluce, Monza, Italy
Measurements: 35 cm high

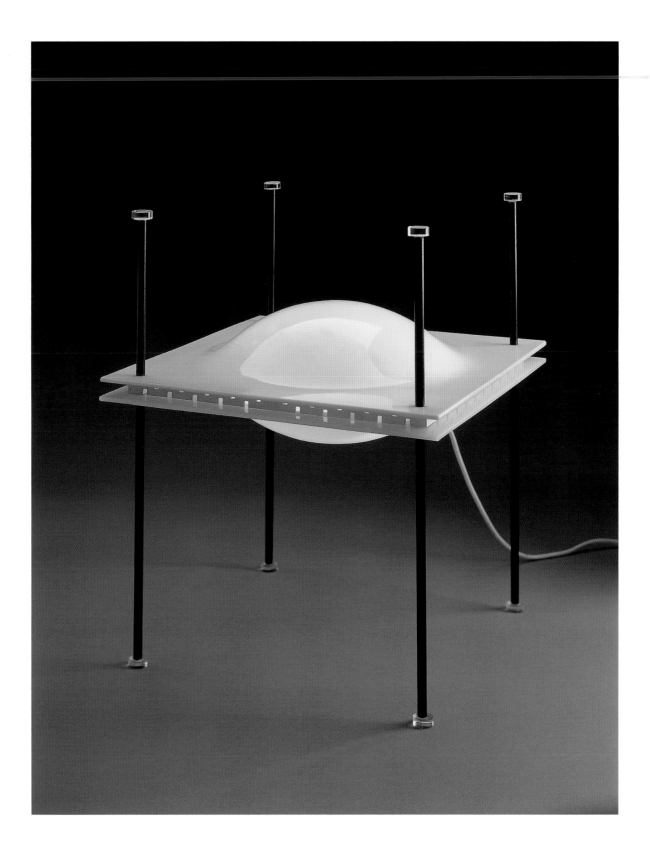

Lily chair
(Invisible Group), 1957

Designers: **Erwine Laverne** (American, 1909–2003) and
Estelle Laverne (American, 1915–1997)
Materials: polymethyl methacrylate (PMMA)
Manufacturer: Laverne Originals, New York (NY), USA
Measurements: 91.5 cm high, 75.5 cm wide, 84 cm deepa

Erwine and Estelle Laverne,
Champagne chair for Laverne
Originals, 1957

American husband-and-wife design team Erwine and
Estelle Laverne may not be as well remembered as
Charles and Ray Eames, but their furniture designs
were every bit as innovative. Like Ray Eames, they
both studied painting under Hans Hoffman (1880–
1966) at the Art Students League in New York. They
subsequently established their own design company,
Laverne Originals, which promoted a modern yet
artistic look for the home. Their New York showroom
was a sparsely furnished, gallery-style space
delineated with walls, half-walls and hidden spaces,
which a nine-page article in *Interiors* magazine
described as: 'extravagantly unfilled', 'a piece of
sculpture', and 'too pure to support any mundane
transactions like selling'. This sense of uncluttered
space was further enhanced by the introduction of
their *Invisible Group* of sculptural, transparent acrylic
chairs in 1957. Comprising the *Lily, Buttercup, Jonquil*
and *Daffodil* chairs, this range was remarkably organic
in form, and had a spatial lightness that predicted the
more art-based furniture designs of the following
decade. The *New York Times* journalist, Rita Reif,
profiled 'The Invisibles' in a 1958 article: 'I knew
immediately what it was, how innovative: it was the
first time we saw full-fledged modern design in acrylic.
Helena Rubenstein had clear plastic furniture in the
30s, but it was more traditional. This was so light and
airy. Dreamlike. And so amusing. Really the most
important thing they ever did.' The couple also
designed other chairs that were noteworthy both for
their form and for their use of synthetic polymers: the
Champagne (1957) with its elegant pedestal base and
transparent, acrylic seat shell; the *Lotus* (1958) with
its cut-away fibreglass seat shell; and the free-form
Tulip (c.1960) with its high-backed moulded fibreglass
seat shell. It was with the *Invisible Group*, however,
that the Lavernes came closest to realising the utopian
Modernist dream of structural de-materialism –
a chair that appears to support its user on nothing
but a column of air.

Laverne Originals advertisement
for 'The Invisible Chair', 1960 –
featuring the *Lily* chair

Kannan
watering can, 1957–1958

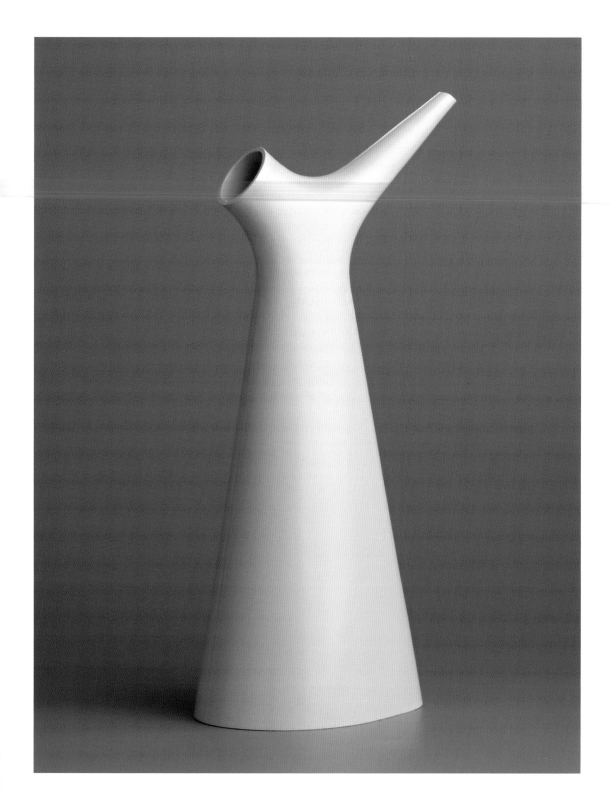

Designer: **Carl-Arne Breger** (Swedish, 1923–2009)
Materials: polystyrene (PS)
Manufacturer: Gustavsberg, Gustavsberg, Sweden
Measurements: 34 cm high, 13.5 cm wide, 11 cm deep

Carl-Arne Breger's most celebrated design is his sculptural *Kannan* watering can of 1957–1958. Unlike traditional models, this slender design was given an innovative form conceived to fit comfortably in the hand while also being easy to fill and pour. Breger's inspiration for the product reputedly came from a vodka bottle that his mother used to stand 'in the old-fashioned way' behind her curtains. Certainly the resulting design, which was intended for the watering of indoor plants, had the advantage of being small enough to be hidden behind drapes or stored easily in a cupboard. As a result of technical difficulties, it took a total of eighteen months and seven different prototypes to arrive at a satisfactory final design. In 1959, it was launched by Gustavsberg as a cutting-edge household product, and was produced in red, black and grey. Although relatively inexpensive at the time, the design is now a much sought-after collector's item thanks to the enduring appeal of its organic form – a form that represents the translation into synthetic polymer of the pioneering organic forms found in Gustavsberg's ceramics from the 1950s. Made of compression-moulded polystyrene, the *Kannan* helped forge Breger's considerable reputation as an industrial designer. In fact, he was to become widely known in Scandinavia as 'Mr Plastic'. This fun and stylish design also became one of the most publicised products of the period, exemplifying the new sculptural direction of 'Swedish Form'. Unfortunately, however, Gustavsberg was forced to suspend production after only a year, when the glue used to join the two plastic mouldings was found to emit toxic fumes. The *Kannan* watering can was Breger's last design as an in-house employee of the company, and he subsequently headed the Stockholm office of the leading Scandinavian industrial design consultancy, Bernadotte & Bjørn, from 1957 to 1958. In 1959, he founded his own office, Breger Design, and continued to develop household objects, such as the *Diavox* telephone (1975) for L.M. Ericsson, notable equally for their functional innovation and alluringly sleek aesthetic. The year Breger's seminal *Kannan* was launched, another similarly progressive Swedish designer, Knut Brinck, registered a design for a larger watering can. This less familiar design made of compression-moulded polyethylene still remains noteworthy because of its engaging fluid form, which allows water to be poured with ease. It is interesting to note that, in Sweden, a designer is referred to as a 'form giver', and certainly both Breger and Brinck produced forms that were both rational and beautiful, even if they were intended for that most mundane of household objects: the humble watering can.

Knut Brinck, Watering can, 1959

LEGO bricks
1958

You never know what's going to come out of a box of LEGO.®...

It could be an aeroplane. Or a windmill. Or the latest thing in space travel. You'll find there's a lot more to LEGO than a collection of brightly coloured building bricks. Every time a little boy (or girl) puts two LEGO bricks together, he's started building something. Something that's all his own work. He can make any shape he likes, play with it, take it to pieces and start again. Every time he builds, he's learning.

As he grows up, he won't grow out of LEGO. It lasts for years, growing into a collection. You can start him building LEGO with Duplo. Large LEGO bricks for small children. When he's three give him this big basic set. It costs less than £4. He can go on collecting until he's nine, when he'll be building bigger models that run on gears and motors. Already every second family in

this country is collecting LEGO. They'll tell you it's cheap at the price. And that you never know what will come out next from a box of LEGO.

LEGO System

9

British advertisement for LEGO
System bricks, 1972

In 1932, a young Danish carpenter, Ole Kirk Christiansen, established his own workshop and began making wooden toys. Two years later, he came up with a name for both his toys and the workshop: LEGO, a contraction of the Danish words *leg godt*, meaning 'play well'. The company grew, and in 1940 it began to manufacture toys in plastic. During the Second World War, research was accelerated into new materials and injection-moulding technologies, and in 1947 LEGO became the first Danish company to invest in plastic injection-moulding machinery, which enabled high-volume mass production. Two years later, LEGO launched its interlocking *Automatic Binding Bricks*, which were based largely on earlier toy bricks produced by the British company, Kiddicraft. These first LEGO bricks were moulded in cellulose acetate, and like traditional wood bricks they could be stacked one on top of the other. However, these plastic bricks also had the added feature of rounded studs on their tops and matching hollows beneath, which allowed them to be snapped together. In 1958, a new and improved LEGO brick was developed and patented by Godtfred Kirk Christiansen, the founder's eldest son,

which featured the distinctive 'stud-and-tube' brick-coupling system. This innovative means of connecting bricks offered greater stability in assembling them, and opened up a world of virtually unlimited constructional possibilities. Over the succeeding years, this universal toy-building system was expanded to include roof tiles (1958), wheels (1961), the LEGO family (1974), mini figures (1978) and a host of other pieces. Since 1963, LEGO has been produced in injection-moulded ABS, which is an ideal material thanks to its good strength-to-weight ratio, impressive resilience and smooth, glossy surface finish. Today, LEGO's engineers use state-of-the-art CAD-CAM software to model new pieces, which enables them to optimise the flow of plastic in the moulding process, and to analyse stress tolerances before committing a new design to mass production. Twice named 'Toy of the Century', the LEGO brick has been in continuous production for over fifty years, during which time it has facilitated countless hours of creative play, while also giving millions of children their first, formative encounter with synthetic polymers.

Designer: **Godtfred Kirk Christiansen** (Danish, 1920–1995)
Materials: cellulose acetate (CA)/1963 to present: acrylonitrile-butadiene-styrene (ABS)
Manufacturer: LEGO, Billund, Denmark
Measurements: Various

Container for liquids
1958

The Italian architect and designer, Roberto Menghi, studied at the Politecnico di Milano, graduating in 1944. He then served briefly as a lieutenant in the Italian infantry, before being interned in a forced labour camp in Czestochowa, Poland, for his refusal to join Benito Mussolini's Repubblica Sociale Italiana. After the end of the Second World War, Menghi returned to Milan and opened a studio there in 1946. He went on to collaborate on architectural projects in 1950 with Marco Zanuso, and in 1953 with Anna Castelli-Ferrieri and Ignazio Gardella. Apart from his architectural commissions and exhibition design work, he was also highly active as an industrial designer and produced designs for a wide range of products including, glassware, car roof racks, radio receivers, furniture and lighting. As a very much materials-led designer, Menghi won much recognition for his product designs in plastic, several of which were manufactured by Kartell, including a polyethylene bucket that was awarded a Compasso d'Oro in 1956. It was, however, his range of stylish containers for transporting liquids, designed for the Milanese tyre manufacturer Pirelli, that stand as his most accomplished designs in plastic. Made of shimmering, silvery-green polyethylene, these jerry cans were designed by Menghi with the assistance of the technicians at Pirelli, who already possessed considerable experience in moulding plastics. The containers, with their integrated handles, were produced in four different sizes – five, ten, fifteen and twenty litres – and were designed to carry not only gasoline, but also acids and other reagent liquids. Their perfect fusion of form and function gave these designs, according to one contemporary commentator, 'a line of natural elegance', and certainly no jerry can before or since has managed to achieve such a level of useful beauty. Above all else, it epitomises the belief in Italy during the 1950s that plastics were the materials of the future, and that architects and designers were duty-bound to apply their talents to the design of everything 'from the city to the spoon'. It would seem that no object was deemed too mundane for the careful consideration of this talented Milanese generation of industrial designers. Menghi demonstrated with his containers that by adopting a thoughtful and rational approach to the design process, and by harnessing the potential of new materials and technologies, real improvements could be made to the objects of everyday life.

Pirelli publicity photograph,
c.1959

Designer: **Roberto Menghi** (Italian, 1920–2006)
Materials: polyethylene (PE)
Manufacturer: Pirelli, Milan, Italy
Measurements: 38.1 cm high, 27.9 cm wide, 12.7 cm deep

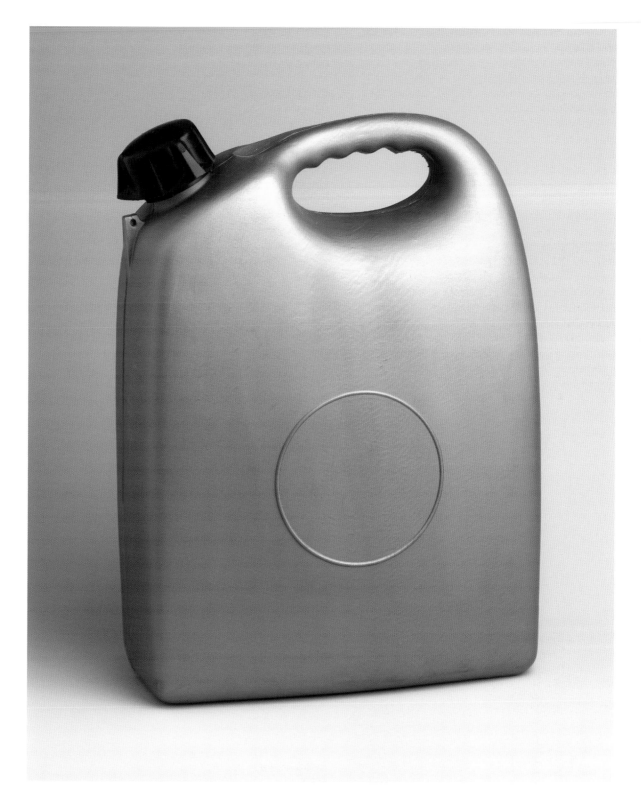

KS 1476
carpet beater, 1959

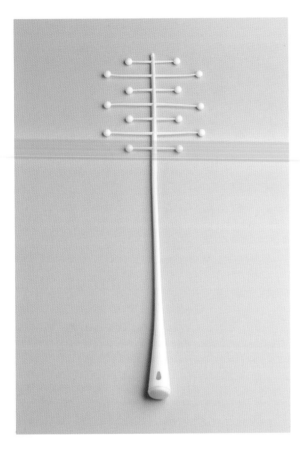

Gino Colombini, *KS 1475* carpet
beater for Kartell, 1957

Between 1953 and 1962, Gino Colombini designed numerous award-winning household products for Kartell, made of newly available injection-moulded plastics. In 1957, he designed his first carpet beater, the *KS 1475*, using steel-reinforced polyethylene. Although it received a Compasso d'Oro special mention, this design, with its molecule-like branches, was not as resilient as his second carpet-beater designed two years later: the *KS 1476*. Replacing the generic bat-like carpet beater traditionally made from sturdy wicker, this revolutionary design with its diamond-shaped head demonstrated the excellent functionality and durability of well-designed plastic products. Like other homewares created by Gino Colombini for Kartell, the *KS 1476* must have seemed startlingly futuristic when it first appeared. Beyond this, though, it exploited beautifully the formal potential of plastics, demonstrating that synthetic polymers could be used to produce designs that were not only practically useful but also visually remarkable. Manufactured from 1960 to 1976, the *KS 1476* was produced in blue, yellow, red and green; and, briefly in 1970, in aquamarine, orange and pale blue. In 1963, Gino Colombini also designed another futuristic-looking plastic carpet beater, with a triangular-shaped head perforated with six holes, for the Swedish manufacturer, Husqvarna Borstfabrik. Beyond any doubt, Colombini's eye-catching, revolutionary and affordable designs helped to refashion cultural attitudes towards synthetic materials.

Designer: **Gino Colombini** (Italian, 1915–)
Materials: steel-reinforced polyethylene (PE)
Manufacturer: Kartell, Milan, Italy
Measurements: 58.5 cm long

Designer: **Verner Panton** (Danish, 1926–1998)
Materials: 1967: glass-reinforced polyester (GRP)/1968–1971: polyurethane hard foam (PU)/1971–1979: acrylonitrile-styrene-acrylate (ASA)/1990–present: polypropylene (PP) or polyurethane hard foam (PU)
Manufacturer: Vitra, Weil am Rhein, Germany
Measurements: 83 cm high, 50 cm wide, 61 cm deep

The *Panton* chair was the first ever single-material, single-piece injection-moulded chair. For this reason, it is one of the most important chairs of all time. The origins of its design can be traced back to an earlier, single-form cantilevered moulded plywood chair that Verner Panton designed in 1956. As plastics became more available during the late 1950s, Panton, like many other designers of his generation, saw that the inherent malleability and resilience of these new materials offered undreamt of functional and aesthetic potentialities. Not least, they held out the possibility of developing a one-piece chair that could be mass produced on a hitherto unimaginable scale. Between 1957 and 1960, Panton produced numerous sketches of a single-form stacking chair that he intended to be injection moulded in plastic. In 1960, a Danish company, Dansk Acyrl Teknik, fabricated a prototype of the chair in vacuum-moulded Polysteron, but this thermoplastic material proved unsuitable for a full-scale production model. Panton subsequently showed the prototype chair to a number of European manufacturers, but the prohibitive development costs involved in taking it from prototype to industrial production meant that he was met with rejection time and again. Eventually, in 1963, Panton contacted a Basel-based furniture manufacturer, Willi Fehlbaum, the founder of Vitra, who immediately spotted the chair's potential and, judging that it was worth the risk, underwrote its development. In the years that followed, Vitra's own technical experts worked alongside Panton to further hone the design, making its form more sinuous, sculptural and to a limited extent, stackable. They also created ten more prototypes, made this time in cold-pressed, glass-reinforced polyester. In 1967, an initial limited edition of approximately 100–150 units of the chair was produced in this material, and the following year the *Panton* chair was officially launched at the Cologne Furniture Fair to immediate and widespread acclaim. Between 1968 and 1971, it was manufactured in moulded Baydur – a hard and inflexible polyurethane foam, which made the chair rather heavy and not particularly comfortable. Later in 1971, however, the chair underwent a slight design modification, adding strengthening ribs under its seat, which enabled it to be injection moulded in Luran S – a styrene acrylonitrile copolymer, or ASA, synthesised by the BASF Corporation – which proved to be the ideal material for its mass production. In fact, this change of polymer heralded the advent of the one-shot plastic chair, ultimately leading to the cheap and ubiquitous plastic monobloc garden chairs that are now produced on a mind-boggling scale all around the world.

Model No. 4999
stacking child's chair, 1960

Kartell publicity photograph showing the way the *Model No. 4999* chair could be used to make children's forts, c.1964

Designed by Marco Zanuso and Richard Sapper, the *Model No. 4999* was the first chair in the world to be made entirely of injection-moulded plastic. The important precedent it set within seating design was acknowledged through the award of a Compasso d'Oro in 1964. Initially, this stacking child's chair was moulded in high-density polyethylene – a resilient thermoplastic with a good strength-to-weight ratio and excellent chemical resistance. It was still relatively difficult to injection mould larger items during the 1960s, and for this reason the chair's ribbed seating section was fabricated separately from its four cylindrical legs, which then slotted into the seat. The designers conceived the chair almost as a lightweight building block, so that a number of chairs could be stacked one on top of the other, or reappropriated by children to construct forts or dens. Produced in either gleaming red, yellow, blue or white plastic, the *Model No. 4999* chair was a radical departure from existing children's seating, typically little more than miniaturised versions of adult-sized chairs. By contrast, Zanuso and Sapper's innovative design was a colourful plaything that invited interaction and imaginative exploration. Weighing just 2.24 kg, the *Model No. 4999* chair could also be scrubbed clean, and its inherent water resistance made it ideal for outdoor use. As a Kartell advertisement emblazoned with child's writing noted, it is 'a beautiful chair that is good for us'. An accomplished, child-centred product, it chimed with Sapper's humanistic design agenda, marked by his desire to make emotional connections and to 'give form meaning'. Its pioneering use of plastics, which shifted from polyethylene to polypropylene in 1975, was consistent with Zanuso's lifelong creativity with materials, and his extraordinary skill in forming them into stylish and groundbreaking objects that were functionally innovative and aesthetically refined.

Designers: **Marco Zanuso** (Italian, 1916–2001) and
Richard Sapper (German, 1932–)
Materials: from 1964: high-density polyethylene (HDPE)/from
1975: polypropylene (PP)
Manufacturer: Kartell, Noviglio, Italy
Measurements: 49 cm high, 28 cm wide, 28 cm deep

Taraxacum
hanging light, 1960

Designers: **Achille Castiglioni** (Italian, 1918–2002) and
Pier Giacomo Castiglioni (Italian, 1913–1968)
Materials: Cocoon/spray-on polyvinyl chloride solution (PVC),
metal wire
Manufacturer: Flos, Bovezzo, Brescia, Italy
Measurements: 60 cm diameter

During the postwar years a new kind of self-skinning, spray-on plastic known as Cocoon was developed in the United States for the mothballing of naval vessels and aircraft. This remarkable plastic webbing polymer was quite literally used to wrap up entire ships and planes in a waterproof, protective skin, defending them from damage and corrosion; yet it could be stripped off in a matter of hours if they were required for further use. For the mothballing of military hardware, around three layers of this gossamer-like polyvinyl chloride compound (administered with a hand-held spray gun) would produce a thin but tough, flexible and joint-less membrane. Unsurprisingly, Cocoon also found applications in the world of design: most notably in the *Bubble* lamps designed in 1952 by George Nelson. It was in Italy, however, that the material was perhaps best exploited in terms of its formal potential. An entrepreneur, Arturo Eisenkeil imported this new wonder material into Italy during the 1950s, and immediately began searching for commercial applications. In 1959, along with Dino Gavina and Cesare Cassina, he founded a company named Flos to produce light fixtures using this

material. This, in turn, led to the Castiglioni brothers designing their landmark series of Cocoon lights for the company, which included the *Taraxacum*, the *Viscontea* (1966) and the *Gatto* (1962). The Castiglionis' self-skinning Cocoon lights were not only some of the first European lighting products to use this state-of-the-art material, but they also helped to establish Flos as a truly innovative lighting company. While the shape of Nelson's earlier lights had been fundamentally determined by their underlying wire structure, these designs possessed freer forms because the plastic webbing was only supported at a few strategic points by their metal frames. The lights' unusual and evocative forms owed to their designers' trial-and-error system of experimentation with the spray gun in the laboratories of Eisenkeil's Merano-based company. The resulting forms of this revolutionary group of lighting designs are reminiscent of seedpods, while the lights' textural surfaces are suggestive of the protective, silky envelopes secreted by insects, from which this remarkable polymer takes its name.

Achille and Pier Giacomo
Castiglioni, Hanging light for
Flos, c.1960 – this design was also
made from self-skinning Cocoon

Polypropylene
side chair, 1960–1963

Designer: **Robin Day** (British, 1915–)
Materials: polypropylene (PP), enamelled tubular metal, rubber
Manufacturer: Hille, London, UK
Measurements: 75 cm high, 53.4 cm wide, 51.5 cm deep

The British designer, Robin Day, came to prominence when he won first prize at the International Competition for Low-Cost Furniture Design held by the Museum of Modern Art, New York, in 1948. This international success brought Day to the attention of Hille, an established British furniture manufacturer that was keen to modernise its product line. Hille subsequently commissioned him to design simple, pared-down furniture within the Modern idiom for the 1949 'British Industry Fair', and the following year he became the firm's chief designer. In 1960, Day was asked to judge a design competition sponsored by Shell, a company that, two years before, had acquired the licence to manufacture polypropylene, a new type of thermoplastic invented in 1954 by Giulio Natta. Having seen the success of the *Plastic Shell Group* chairs (1948–1950), by Charles and Ray Eames, Day decided to use this new plastic material for his own seating system, similarly conceptualised as a standardised plastic seat shell that could be used with different bases. Made of injection-moulded poly-propylene, the resulting *Polypropylene* chair, with its universal seat shell, was developed between 1960 and 1963. In a press release, Day asserted that it answered 'the need for a multi-purpose side chair at a very low cost', continuing that its form evolved from 'considera-tions of posture and anatomy'. Also referred to as the

Polychair, it was one of the first seating designs that fully exploited the high-volume manufacturing potential of thermoplastics and, as such, it was far more commercially successful than the *Plastic Shell Group* chairs, because it could be produced at a fraction of the unit cost. Strong and durable, poly-propylene had the added benefit of being a resilient yet malleable polymer, which meant that Day's seat shells had a degree of flexibility, ensuring comfort without the need for upholstery. Developed as a system with two standard seat shells – the side chair shown here, and an armchair launched in 1967 – and a variety of interchangeable bases, the *Polychair* had numerous possible applications, including airport and stadium seating. In the years that followed, Day also designed other seat shells for the *Polychair* range, notably the *E-Series* (1972) for school children, and the *Polo* (1973) for outdoor use. In Britain, virtually every school, hospital and church hall has, at some stage, been furnished with the tough, light and stackable *Polychair*, and Hille has exported this landmark utilitarian design around the globe. Since its debut in 1963, over 14 million *Polychairs* have been sold worldwide, and Hille still produces 500,000 annually – demonstrating the continuing demand for reasonably priced, durable, practical and multi-functional plastic chairs.

Hille's 'World-Wide Chair Programme' of *Polypropylene* chairs, 1960s

Acrilica
table light, 1962–1963

In 1962, Joe Colombo designed interiors and fittings for a remote Sardinian hotel, including ceiling fixtures made of acrylic prisms for its lobby. These early Perspex lights hung down like futuristic stalactites from the wooden panelling and diffracted the light in an interesting manner, with the edges of the polymer blocks glowing brighter than the rest – an optical phenomenon known as 'live edge'. The fixtures' methacrylate also diffused the light to produce a pleasant, indirect glow. With his brother Gianni, Colombo eventually evolved this idea into the design of the *Acrilica* table light, manufactured by OLuce. Awarded a gold medal at the XIII Milan Triennale in 1964, this elegant design can be seen as the culmination of Colombo's studies into the thermoplastic and optical properties of PMMA. Easily moulded using heat and pressure, the acrylic was formed into a C-shaped curve that eloquently revealed the material's extraordinary ability to carry light even round bends. A naturally transparent and colourless polymer with a high transmission level for visible light, the substance known as PMMA, polymethyl methacrylate or acrylic glass is sold under numerous trade names, including: Plexiglas, Lucite, Acrylex and Perspex. Although discovered by the German chemists Fittig and Paul as early as 1877, this remarkable plastic material did not go into viable commercial production until 1936. During the ensuing decades it was favoured mainly for its decorative potential, especially in the manufacture of costume jewellery and glitzy Lucite handbags. It was, however, the early 1960s that really saw the expressive potential of PMMA being fully exploited, and Joe Colombo's landmark design visually articulated the optimistic *zeitgeist* of the period through its glowing, futuristic presence.

Designer: **Joe Colombo** (Italian, 1930–1971)
Materials: polymethyl methacrylate (PMMA), lacquered metal
Manufacturer: OLuce, San Guiliano, Italy
Measurements: 23.5 cm high, 24 cm wide, 23 cm deep

Heller Compact
Stacking Dinnerware
1964

This well-known melamine dinnerware range was initially named *Max 1*, and was manufactured by Articoli Plastici Eletrici in Cologno Monzese, Italy. It was, according to Massimo Vignelli, 'designed to be stackable in a compact way... and won our first Compasso d'Oro for good design in 1964'. It was originally manufactured in bright yellow melamine resin. However, when Heller licensed its production in the United States, a rainbow of bright, mix-and-match colours was introduced, which was undoubtedly responsible for its ensuing popularity. The virtually unbreakable *Heller Compact Stacking Dinnerware* range initially comprised two covered bowls, two lipped plates, a square tray and a rectangular tray, which all stacked together perfectly. Inexpensive to manufacture and highly durable, this practical dinnerware was perfect for everyday use, as well as for casual indoor or outdoor entertaining. In 1970, matching stacking cups and saucers were introduced, with the former featuring handles that were, 'conceived as a projection of the cup's walls'. Two years later, elegant stacking mugs with the same D-shaped handles were also launched, joined in 1978 by a pitcher that was ready to pour when its lid was correctly aligned to the handle. In perfect harmony with the prevailing taste for brightly coloured polymers and bold geometric forms, *Hellerware* (as it became widely known) was *the* plastic dinnerware service of the 1970s, and remains in production to this day – a testament to the enduring appeal of its essentialist design. As Massimo Vignelli puts it: 'I like design to be semantically correct, syntactically consistent, and pragmatically understandable. I like it to be visually powerful, intellectually elegant, and above all timeless.' The Vignellis' classic designs for Heller give form to these sentiments, proving in the process that, while plastic dinnerware might be cheap and practical, it can also be incredibly stylish.

Heller Compact Stacking Dinnerware stacking mugs, 1972

Heller Compact Stacking Dinnerware plates and bowl, 1964

Designer: **Massimo Vignelli** (Italian, 1931–) and **Lella Vignelli**
(Italian 1934–)
Materials: melamine formaldehyde (MF)
Manufacturer: Heller, New York (NY), USA
Measurements: various

Heller Compact Stacking
Dinnerware covered bowl, 1964

Designer: **Helmut Bätzner** (German, 1928–)
Materials: glass-reinforced polyester (GRP)
Manufacturer: W. Bofinger, Ilsfeld, Germany
Measurements: 73 cm high, 49 cm wide, 39 cm deep

An acknowledged masterpiece of German design, the *BA 1171* chair debuted at the Cologne Furniture Fair in 1966 as the first glass-reinforced polyester chair to be moulded as a single piece. The manufacturing process behind this technical breakthrough involved placing several layers of fibreglass matting over a steel die, forming a matrix where the design needed greatest strength: the seat and back sections. Next, a layer of polyester was laid up over the die and compressed at temperatures of more than 100° Celsius and at a pressure of approximately 350 kg per square centimetre. Often referred to through the contraction 'prepreg', it is a technique known as pre-impregnation compression moulding. The steel mould used to make the *BA 1171* chair weighed more than 11,000 kg, and could produce around 200 chairs a day with a cycle time of four minutes per unit. Once the cooled chair was extracted from the mould, any excess polyester could be easily removed by scraping. As its manufacturer noted, 'There were plenty of stacking chairs jostling for the attention of the consumer, but both in technique and function the Bofinger chair was a vast improvement in GRP as a material for furniture.' This hard and stable composite plastic also ensured that Helmut Bätzner's durable stacking chair was ideal for both indoor and outdoor use. Available in a number of colours, the *BA 1171* was produced in high volumes by Bofinger-Produktion, with around 120,000 units being manufactured during the late 1960s and 1970s. Significantly, the 'Bofinger chair' can be seen as the progenitor of the myriad one-piece plastic garden chairs produced over the succeeding decades.

Series of photographs showing the manufacture of the *BA 1171* chair, c.1966

Land Camera
Swinger Model 20, 1965

One of the greatest industrial design consultants of his generation, Henry Dreyfuss was responsible for the creation of numerous landmark products, from his ubiquitous telephones for the Bell Telephone Company to his stylish vacuum cleaners for Hoover. One of his office's most important corporate clients was the Polaroid Corporation, with which it enjoyed a fruitful working relationship from 1961. The office's first design for the company was the *Automatic 100 Land Camera* of 1963, which saw the introduction of an easy-to-use film pack. That same year, Henry Dreyfuss Associates' team of designers, headed by Jim Conner, began work on developing a camera with a more structurally unified and ergonomically designed plastic casing. The team's goal was to come up with a design that was easy to operate, and that would introduce 'absolute one-step photography'. The resulting production camera, the revolutionary *Swinger Model 20*, was introduced in 1965 and set a new standard for simplicity of operation and stylish good looks. It was also the Polaroid Corporation's least expensive camera ever, retailing at a mere $19.95, and quickly became one of the fastest selling cameras ever with four million units sold within two years of its debut. With its funky black and white casing the *Swinger* was essentially a 'fun' product and was targeted at a youthful audience through a stylish advertising campaign featuring groups of hipsters enjoying themselves. The camera could be casually slung over an arm when not in use, and gave its young owners instant gratification with on-the-spot images. In fact the act of taking a Polaroid photo was an exciting event in itself, with the image slowly appearing in the slightly damp, chemical-smelling paper. The *Swinger* camera was perfectly in tune with the hedonistic, 'want-it-now' *zeitgeist* of the mid-Sixties and with its revolutionary ABS body it powerfully demonstrated that thermoplastics could improve the handling properties of a product, while also making it more visually appealing to a younger market. As far as consumer goods were concerned, they were the materials of the future.

THE SWINGER the new Polaroid Land camera that gives you a black and white picture in 15 seconds.

Polaroid advertisement for
The Swinger camera, c.1965

Designer: **Henry Dreyfuss Associates** (American, est. 1929)
Materials: acrylonitrile-butadiene-styrene (ABS)
Manufacturer: Polaroid Corporation, Concord (MA), USA
Measurements: 12.5 cm high, 15 cm wide, 13 cm deep

Dalù
table light, 1965

Designer: **Vico Magistrett**i (Italian, 1920–2006)
Materials: acrylonitrile-butadiene-styrene (ABS), metal
Manufacturer: Artemide, Pregnana Milanese, Italy
Measurements: 26 cm high

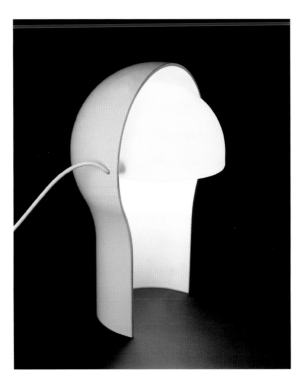

Vico Magistretti, *Telegono* table
light for Artemide, 1968

One of the central goals of Modern design has been the realisation of single-medium, single-piece constructions – the idea being that material and structural unity within a design pays dividends in manufacturing efficiency: fewer parts make for ease of assembly. Incorporating an innovatively cantilevered form and made from a single sheet of plastic, Vico Magistretti's diminutive *Dalù* light represented this Holy Grail of design. Magistretti's vision was to mould the plastic sheet into two conjoined segments of a sphere: one formed into a hood-like shade, while the other acts as a base. Originally made of ABS, the *Dalù* light's high-gloss surface emphasised its sculptural qualities and dramatic backwards swoop. This small and elegant design can be seen as the lighting equivalent of Verner Panton's groundbreaking single-form, single-material plastic *Panton* chair of 1959–1960. Originally manufactured in opaque red, orange, black and white, the *Dalù* has recently been reissued by Artemide, using PMMA to achieve an array of translucent colours. In 1968, Vico Magistretti designed another light for Artemide, the *Telegono*, which like his earlier design incorporated a self-supporting ABS body. The *Telegono*, however, did not possess the material or structural unity of the Dalù light. Instead, it had a two-piece, two-material construction with a hemispherical, eyelid-like shield made of opalescent PMMA that could be angled to regulate the amount of emitted light. Thanks to Magistretti's choice of state-of-the-art materials, both of these designs had a refreshing formal simplicity that was the very antithesis of the traditional shaded lamp.

Playplax
constructional toy, 1965–1966

Contemporary photograph showing young girl playing with various toys designed by Patrick Rylands, 1970

Whilst studying ceramics at the Royal College of Art in London, Patrick Rylands worked on a number of designs based on the concept of interlocking tiles, two of which were produced and marketed in wood by Spiel Naef of Switzerland. He also translated his ideas into a prototype constructional toy made from a sheet of acrylic, which he hand cut and slotted using a router. Over the summer holidays, while he was working at the Hornsea Pottery in his native Yorkshire, Rylands showed this early working model to the owner of Trendon, a trade moulder that made bungs for the pottery's salt pots. The firm immediately put his design into production and, branded the *Playplax* constructional toy, it proved an immediate commercial success from its launch in 1966. With its interlocking squares and tubes of coloured acrylic it expressed the almost magical optical qualities of Perspex. Beyond this, and as Rylands himself observes, *Playplax* was 'stuff' that was intended to stimulate interaction and play, and was essentially 'one unit that could build anything'. Absolutely in tune with the creative *zeitgeist* of the mid-1960s, *Playplax* invited interaction but was not prescriptive in how it should

be used. Just what was built out of the pieces of clear, red, blue, yellow and green translucent plastic was up to the child, who was also free to experiment with the colours themselves, layering the component elements to create a kaleidoscopic array of new shades. Looking like a playful Pop interpretation of a Constructivist sculpture, *Playplax* squares and tubes, with their glowing live edges, could be endlessly and imaginatively joined together into different tower-like configurations. It was quite simply *the* plastic toy for a new generation of children born into the 1960s – the Age of Plastics. In 1970, Rylands was awarded the Duke of Edinburgh's Prize for Elegant Design for his children's toys. In the opinion of the judges – who included the fashion designer Mary Quant and the industrial designers Robin Day and Robert Heritage – he had shown 'how toys can be designed to amuse, to stimulate creative talent and to educate'. They specifically commended *Playplax* for its abstract qualities that, 'encourage children to use their imagination and introduce them to ideas of structure, form, colour and balance'.

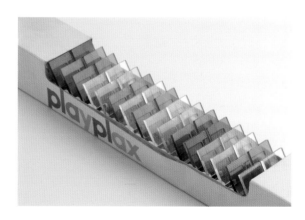

Designer: **Patrick Rylands** (British, 1942–)
Materials: polystyrene (PS)
Manufacturer: Trendon Ltd., Malton, Yorkshire, UK (later manu-
factured under licence by James Galt & Company, Cheadle, UK)
Measurements: 5 cm high, 5 cm wide, 0.3cm deep

KD29
table light, 1965

During the 1960s, Kartell produced a number of
innovative lighting designs, including several by Joe
Colombo, that employed state-of-the-art polymers
and manufacturing techniques. In the mid-1960s,
Colombo designed the *KD28* table light for the
company, which used for its base the top half of Gino
Colombini's well-known *Model No. 4610* waste-bin
(1965). Colombo then developed a variation of this
quintessential Pop lighting design, the *KD29* table
light (produced by Kartell from 1966), which
incorporated an integral ABS tray, intended for storing
items such as pens or pipes. The main structural
element of this eye-catching and futuristic design was
made of coloured Cycolac ABS, and had a chamber
running up its neck that hid the electric cabling.
Into this main body were placed the two acrylic
diffusers, one opaque white and the other transparent,
and the concealed bulb was switched on and off with
a pull cord that hung from beneath this shade section.
The light's white ABS tray, with its three hollowed
storage compartments, also slotted efficiently into the
coloured supporting structure. This highly rational yet
visually striking design essentially comprised just four
plastic mouldings, which made it relatively easy to
manufacture and assemble. Like Colombo's related
KD28 table light, the *KD29* was intended for high-
volume, low-cost production, which could only be
achieved by employing injection-moulded polymers.
Intrigued by the notion of futuristic habitats, Joe
Colombo was a visionary designer who recognised the
nobility of synthetic materials, and exploited their
functional and aesthetic potential to create highly
innovative objects with a utopian Space Age sensibility.

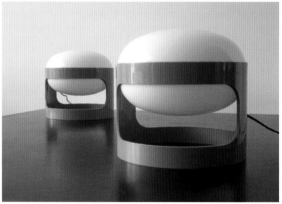

**Joe Colombo, *KD28* table light for
Kartell, 1965**

Designer: **Joe Colombo** (Italian, 1930–1971)
Materials: acrylonitrile-butadiene-styrene (ABS), polymethyl
methacrylate (PMMA)
Manufacturer: Kartell, Noviglio, Italy
Measurements: 33 cm high, 25 cm diameter

Universale, Model No. 4860
chair, 1965–1967

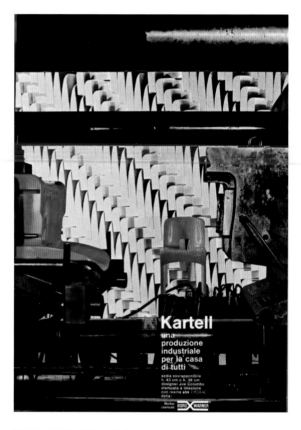

Kartell publicity photograph for
Universale chair, c.1967

The most influential Italian designer of his generation, Joe Colombo wove the future into the present with his Space Age furnishings and 'living cells' microenvironments. He also enthusiastically embraced the concept of large-scale mass production, and was captivated by the possibilities presented by new synthetic materials and advanced manufacturing technologies. Throughout his short yet highly productive career, Colombo continually experimented with different polymers and moulding techniques, resulting in the creation of several landmark product designs in plastic. Perhaps the most influential was his *Universale* chair, developed between 1965 and 1967 for the Milanese furniture company Kartell. The *Universale* was the first adult-sized, single-material plastic chair manufactured entirely in an injection-moulded thermoplastic – in this case Cycolac ABS. As with his other designs, function and materials ultimately determined the bold and sturdy form of the *Universale*, and because it was pushing the boundaries of both it took two years of painstaking development: from die-cast aluminium prototype to final production model. As its name suggests, Colombo was searching for a universal seating solution – a goal that to some extent he achieved with a seating section that could be used with three different and interchangeable leg heights, producing a bar stool, a dining chair or a low lounger. This quintessential Pop design also stacked relatively well, and the hole in its back section not only made it easy to remove from the mould but also functioned as a handhold, allowing the design to be carried effortlessly. Unfortunately, ABS proved less than the ideal material because it became brittle if the chair was left outside. Between 1971 and 1975, Bayer's Durethan nylon was adopted instead, but was to prove too expensive and insufficiently resistant to water. Since 1975, the design has been made in polypropylene, an altogether more resilient and durable polymer. Ultimately, Colombo can be seen as a true design visionary. His iconoclastic modular products were charged with his optimistic dreams of a futuristic utopia while remaining grounded in the availability of inexpensive and colourful plastics.

Designer: **Joe Colombo** (Italian, 1930–1971)
Materials: 1967–1970: acrylonitrile-butadiene-styrene (ABS)/1971–
1975: polyamide (PA – nylon)/1975–present: polypropylene (PP)
Manufacturer: Kartell, Noviglio, Italy
Measurements: 71 cm high, 42.5 cm wide, 43 cm deep

Grillo

telephone, 1965

Designers: **Marco Zanuso** (Italian, 1916–2001) and
Richard Sapper (German, 1932–)
Materials: acrylonitrile-butadiene-styrene (ABS)
Manufacturer: Società Italiana Telecomunicazioni Siemens SpA,
Milan, Italy
Measurements: 6.5 cm high, 16.5 cm wide, 7 cm deep (closed)

Società Italiana Telecomunicazioni Siemens advertisement
showing the different colour
options of the *Grillo* telephone,
1975

Awarded a Compasso d'Oro in 1967, the *Grillo* was a revolutionary telephone design that folded in on itself to create a compact sculptural form. Its name, means 'cricket' in Italian, and refers not only to its unusual springing action when picked up, but also to its curious chirping ringtone. The *Grillo* also had a rotary dial integrated into its main body – an innovative feature that was to prove highly influential for the design of subsequent telephones. The origins of this landmark product can be traced to an earlier design for a folding telephone patented by Marco Zanuso in 1963, the rights to which were held by the Società Italiana Telecomunicazioni Siemens. This design, which never made it into production, was less ergonomically refined than the later *Grillo*, and had a harder-edged aesthetic. SIT Siemens' goal was to devise a new, smaller telephone that was less cumbersome than earlier models, and which could be moved around rather than staying fixed to a wall. It was in response to this brief that Zanuso and Sapper developed the *Grillo* – a compact design with its functional elements encased in a single, shell-like body. Made feasible by the availability of new thermoplastics and the increasing miniaturisation of technology, the *Grillo* was a highly integrated design that could be held in the hand as a single unit. When at rest, the closed *Grillo* looked like a smooth pebble with its fluid lines inviting interaction, but, when opened for use, its earpiece and mouthpiece were perfectly ergonomically placed. Made of injection-moulded ABS, the *Grillo*'s casing was only one millimetre thick, yet the intrinsic resilience of this polymer made the telephone strong enough to withstand years of use. Moreover, this seminal design not only exploited the strength and tactile smoothness of this wondrous new thermoplastic, but also the fact that it could be easily dyed to produce a number of attractive colours: white, red, orange, khaki green, and mid-blue. This, of course, made the telephone still more appealing, especially to younger and more fashion-conscious consumers.

Chimera

floor light, 1966

Designer: **Vico Magistretti** (Italian, 1920–2006)
Materials: polymethyl methacrylate (PMMA), enamelled metal
Manufacturer: Artemide, Pregnana Milanese, Italy
Measurements: 180 cm high (*Mezzochimera*: 78 cm high)

Vico Magistretti, *Mezzochimera*
for Artemide, 1966

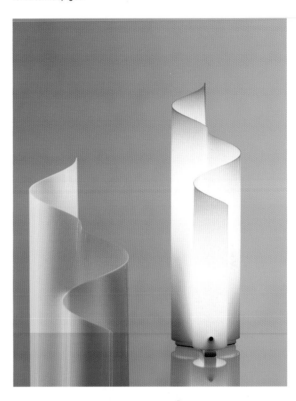

Throughout his long and prolific career, Vico Magistretti created numerous products that were both functionally and formally innovative, and which also ingeniously employed advanced polymers to achieve optimal solutions. A veritable maestro of Italian design, Magistretti's thoughtful, sensitive and stylish use of plastics helped to raise the status of materials all too often perceived by the general public as low value and disposable. Magistretti also demonstrated that plastics such as PMMA could have a poetic and sculptural quality. For instance, the innovative, wave-like form of his *Chimera* floor light not only provides the design with a self-supporting structure, but also radiates the emitted light along its rippling translucent diffuser, transforming a relatively straightforward product into a light sculpture. Among the defining characteristics of Magistretti's work is his use of strong graphic outlines that give his designs a powerful visual presence. As he admitted, 'I love geometric shapes. I love creating essential shapes that seem mere wisps.' And it was frequently the case that only plastic compounds could be moulded into the bold yet graceful forms conjured by his imagination. Artemide produced a smaller table light version of this sinuous design, known as the *Mezzachimera* (1966), which was also thermo-formed from a sheet of white opalescent polymethyl methacrylate. The undulating, single-form acrylic structures of these two products pleasantly soften and filter the emitted light, while also conferring an engaging identity. Magistretti also exploited the structural potential of serpentine shapes in moulded plastics in furniture design, most famously with his *Selene* chair (1969), *Gaudí* armchair (1970) and *Vicario* armchair (1971).

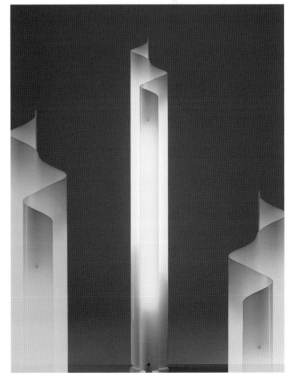

Dedalo

umbrella stand, 1966

Designer: **Emma Gismondi Schweinberger** (Italian, 1934–)
Materials: acrylonitrile-butadiene-styrene (ABS)
Manufacturer: Artemide, Pregnana Milanese, Italy
Measurements: 32 cm high, 38 cm diameter

Artemide publicity photograph,
c.1966

In 1960, the design entrepreneur Ernesto Gismondi, together with the designer Sergio Mazza, founded Artemide, a new lighting and furniture manufacturing company named after Artemis, the daughter of Zeus and Leto, the twin sister of Apollo, and the Greek goddess of hunting. Over the next decade, this Milanese firm would produce some of the most progressive objects in plastics, many of which are now widely seen as classics of modern design. The first products manufactured by Artemide were made of reinforced plastics; however, by the mid-1960s, the company was beginning to exploit the potential of ABS. One of their first designs made in this new, injection-moulded thermoplastic was the *Dedalo* umbrella stand, designed by Gismondi's talented wife, Emma Schweinberger. Its name is also derived from Greek mythology, being the Italian name for Daedalus, the Athenian craftsman and architect who, so the story goes, constructed the famous labyrinth on the island of Crete. Certainly the *Dedalo*, with its dome-shaped form and its seven holes set in a daisy-like pattern, has a distinctive, cavern-like presence. Produced in red, white or black thermoplastic, the exact form of the *Dedalo* was also repeated on a smaller scale in Schweinberger's *Dedalotto* vase (1966), and her diminutive *Dedalino* pencil-holder (1966). Emma Gismondi Schweinberger also designed lighting for Artemide, as well as other furnishings made from advanced polymers, including her well-known *Giano Vano* bedside table of 1966, which was also manufactured in injection-moulded ABS.

Sinus, Model No. 95
ashtray, 1966–1967

The Austrian designer and lecturer Walter Zeischegg initially studied at the Bundesanstalt für das Baufach und die Kunstgewerbeschule (the Federal Institute for Building and the School of Decorative Arts) in Graz, and later went on to study sculpture at the Akademie der Bildenden Künste (the Academy of Fine Arts) in Vienna. After military service during the Second World War, he resumed his training under the Austrian sculptor, Fritz Wotruba (1907–1975). Throughout his studies, Zeischegg had also worked as a freelance designer, developing handles for tools, surgical instruments and machinery. While on a trip to Switzerland in the early 1950s, he met Max Bill, an encounter that was to have a profound influence on the direction of his career, as Bill urged him to focus on design. To this end, Zeischegg co-curated an exhibition with Carl Auböck entitled 'Hand und Griff' ('Hand and Grip') at the Ausstellung Wien in 1951. He subsequently became a lecturer at the Hochschule für Gestaltung in Ulm – Bill's 'New Bauhaus' academy of design founded in 1953. From then, until the closure of the Ulm school in 1968, Zeischegg taught product design, ultimately becoming the longest serving member of staff. After its closure, Zeischegg

established his own design office in Ulm, working mainly as a designer for Helit, a company known for manufacturing innovative office accessories. The company had been making products in Bakelite and other thermoset plastics since the 1920s and, in 1958, had switched to injection-moulded thermoplastics. Zeischegg's best-known design for Helit was his stacking *Sinus* ashtray, produced in 1966–1967 from heat-resistant melamine. Its eye-catching sine form is reminiscent of a Max Bill sculpture, and bespeaks Zeischegg's exploratory studies in geometric form. The ashtrays were produced in two different sizes (the larger model having a diameter of twenty-one centimetres), and came in a number of colours, including black, orange, white, grey, brown, yellow and blue. This iconic Ulm design influentially demonstrated that the form-giving potential of plastics could be harnessed to create useful, everyday objects of high aesthetic merit. Zeischegg's other designs for Helit – among them a tray, a magazine rack, a fruit dish and bookends – shared a similar fusion of form and function, achieved through the thoughtful and artistic handling of synthetic polymers.

Designer: **Walter Zeischegg** (Austrian, 1917–1983)
Materials: melamine formaldehyde resin (MF)
Manufacturer: Helit, Ulm, Germany
Measurements: 5.1 cm high, 13.4 cm diameter

Timor
desk calendar, 1967

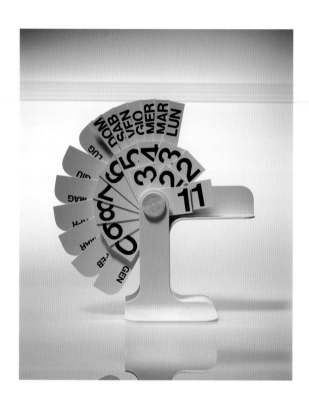

An acknowledged icon of Italian design, the *Timor* perpetual desk calendar is one of Enzo Mari's best-loved designs. Unlike traditional desk calendars, this design has a stylish sophistication attributable not only to the designer's understanding of form, function and materials, but also to Danese's commitment to 'simple objects of great quality'. From its beginnings in 1957, this Milan-based company has dedicated itself to excellence in manufacturing, and has always succeeded in creating superlative objects irrespective of the materials involved. In this case, Mari chose either white or black ABS for the stand, and for the thirty-two fan-like elements adorned with PVC lettering in Italian, English, French or German. The inverted 'J' form of the calendar perfectly complements the bold lettering – it is an object where product design and typographic design are harmoniously married. Although the *Timor* was designed more than forty years ago, it still looks as fresh and innovative as the day it was created showing that, when handled sensitively and intelligently, plastics can imbue a product with both functional and aesthetic longevity. As Enzo Mari has noted, 'When I make something for Danese I take the view that it has to outlive the current design trend… the idea being that something that is relevant today will be relevant in three hundred years' time.' It is a viewpoint that more designers and manufacturers will need to take seriously if designed objects, and especially those made of plastics, are to be sustainably produced in the future.

Designer: **Enzo Mari** (Italian, 1932–)
Materials: acrylonitrile-butadiene-styrene (ABS), lithographed
polyvinyl chloride (PVC)
Manufacturer: Danese, Milan, Italy
Measurements: 16 cm high, 17 cm wide, 9 cm deep

Duett
citrus press and pitcher, 1967

Designer: **Carl-Arne Breger** (Swedish 1923–2009)
Materials: polypropylene (PP)
Manufacturer: Gustavsberg, Gustavsberg, Sweden
Measurements: citrus press: 14 cm high, 15 cm wide, 10.5 cm
deep | pitcher: 22 cm high, 15 cm wide, 10.5 cm deep

Carl-Arne Breger was perhaps the most accomplished of all the Swedish designers who turned to the form-giving potential of plastics in their household product designs. Between 1943 and 1948, he had studied decorative painting and model making at the Konstfackskolan, Stockholm, before briefly working as a billboard painter for Svensk Filmindustri. Then, in 1953, he joined the in-house design studio of the Gustavsberg porcelain factory, where he worked alongside Stig Lindberg. Initially, Breger worked on decorative ceramic designs, but he grew disillusioned and later joined Gustavsberg's more engineering-based sanitary division instead. In this capacity, Breger designed sanitary wares and, like Lindberg, also a number of homewares using newly available plastics, including his acclaimed square bucket of 1955, out of which water could be poured more easily than from a traditional bucket, and which also had a cover. This design was named best plastic product of the 1950s by the Swedish Plastics Association, and led Breger to become known at the Gustavsberg factory as: 'him with the bucket'. Like this earlier design, Breger's

stylish *Duett* pitcher and matching citrus press of 1967 were not only well engineered for mass production in thermoplastic, but were also functionally innovative. Produced in either bright orange or yellow injection-moulded polypropylene, they also anticipated the early 1970s predilection for bright colours and bold forms. Together, they were refined contemporary products with appealing futuristic connotations, while nonetheless remaining affordable to the average consumer – objects which, in other words, exemplified the Swedish design community's consistent advocacy of sophisticated yet democratic consumer goods. Thanks to his in-depth understanding of the technical demands of large-scale mass production, as well as his careful consideration of consumers' needs, Carl-Arne Breger went on to become one of the leading pioneers of Scandinavian industrial design during the 1960s. His design consultancy, Breger Design, was ultimately responsible for the creation of more than 5,000 products, many of which Swedish people used on a daily basis: from telephones and butter dishes to coffee makers and food storage containers.

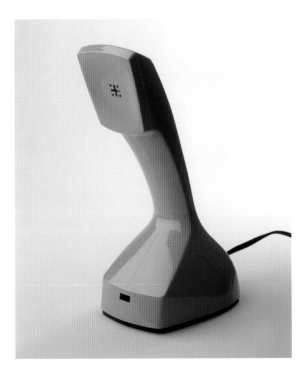

Carl-Arne Breger, *Ericofon 700*
telephone for Ericsson, 1976
– another landmark design by
Sweden's 'Mr. Plastic'

Pastil
chair, 1967

Eero Aarnio was one of the great pioneers of plastics in furniture design, creating seating forms that powerfully expressed the optimistic *zeitgeist* of the 1960s Plastics Age. Looking like a gigantic tablet or candy, his *Pastil* chair was an iconoclastic reinterpretation of the traditional rocking chair and was meant to be used indoors and outdoors. In fact, its hollow, fibreglass construction meant that it even floated in water. In 1968, it received an AID award that helped to forge Aarnio's Pop Design credentials beyond the shores of his native Finland. According to Aarnio, the *Pastil* would have fitted inside the space occupied by his earlier, globe-like *Ball* chair (1962). In his words, 'The *Pastil* shape can be looked at from many angles. The initial idea [for] the product shape comes from a small sweetie, a pastille. I made the first prototype out of polystyrene, which helped me to verify the measurements, ergonomics and rocking

ability. Because fibreglass is always laminated by hand on a smooth mould, the visible surface is perfectly shiny but the other surface slightly rough. I have always wanted to cover or to hide this side of my fibreglass products. In the *Pastil* it is ideally on the inside and thus totally invisible.' Unlike most Pop furniture from the 1960s, Aarnio's designs did not link plastics to the concept of disposability, but were instead intended to be long-lasting, a quality achieved through the skilful use of this durable material. Since its debut in 1967, the *Pastil* has become a much-loved icon of Scandinavian design, and has comfortably rocked forwards, backwards and sideways throughout the intervening decades. It demonstrates that exploiting the inherent sculptural potential of synthetic materials can produce landmark designs that stylishly redefine existing typologies.

Asko Oy publicity photograph showing *Pastil* chairs being used outside, c.1967

Eero Aarnio, *Bubble* chair for Asko Oy, 1968

Designer: **Eero Aarnio** (Finnish, 1932–)
Materials: glass-reinforced polyester (GRP)
Manufacturer: Asko Oy, Lahti, Finland (later reissued by Adelta
International, Dinslaken, Germany)
Measurements: 52 cm high, 90 cm diameter

Blow
chair, 1967

The origins of vinyl resins go back to 1838, when a French chemist, Henri Victor Regnault, observed the formation of a white powder when sealed tubes of vinyl chloride were left in the sunlight. In 1872, a German chemist, Eugen Regnault Baumann, polymerised this compound into a white substance that was 'unaffected by solvents or acids'. The new material was, however, a rather brittle compound, and not particularly suitable for commercial applications. In 1926, though, the American inventor Waldo Semon developed a way of plasticising the compound by blending it with additives, resulting in a commercially viable plastic with good elastic properties and a remarkable degree of flexibility. Moreover, this extraordinary new vinyl plastic was relatively easy to process, and within a few years was being used for a wide variety of commercial products, from records and dentures to food packaging and shoes. As *Modern Plastics* magazine noted in October 1936: 'The commercial development of this group of vinyl resins indicates the diversified possibilities of these materials and their extreme versatility... On the basis of performance and probable cost it is reasonable to expect that this group of resins will play an important part in the rapidly expanded field of plastics.' And, of course, this prediction proved to be right, especially during the post-war years as vinyl polymers became more widely available once wartime restrictions had been lifted. All the same, it was not until the middle and later years of the 1960s that flexible and transparent PVC reached the zenith of its popularity. In fact, high-frequency electronically welded PVC offered a whole new world of design possibilities, summed up in one word: inflatables. Although numerous blow-up chairs and sofas were created during this period of intense design experimentation, the *Blow* chair designed for Zanotta by the Milanese design trio, Jonathan De Pas, Donato D'Urbino and Paolo Lomazzi, stands out not only as one of the first mass-produced inflatable chairs from Italy, but also as one of the most commercially successful and widely disseminated seating designs of the period. As a veritable icon of 1960s Pop culture, the *Blow* chair's expendability playfully dismissed the traditional associations of furniture with costliness and permanence. Importantly, it also heralded a more youthful and carefree spirit in design and manufacture. The *Blow* chair celebrated the ephemeral novelty as well as the aesthetic and functional potential made possible by new polymers – and what could be more transient than an inexpensive chair made of transparent PVC that is filled with air.

Zanotta publicity photograph showing the *Blow* chair in use, c.1967

Designer: **Jonathan De Pas** (Italian, 1932–1991), **Donato D'Urbino**
(Italian, 1935–) and **Paolo Lomazzi** (Italian, 1936–)
Materials: polyvinyl chloride (PVC)
Manufacturer: Zanotta, Milan, Italy
Measurements: 83 cm high, 110 cm wide, 102 cm deep

Designer: **Anna Castelli-Ferrieri** (Italian, 1920–)
Materials: acrylonitrile-butadiene-styrene (ABS)
Manufacturer: Kartell, Noviglio, Italy
Measurements: 65 cm high (tall unit), 40 cm high (low unit),
42 cm diameter

Although Anna Castelli-Ferrieri was at the forefront of Italian design and architecture from the 1950s to the 1980s, her remarkable contribution as one of the pioneers of plastics in design is often overlooked. Having studied architecture at the Politenico di Milano, she married the chemical engineer Giulio Castelli in 1943, who subsequently went on to establish Kartell in 1949 to produce high-quality household products from newly developed polymers. While the fledging company grew, Anna collaborated on a number of important architectural and urban planning projects with the architect Ignazio Gardella, including a headquarters building and manufacturing complex for Kartell in the industrial suburbs of Milan. In 1964, she also turned her attention to industrial design, and co-designed with Gardella her first product for Kartell: the *Model No. 4991* table made of glass-reinforced polyester. This was followed in 1967 by her revolutionary *Model No. 4970* system, which comprised square storage devices in two sizes that could be stacked with their openings facing in any of four directions, and that were topped with a tray-like element. These units could also be used in conjunction with optional doors and castors. Launched in 1968 and also known as the *Multi Box System*, this range became the world's first storage system made entirely of injection-moulded ABS. Designed at around the same time but appearing a year later, Castelli-Ferrieri's cylindrical *Model No. 4965–6–7* stacking storage units had a similar construction, and were also injection moulded in an ABS developed by Beylerian. The doors of this range, however, were sliding rather than hinged, which made them easier to install and use. Originally produced in white, red, black, yellow and green, these units could be used singly as side tables or bedside cabinets, or alternatively they could be stacked to make useful, tower-like containers for almost any part of the home – even kitchens and bathrooms thanks to their waterproof, wipe-clean, gleaming surfaces. Inexpensive to produce yet extremely durable, the multi-functional *Model No. 4965–6–7* units have remained popular for over forty years – a testament to Castelli-Ferrieri's remarkable ability to create stylish, practical and enduring furniture designs that express the nobility of synthetic materials.

Anna Castelli-Ferrieri, *Model No. 4965–6–7* cylindrical stacking storage units for Kartell, 1967

Anna Castelli-Ferrieri, *Model No. 4970* 'Multi Box System' of storage units for Kartell, 1967

Gherpe
table light, 1967

Superstudio was a leading Anti-Design group, founded in Florence by the architecture students Adolfo Natalini and Cristiano Toraldo di Francia in the year of that city's great flood, 1966. Subsequently, Alessandro Magris, Roberto Magris and Piero Frassinelli also joined, and during the next twelve years Superstudio created work that continually challenged and contested preconceived notions about the role of design and architecture in society. The group questioned the validity of rationalism, overtly criticised consumerism, and advocated a 'design of evasion', involving objects that were industrially produced, yet poetic and irrational. Attempting to counter the orthodoxy of the Modern Movement, the group initially designed objects for serial production that met their goal of anti-consumerist artistic freedom. One such design was their futuristic *Gherpe* table light, made from an arching fan of looped acrylic bands. Though relatively low-tech in its construction, this experimental design took full advantage of the extraordinary optical qualities offered by new synthetic materials, with the acrylic elements in either translucent fluorescent pink, translucent fluorescent yellow or milky white PMMA diffusing the light in an other-worldly manner. The Italian word *gherpe* is the name of a child-scaring monster, and this futuristic design certainly has a strong spectral quality that adds to its undeniable sculptural presence. The *Gherpe* was one of the most beautiful lights to be produced during the golden age of Italian design, which lasted from the mid-1960s to the early 1970s. It also reflected Superstudio's interest in the idea of 'mutation' in an object, in which the same component was used over and over again – in this case, the loops of plastic that could be moved over each other to control the intensity of the emitted light. A stunning expression of the utopian ideals projected by Superstudio, the *Gherpe* was a visionary design that poetically captured the idealistic and futuristic *zeitgeist* of the Plastics Age.

Launch of a new range of lighting designs on the Poltronova stand at the Design Centre, Florence, 1968 – including the *Gherpe* light

Design Group: **Superstudio** (Italy, est. 1966)
Materials: polymethyl methacrylate (PMMA), acrylonitrile-
butadiene-styrene (ABS), chromed steel
Manufacturer: Francesconi, Ronacadelle, Italy for Design Centre/
Poltronova, Agliana, Italy
Measurements: 39 cm high, 51.5 cm wide, 30 cm deep

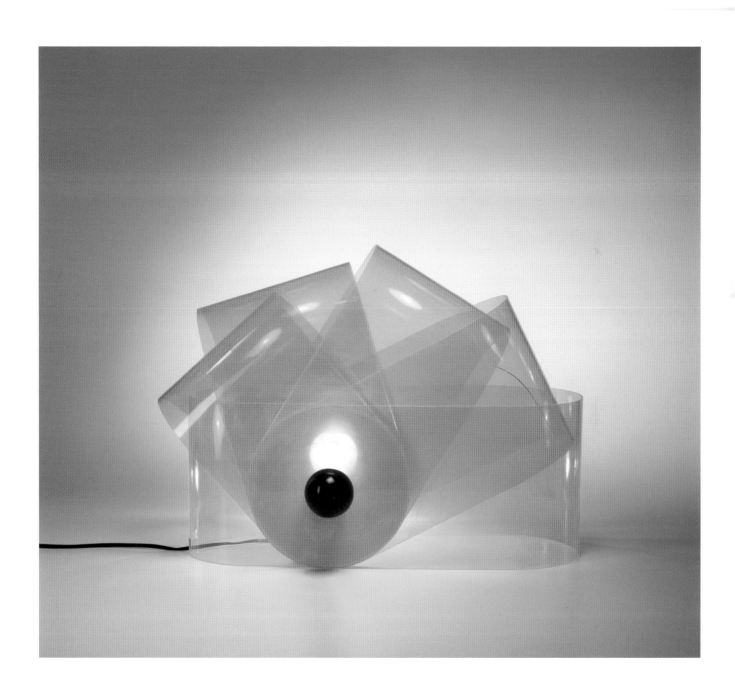

Dondolo
rocking chaise longue, 1967

Cesare Leonardi and Franca Stagi,
CL9 Ribbon chair for Bernini
(later Elco), 1961

In 1961, Cesare Leonardi and Franca Stagi designed the eye-catching *CL9* chair for Bernini, which incorporated a continuous band of moulded fibreglass that formed a sculptural seating section attached to a cantilevered tubular metal base with rubber shock mounts. Their *Dondolo* rocking chaise longue – a veritable sculptural and constructional *tour de force* – followed this structurally innovative chair six years later. According to Helen Quin, writing in *Design* magazine: 'When Cesare Leonardi approached Bernini with an idea for an all-in-one S-shaped rocking chair, he literally hadn't a clue as to how it could be made. His only solo contribution was a form sketch on a piece of paper. The technical aspects of putting this shape into physical form – and the decision to press it out of a continuous sweep of hollow fluted glass-reinforced polyester – was made by technicians on Bernini's factory floor. The first prototype, therefore, was not only worked out by the factory but financed by Bernini as well.' The resulting form was a continuous, looping, single-material, one-piece fibreglass construction, strengthened on its underside by ribbing. Like the vault of a Gothic cathedral, this fluted moulding gave the rocking chair structural support and enhanced its load-bearing capabilities with the minimum of material. The ribbing also heightened the design's sinuous aesthetic, giving it an almost serpentine quality. Importantly, the glass-reinforced polyester resin had a degree of resiliency, which ensured that the chaise was more comfortable than if it had been completely rigid. This beautiful and fluid design was produced in three colours – white, grey and light blue – and dramatically redefined the notion of the rocking chair. Its manufacturer, Bernini, specialised in furniture made of GRP and other plastics, and produced other noteworthy designs including Fabio Lenci's remarkable knock-down table and chairs made of polyester-skinned polyurethane (1971).

Designers: **Cesare Leonardi** (Italian, 1935–) and **Franca Stagi**
(Italian, 1937–2008)
Materials: glass-reinforced polyester (GRP)
Manufacturer: Bernini, Figline Valdarno, Italy (1967–1969) and
Elco, Venice, Italy (after 1969)
Measurements: 85 cm high, 170 cm long, 39 cm wide

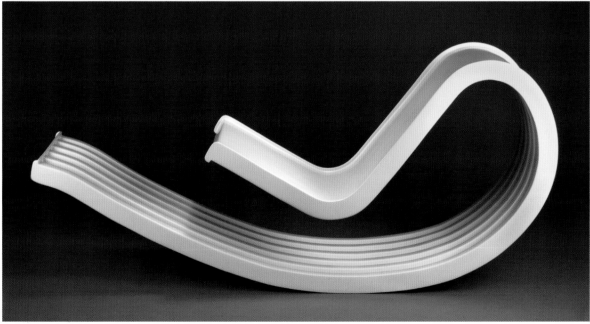

Tam Tam
stool, 1967

Launched in 1968, Henry Massonnet's *Tam Tam* stool enjoyed enormous sales success during the 1970s, and has long been recognised as a design classic. As a designer and entrepreneur, Massonnet owned a small plastics manufacturing company in Nurieux called Stamp, which made cold boxes and buckets for the local fishermen. He originally designed the *Tam Tam* as a fisherman's stool, but it did not sell particularly well. This changed spectacularly, however, when Brigitte Bardot was photographed sitting on one for a magazine article about her home in Saint-Tropez which of course made it appear instantly fashionable and stylish to the wider public. The ensuing sales of this practical, ergonomic and inexpensive stool reached a truly extraordinary level – twelve million units were sold in the five years following its creation. Certainly, its choice of bright colours, its clean and uncluttered lines, unusual hour-glass shape and gleaming surfaces must have made it seem startlingly contemporary in comparison with other stools on the market during this period. A further reason for its success lay in the fact that the *Tam Tam* was (and still is) extremely cheap to manufacture, thanks to its simple and highly rational three-piece construction – two identical mouldings fit together to form the hourglass stem, and one disc-shaped moulding snaps onto its top, forming the seat. With no need for screws or glue, the stool could be self-assembled in a matter of seconds, and could also be easily transported in its dismantled state. Manufactured in injection-moulded polypropylene, the *Tam Tam* was also durable and easy to clean, as well as water-resistant, which made it equally appropriate for indoor or outdoor use. This inexpensive design encapsulated Massonnet's guiding motto, 'Innovative ingenuity coupled with a dynamic approach', and predicted his development in 1973 of the world's first single-piece, injection-moulded armchair in polypropylene – a major technical achievement that heralded the advent of the cheap yet practical monobloc plastic chair which, for better or worse, is now such an omnipresent feature of the urban landscape throughout the world.

Tam Tam stool shown
disassembled

Designer: **Henry Massonnet** (French, 1922–)
Materials: polypropylene (PP)
Manufacturer: Stamp, Nurieux, France (reissued by Branex
Design, Paris, France)
Measurements: 45cm high, 30 cm diameter

Model No. 4905/6/7
nesting tables, 1967

Apart from his various architectural commissions, designed in conjunction with his partners Vittorio Gregotti and Lodovico Meneghetti, Giotto Stoppino also created some interesting furniture and lighting. His work in these fields was characterised by the use of the latest thermoplastics, and a quirky Space Age aesthetic. One of his most widely celebrated designs was a set of three nesting tables, manufactured from 1968 by Kartell in shiny, injection-moulded ABS. Available in either white, red, yellow or orange colours, these tables were not only designed to stack together efficiently, but their fluid, single-piece construction was also conceived so that they could be easily extracted from their moulds during the manufacturing process. While the legs of each table flow seamlessly like a cascade from the top surfaces, their 'folded' edges provide additional stability and strength. Like many other progressive Italian designs in plastic, the *Model No. 4905/6/7* tables were included in a section devoted to objects selected for their 'formal and technical means' at the landmark 1972 exhibition, 'Italy: The New Domestic Landscape', held at the Museum of Modern Art in New York. With these tables, Stoppino undeniably created beautiful yet functional forms that were logically derived from a process-driven approach to design. His *Model No. 4905/6/7* tables were radically different from preceding designs, as was his highly successful *Model No. 4675* magazine rack of 1971, also produced by Kartell. Quite simply, new materials were permitting new forms, and heralding the birth of a bold new synthetic aesthetic.

Giotto Stoppino, *Model Nos. 4675* and *4676* magazine racks for Kartell, 1971

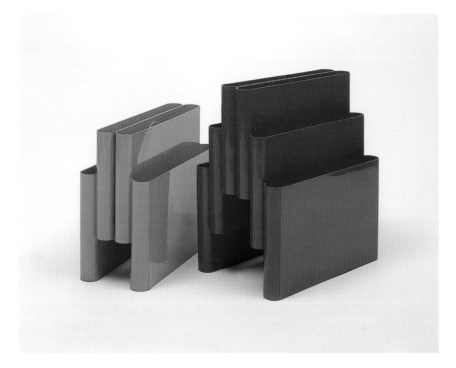

Designer: **Giotto Stoppino** (Italian, 1926–)
Materials: acrylonitrile-butadiene-styrene (ABS)
Manufacturer: Kartell, Noviglio, Italy
Measurements: 32 cm high, 37 cm high, 42 cm high,
43 cm diameter

Plia
folding chair, 1967

Designer: **Giancarlo Piretti** (Italian, 1940–)
Materials: polymethyl methacrylate (PMMA)/later cellulose triacetate (CT), chrome-plated steel, cast aluminium
Manufacturer: Anonima Castelli, Bologna, Italy
Measurements: 77 cm high, 47 cm wide, 47 cm deep

The *Plia* was a truly revolutionary folding chair. Made of transparent plastic, its see-through back and seat were set into a minimalist steel frame that boasted an innovative three-disc hinge, allowing the chair to be folded in one simple movement. It was Giancarlo Piretti's first design in plastics for Anonima Castelli, and used thermo-formed elements initially made of acrylic (PMMA). However, this material was soon changed to Cellidor, a medium-rigidity cellulose triacetate developed by Bayer, with greater resilience and excellent resistance to weather and heat. The chair was offered in clear, smoky grey or opaque colours, and was extremely popular thanks to its clean, elegant and progressive aesthetic, which predicted the Neo-Modernism of the 1970s. Essentially a modern reworking of a traditional wooden folding chair, the *Plia* was a highly space-efficient design, which when collapsed was only about 2.5 centimetres (one inch) in depth (excluding the central hub). The design won numerous awards, including Germany's Bundespreis Gute Form (Federal Prize for Good Form) in 1973 and was also included in the 'Objects Selected for their Formal and Technical Means' section of the landmark exhibition, 'Italy: The New Domestic Landscape', held in 1972 at the Museum of Modern Art, New York. Interestingly, the exhibition's curator, Emilio Ambasz, went on to form a design collaboration with Piretti, resulting in a number of seminal chair designs, including the influential and ergonomically responsive *Vertebra* office chair (1977). The *Plia* chair has also been a great commercial success, with more than seven million units being sold since its launch in 1969. During his twelve-year stint working as a designer for Anonima Castelli, Piretti produced other important furniture designs in thermoplastics, including his *Platone* folding desk/table (1971) and the *Plona* folding armchair (1970), the latter featuring a one-piece seating section that, like the *Plia*, was formed from glossy surfaced Cellidor.

Anonima Castelli publicity photograph for the *Plia* chair, 1970

Cespuglio
table light, 1968

Designer: **Ennio Lucini** (Italian, 1934–1997)
Materials: polymethyl methacrylate (PMMA), aluminium
Manufacturer: DH Guzzini, Recanati, Italy
Measurements: 32 cm high

Ennio Lucini's *Cespuglio* table light ranks among the most stunning Italian Pop designs of the late 1960s. It powerfully expresses the confidence with form that emerged in product design during this period thanks to the availability of new and colourful plastics. The *Cespuglio*'s hauntingly beautiful play of light is achieved through jagged sheets of acrylic, which not only diffuse the light effectively, but also produce the other-worldly optical effect known as 'live edge', which occurs when the acrylic glows more brightly along its extremities. Although the design works well as a light, it is also a highly sculptural composition and, like so many Italian lights from this period, it reflects the playful and futuristic experimentation of the late 1960s, and the beguiling currents of optimism and utopianism associated with that era. In Italian, *cespuglio* means 'bush', and certainly this extra-ordinary light appears to have been plucked from some psychedelic sci-fi landscape. Available in milky white, yellow, magenta or green, the *Cespuglio* was a highly innovative yet structurally simple design, with a strong diagramatic quality that produced a powerful sense of three-dimensionality. Provocative products of this kind came to define the 'golden age' of Italian design between 1968 and 1973 – a period inextricably linked to a bold experimentation with plastics that spectacularly expanded their functional and aesthetic boundaries.

Yellow translucent version of the
Cespuglio light

Egg
garden chair, 1968

Born in Budapest, Peter Ghyczy fled to West Germany as a teenager in 1956. After completing his schooling, he attended sculpture classes at the Staatliche Kunstakademie in Düsseldorf, before training as an architect at the University of Aachen. Shortly after finishing his studies, he was hired as a furniture designer by a German plastics manufacturer, Elastogran/Reuter, becoming the head of the firm's design department in 1968. In this capacity, his primary aim was to create 'independent and unique pieces of furniture' – a worthy goal that he resoundingly achieved with the design of his *Egg* garden chair. An iconoclastic plastic outdoor seating design with true cult status, the weather-resistant *Egg* opened and closed like a clamshell. Its hinged top could be folded down when not in use to create a completely waterproof pod that concealed and protected the detachable, upholstered cushions within. During his time at Elastogran/Reuter from 1968 to 1972, Ghyczy also designed other eye-catching furniture pieces in plastic, most notably the *GN2* chair (1970) that was similarly constructed of polyurethane. Despite the critical success of these progressive products, Ghyczy felt creatively limited at Elastogran/ Reuter, and left in 1972 to establish his own manu- facturing company, Ghyczy Novo, in the Netherlands. In 1998, this venture reissued the *Egg* chair, which had also been produced for a number of years by VEB- Synthese-Werk in East Germany. Unlike the original version, which was moulded in polyurethane resin as a small limited edition, today's unlimited production edition is made of a superior and recyclable, high- impact polystyrene instead.

Egg chair in use, contemporary photograph

Designer: **Peter Ghyczy** (Hungarian, 1940–)
Materials: polyurethane (PU), jersey-covered flexible
polyurethane foam, metal
Manufacturer: Elastogran/Reuter Lemförde, Germany (later
VEB-Synthese-Werk, Schwarzheide, Germany and from 1998
reissued by Ghyczy Novo, Swalmen, Netherlands in high-impact
polystyrene (HIPS)
Measurements: 45 cm high (closed), 101 cm high (open), 75 cm
wide, 84 cm deep

Pillola
table light, 1968

Designer: **Cesare Casati** (Italian, 1936–) and **Emanuele Ponzio** (Italian, 1923–)
Materials: acrylonitrile-butadiene-styrene (ABS), polymethyl methacrylate (PMMA)
Manufacturer: Ponteur, Bergamo, Italy
Measurements: 55 cm high, 13 cm diameter

One of the great defining features of Pop Art and its close counterpart, the Italian Radical Design movement, was the creation of oversized and de-contextualised objects. Cesare Casati and Emanuele Ponzio's *Pillola* lights exemplify this eccentric phenomenon, looking as though they have just spilled from a gigantic pill bottle. As an archetypal Pop design, the out-of-scale *Pillola* lights drew direct inspiration from the iconoclastic work of Andy Warhol (1928–1987) and Claes Oldenburg (b.1929), which explored the nature of the banal object and reappropriated it as art, thereby challenging our perceptions of both. Casati and Ponzio's five 'pill' lights were made from half-mouldings of opaque ABS and translucent PMMA, which were joined together just like the pharma-ceutical capsules that inspired them. The little holes evenly spaced along these capsules provided the necessary ventilation, so that the plastic diffusers would not be overheated by the bulbs illuminating them. The lights were also weighted in such a way that they could be variously positioned on their transparent acrylic bases, affording a degree of creative control and interaction to the user – another defining feature of Italian design from the 1960s. Quintessentially of their time, the *Pillola* lights were a bold statement, subverting existing preconceptions about lighting design and, in some ways, functioning more as an 'art multiple' than as a functional design solution. At the same time, these giant, gleaming pills also gloriously celebrated the candy-like allure of coloured plastics. Of course, they referred equally to the flourishing drugs culture of the 1960s, and it is no surprise that in 1968, the year of their design, Valium became the most prescribed drug in America. That epoch-defining year marked a cultural and political watershed, and these Plastic Age lights reflect the rebellious transitions occurring within society, and the quirky, anything-goes Pop aesthetic of the Swinging Sixties – a sensibility spurred on by utopian visions of the future that enthusiastically embraced state-of-the-art plastics.

Cesare Maria Casati and Emmanuele Ponzio, Perspex furniture group designed for Il Grifoncino discothèque at the Hotel Grifone, Bolzano, 1968 – the table could be illuminated

Sacco
beanbag, 1968–1969

From 1965 onwards, Piero Gatti, Cesare Paolini and Franco Teodoro worked in various fields of creative activity: architecture, interior design, industrial design, urban planning, corporate identity and graphic design. It was, however, the design of their *Sacco* beanbag that would bring them the greatest acclaim. As Piero Gatti recalled in a later interview, 'Between 1967 and 1968 ergonomics was in fashion... Many of us were interested in designing objects as flexible as possible, which could adapt to different situations, not just to forms of behaviour but also different physical structures. So we said: think of a chair that will allow these functions. We began to think about a material that would allow this adaptability, both for the body and its positions... In the end we thought about the old mattresses stuffed with chestnut leaves, widely used by peasants: you take a sack, you fill it with leaves or similar materials, and this moulds itself to fit the body... From this ... we got the idea of something, like marbles or balls, that would mould themselves to the body, i.e. behave like a semi-fluid... Then we found a material used in the building trade, foam polystyrene for sound- and heat-proofing. So we cut out an envelope, put these little balls inside and saw it worked.' The design trio then made several prototypes with electro-welded vinyl covers, took some photographs of these beanbags and then left the prototypes lying in their office, presuming that 'no one would ever want to make this thing'. However, the pictures were included with images of other designs sent to an American magazine, and this led to an enquiry from the Italian branch of Macy's, which wanted to place an order for 10,000 units. In the meantime, Gatti, Paolini and Teodoro had mentioned their beanbag design to Aurelio Zanotta, who they knew from the Eurodomus exhibition held in Turin in 1960. After examining their prototype, Zanotta made three 'production' models and took them to the Paris Furniture Show, where they were an instant success. The revolutionary *Sacco*, with its PVC or leather envelope filled with thousands of tiny polystyrene beads, captured the youthful *zeitgeist* of the laid-back 1960s, with its low yet extremely comfortable sitting position perfectly aligned to the more relaxed and casual lifestyle of the period. Naturally, its commercial success spawned a host of inferior copycat designs, but they were never able to equal the incredible comfort or stylish good looks of Gatti, Paolini and Teodoro's original – the vinyl version of which was an entirely synthetic seating solution. The *Sacco* can be judged a true design of the 1960s Plastics Age – it would have been impossible to develop without access to polystyrene beads, which were the ideal material because of their feather-like lightness and fluid movement, cascading over each other like tiny, almost weightless ball bearings.

Zanotta publicity photographs
showing *Sacco* beanbag, c.1969

Designers: **Piero Gatti** (Italian, 1940–), **Cesare Paolini** (Italian, 1937–1983) and **Franco Teodoro** (Italian, 1939–2005)
Materials: polyvinyl chloride (PVC) or leather, beaded semi-expanded polystyrene (XPS)
Manufacturer: Zanotta, Milan, Italy
Measurements: 114.3 cm high, 83.8 cm diameter

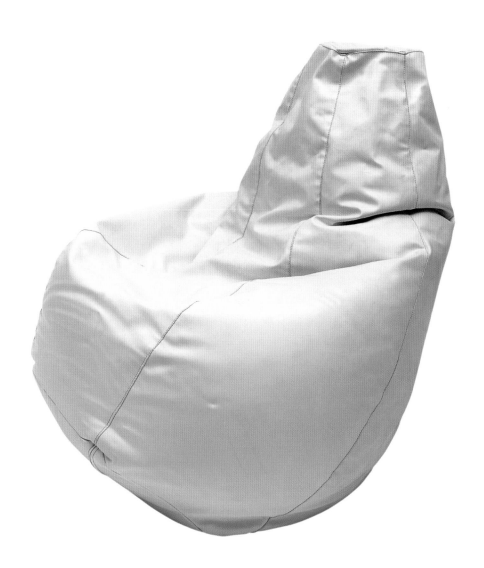

Designer: **Sergio Mazza** (Italian, 1931–)
Materials: glass-reinforced polyester (GRP)
Manufacturer: Artemide, Pregnana Milanese, Italy
Measurements: 64 cm high, 80 cm wide, 80 cm deep

Artemide publicity photograph,
c.1968 – showing *Toga* chair with
Nesso table light (designed in
1962 by Giancarlo Mattiolo and
Gruppo Architetti Urbanisti Città
Nuova)

Sergio Mazza graduated in 1954 from the school of architecture in Lausanne, Switzerland, and two years later established his own Milan-based design office, Studio SMC Architettura. In 1960 he went on to co-found Artemide, and subsequently designed numerous innovative lighting products for the company as well as several important furniture pieces using newly available plastics – including his well-known *Toga* chair. This sculpturally organic design from 1968 (produced from 1969) appears to have been the first single-form plastic stacking chair manufactured in Italy, and as such it set an important precedent for the nation's furniture industry. Made of compression-moulded glass-reinforced polyester, the *Toga* chair had a simple construction that was straightforward to produce, while its ergonomic form made it relatively comfortable despite its lack of upholstery. A year before designing it, Mazza had created the similarly constructed *Mida* chair and sofa (also made by Artemide) from a moulded glass-reinforced plastic composite, with the addition of upholstered seat and back sections. Also in 1967, he designed the well-known *Bacco* minibar – one of the first Artemide products to be made of injection-moulded ABS. Like the Toga, this single-form bar unit on rolling castors broke new ground in plastics manufacturing technology. At the time of its launch it was, in the words of Mazza's long-time colleague Giuliana Gramigna, 'One of the first examples in the world of injection moulding so large an item.'

Luigi Colani is a true design visionary who, throughout a prolific career spanning over five decades, has created numerous innovative and provocative products characterised by his pioneering use of biomorphic and sculptural forms. Having studied sculpture at the Akademie der Künste in Berlin, Colani went on to study aerodynamics at the Sorbonne in Paris, before in 1953 heading the New Materials Project Group at McDonnell Douglas in California. Since then, he has specialised in the design of various modes of streamlined transportation, from catamarans and sports coupés to aeroplanes and trucks. He has also designed numerous futuristic products – including furnishings, ceramics, cameras, electronic equipment and bathroom fittings – all of which demonstrate his use of soft, almost melting forms. Not surprisingly, plastics have long been Colani's materials of choice, with their inherently mouldable and form-giving nature. In 1969, for instance, he designed a baby's bath and matching potty that exploited the functional, formal and high-volume manufacturing possibilities of injection-moulded polypropylene. Unlike similar baby accessories, these designs have dynamic, fluid shapes that echo the human form and are, therefore, more ergonomically refined. Produced in a number of bright colours, Colani's baby's bath was awarded the prestigious Bundespreis Gute Form prize in 1971 – the official 'good design' award of the West German Federal Republic. It remained in production for many years, thanks to a functional yet attractive form that was easy and relatively cheap to manufacture in thermoplastic.

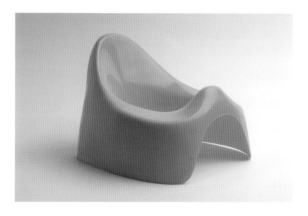

Luigi Colani, *Model No. 044530*
child's potty for Sulo, 1969

Designer: **Luigi Colani** (German, 1928–)
Materials: polypropylene (PE)
Manufacturer: Sulo (Eisenwerk Streuber & Lohmann), Neustadt,
Germany and OKT, Stemwede, Germany (from 1986)
Measurements: 83 cm long, 26 cm high, 48 cm wide

Valentine
portable typewriter, 1969

Designers: **Ettore Sottsass** (Austrian/Italian, 1917–2007) and
Perry King (British, 1938–)
Materials: polyethylene (PE), acrylonitrile-butadiene-styrene
(ABS), metal
Manufacturer: Olivetti, Ivrea, Italy
Measurements: 35 cm deep, 34.5 cm wide, 11.5 cm high

In 1969, Olivetti launched a new portable typewriter called the *Valentine*, designed by Ettore Sottsass and Perry King, which would become one of the most influential designs of the 20th century. As *Domus* magazine noted in its June 1969 issue, 'The case is a bucket into which you put the typewriter, and the handle is attached to the machine and not to the bucket; you thus carry the machine with the bucket attached to it. The general idea is that a portable typewriter is no longer a special object, but an everyday tool.' Sottsass also expressed this new concept of the portable typewriter in his choice of colourful polyethylene and ABS, in the machine's chunky yet playful form, and in its catchy name prominently moulded in a Pop-Deco font above the keyboard. With its bright red plastic casing and cover, and its orange plastic ribbon spools, the *Valentine* had a distinctive, toy-like quality that spoke directly to a younger and more fashion-conscious audience, keen to reject the stuffy, grey hierarchies of traditional office life. The *Valentine* was a quintessential Pop

design that celebrated the Plastics Age of the 1960s through a bold ergonomic form that showcased the intrinsic, form-giving qualities of the polymers used in its manufacture. As Sottsass noted, the design was, 'the sort of thing to keep lonely poets company on Sundays in the country', and its playful aesthetic certainly did establish a strong emotional connection between object and user, with huge implications for the later design of consumer electronics. Above all, the *Valentine* proved that if the design of office equipment could be given a treatment that actively endeared it to its users, then this entire product category could be transformed into a context for desirable, fashionable, must-have items – a lesson Jonathan Ive clearly absorbed in designing the *iMac* computer some thirty years later. The success of the *Valentine* also revealed that consumers were prepared to pay a premium for objects that brought a touch of modish glamour into their daily lives, and eloquently confirmed that, when handled as noble materials, plastics were ideally suited to this purpose.

Black ST201
television set, 1969

During the 1960s and 1970s, Marco Zanuso and Richard Sapper developed a number of iconic products that relied on the innovative use of synthetic polymers. Many of these landmark designs were created for the Italian company Brionvega, founded in 1945 by Giuseppe Brion and the engineer Leone Pajetta, with the original intention of manufacturing radios. The company ultimately diversified its product line to incorporate hi-fi equipment and televisions, the latter in response to the birth of Italy's television network in the early 1950s. During the next two decades, and not least thanks to its collaboration with Zanuso and Sapper, Brionvega became the most progressive consumer electronics company in Italy, consistently introducing groundbreaking, design-led products that redefined the parameters of electronics design. Made of semi-transparent black acrylic, the *Black ST201* television, designed by Sapper and Zanuso in 1969,

marked a paradigm shift in the design of televisions, rejecting the veneered, furniture-like boxes of the past and charting a brave new world of stylish minimalism. This truly remarkable television was conceived as a cube and, when not in use, the semi-transparent PMMA concealed the screen giving it the appearance of a simple, sculptural box. The year before it was designed saw the release of Stanley Kubrick's *2001: A Space Odyssey*, and it is inconceivable that the mysterious, slab-like black monolith that appears in this cinematic masterpiece did not in some way inspire the *Black ST201*. The television was meant to be portable and came with a carrying cover and detachable aerials. Significantly, this aesthetically sophisticated design was only achievable through the technical mastery of acrylic, and was a fitting design for the crescendo of the Plastic Age that immediately preceded the oil crisis of 1973.

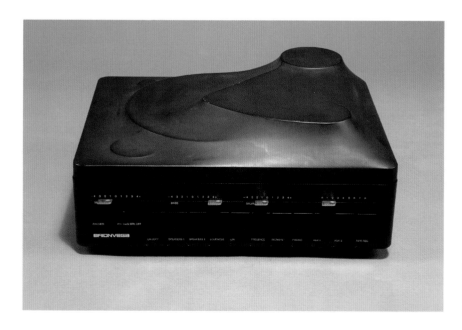

Marco Zanuso, Roberto Lucci and Paolo Orlandini, *Concetto 101* hi-fi system for Brionvega, 1974 – a minimalist electronics design that again used synthetic polymers in an unusual way

Designers: **Marco Zanuso** (Italian, 1916–2001) and
Richard Sapper (German, 1932–)
Materials: polymethyl methacrylate (PMMA), metal,
other materials
Manufacturer: Brionvega, Milan, Italy
Measurements: 25.4 cm high, 29.2 cm wide, 30.5 cm deep

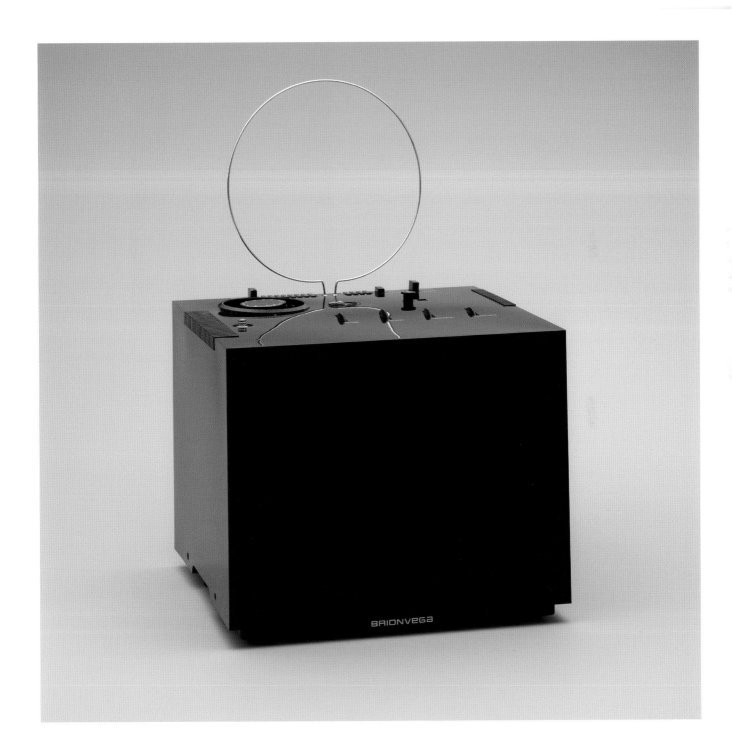

TYP F
pendant light, 1969

One of the great success stories of Germany's post-war economic miracle was the reconstruction and expansion of the Bayer chemical company. By the early 1960s, it was one of the leading developers of new plastics and other man-made fibres, and one of its many products was a new thermoplastic known as cellulose triacetate, sold under the trade name Cellidor. This advanced polymer had a high-gloss surface finish, and as a naturally transparent plastic it could be easily dyed to create bright colours. In 1969, Verner Panton used spheres of Cellidor to create a new lighting range, known as Kugel-Lampen ('Ball Lamps'). This quintessential Pop lighting range comprised seven different designs, including the *TYP F* pendant, and came in a variety of colour options: pink/red, purple/blue, cream/white and chromium-plated silver. Suspended on invisible nylon threads, the translucent ping-pong-like balls diffused and tinted the emitted light in an almost magical way. Certainly, these clustered ball lights must have seemed incredibly progressive when they were shown as part of *Visiona 2*, the futuristic installation designed by Panton, sponsored by Bayer and staged at the Cologne Furniture Fair in 1970. For this landmark design event, Panton also created his similarly festive *Spiral Lampen* series of hanging lights that incorporated clustered Cellidor spirals. These two extraordinary lighting ranges playfully exploited the formal potential of this new thermoplastic and, in so doing, helped to create Panton's very personal vision of the future – an unforgettable utopian landscape of kaleidoscopic colours and extraordinary sculptural forms.

J Lüber promotional poster, c. 1969

Verner Panton, *SP01 Spiral* hanging light for J Lüber, 1969

Designer: **Verner Panton** (Danish, 1926–1998)
Materials: cellulose triacetate (CT), polyamide (PA/nylon), metal
Manufacturer: J. Lüber, Basel, Switzerland
Measurements: 46 cm high, 44 cm diameter

Uten.Silo II
wall-mounted organiser, 1969–1970

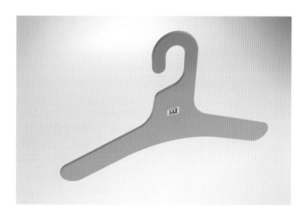

Ingo Maurer, plastic clothes
hanger for M Design, 1968

Born in Germany, Dorothée Maurer-Becker studied
languages and then lived for a time in London and
Paris, before moving to California in 1960. She
eventually returned to Germany in 1963 with her
husband, the well-known lighting designer Ingo
Maurer, and three years later they established Design
M, a design and manufacturing company based in
Munich. Although Ingo Maurer was responsible for
the majority of the designs produced by this enterprise, Maurer-Becker also created a number of
innovative products, including her iconic *Uten.Silo I*
wall-mounted organiser from 1969. The following year,
she designed a smaller version of this stylish 'wall
tidy' known as the *Uten.Silo II*, which was similarly
produced from two panels of injection-moulded ABS
and polystyrene. These striking plastic storage units
were based on earlier experimental wooden designs
that Maurer-Becker had executed in the 1960s.
With their differently shaped and sized containers,
and their numerous metal hooks and clips, the
Uten.Silo I and *Uten.Silo II* were intended to be used
as organizers in kitchens, bathrooms, offices or
children's bedrooms. These highly useful products
were also marketed under the name *Wall-All*, while
another related design for a smaller organizer, known
as the *Wall-All III*, was manufactured by Format
Sales in the United States. Design M produced other
household products in colourful ABS, including some
stylish yellow coat hangers designed by Ingo Mauer in
1968. The company's innovative and modish designs
in shiny, durable thermoplastic not only captured the
optimistic spirit of the times, but perfectly suited the
increasingly casual lifestyle of the 1960s.

Designer: **Dorothée Maurer-Becker** (German, 1938–)
Materials: acrylonitrile-butadiene-styrene (ABS), polystyrene (PS), metal
Manufacturer: Design M, Munich, Germany (reissued in
2000: Vitra, Weil am Rhein, Germany)
Measurements: 68 cm high, 51 cm wide (larger version: 87 cm
high, 66 cm wide)

Pago Pago
reversible vase, 1969

This iconic design reflects the way in which Italian designers and manufacturers of the 1960s pushed the aesthetic and formal parameters of synthetic polymers to create objects of intrinsic value and beauty. The *Pago Pago* vase was designed by Enzo Mari, one of the great masters of 20th-century Italian design, whose long and illustrious career is replete with rationally conceived products that are both functionally and formally provocative. A single-piece injection moulding in glossy ABS, the *Pago Pago* has two juxtaposed cavities, of different sizes, with the smaller, cone-like cavity fitting into the second, larger one. This cleverly designed configuration means that the *Pago Pago* effectively functions as a reversible double vase. In one orientation, it flares out to hold a large bouquet of flowers, yet when inverted the design becomes an elegant, tapering vessel that holds fewer blooms. So skilful was Mari's handling of plastics, that many of the designs he created for Danese in the late 1960s possess a strong sense of sculptural fluidity and sensual tactility. At around this time, Mari also created two further ranges of vases, innovatively made of pressure-moulded PVC tubing: the *Bambù* and the *Torciglione* (which translate as 'bamboo' and 'clover' respectively). As their manufacturer, Bruno Danese explained, 'A good design and consequently a good product are achieved when the use (function), quality of material, execution (technology) and form (aesthetics) are combined in perfect proportion. It has, in addition, always been specifically intended that our objects have characteristics than can be realised only in plastic.' Certainly, Mari's designs for Danese, and especially the elegant *Pago Pago* vase, were widely regarded among critics as playing a significant role in persuading the public that plastic products could possess high quality, originality and style, and in countering the perception that they were inevitably tacky, cheap and disposable.

Enzo Mari, *Bambù* vases for Danese, 1969 – made by pressure moulding a PVC tube

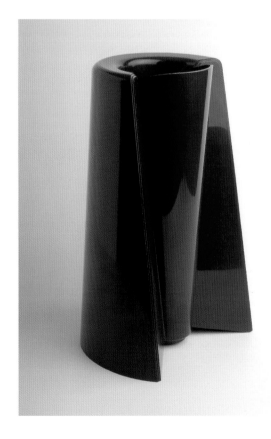

Designer: **Enzo Mari** (Italian, 1932–)
Materials: acrylonitrile-butadiene-styrene (ABS)
Manufacturer: Danese, Milan, Italy
Measurements: 30 cm high, 20 cm wide

Model No. **9644** mugs
and **Model No. 1099** pitcher
1969–1970

From the mid-1950s until the early 1970s, many Swedish companies focused on the mass-manufacturing potential of plastics, which were seen as suitably modern and democratic materials with which to shape the nation's progressive welfare state. For decades, there had been a widespread belief in Sweden that good design was a birthright for all, and that well-designed goods should be an enhancing aspect of individual and community life. During this period, companies such as Gustavsberg, Husqvarna and Hammarplast subscribed to this conviction that properly conceived products could promote these civic-minded goals among the masses, and designed their plastic household products accordingly. Sven-Eric Juhlin's *Model No. 9644* mugs and *Model No. 1099* pitcher exemplify the extraordinary level of design and engineering refinement consequently found in Swedish plastic housewares from this period. These useful and beautiful objects were made of styrene acrylonitrile copolymer (SAN), which has a molecular structure similar to ABS, but possesses quite different thermal and resistance properties. Generally, SAN polymers contain between twenty and thirty percent acrylonitrile, and the higher this percentage, the greater the resulting tensile strength and heat resistance. Although they have very similar properties to polystyrene, the superior heat and chemical resistance of SAN plastics make them the ideal materials for food containers, kitchenwares, computer casings and packaging. According to Gustavsberg, this odourless plastic could withstand a temperature range between minus 40° and plus 90° Celsius; nonetheless, the company did recommend washing its mugs and pitcher by hand. The two-tone mugs could be used either for hot or cold drinks, and came in a range of colours, including yellow, red, orange, green, blue, purple and brown. Immensely successful in terms of sales, approximately 2.5 million mugs were produced, and Juhlin designed a matching child's beaker and bowl that also proved popular. As he explained, 'Plastics only came to have their own value when the choice of material was guided by requirements. We realised that certain plastics allow the creation of designs, which are not possible in any other materials.'

Sven-Eric Juhlin and Maria Benktzon (Ergonomi Design Gruppen), slicing knife for Gustavsberg, 1974 – intended for disabled users

Designer: **Sven-Eric Juhlin** (Swedish, 1940–)
Materials: styrene acrylonitrile copolymer (SAN)
Manufacturer: Gustavsberg, Gustavsberg, Sweden
Measurements: 10 cm high (mugs) | 20.6 cm high (pitcher)

Boby
storage trolley, 1970

One of Joe Colombo's most enduring designs, the *Boby* trolley is a highly versatile mobile storage unit, that was specifically designed for use by architects needing to store drawing materials, drafting equipment and blueprints. It can also, however, be used in the home, the office, doctors' examination rooms, laboratories and even hairdressing salons. The *Boby* trolley epitomised Joe Colombo's love of modular design systems, which also had strong Space Age connotations. Like his other designs produced in plastic, the *Boby*'s form was dictated by functional and manufacturing considerations, while at the same time the expression of a bold and futuristic aesthetic that appealed to a young audience. It was also designed to be highly flexible in that it could be extended vertically to provide further storage capacity. The B*oby*'s structural modules and drawers were made of injection-moulded ABS, and these elements were held in place with concealed stainless steel tie-rods and screws that allowed the drawers to swing out. On its upper surface, the *Boby* also had a removable oblong cover with a finger-hole, which gave easy access to a hidden storage space running the whole way down one of its sides, which was the space intended for scrolled plans or blueprints. This practical and stylish portable storage system was awarded first prize at SMAU in 1971, and has since entered the permanent collections of design museums all over the world as a bold icon of Italian Pop design. Above all, the *Boby* trolley can be seen to symbolise the utopian aspirations of 1960s popular culture, which not only celebrated synthetic materials but also (if somewhat naïvely) a belief in humanity's salvation through the advancement of technology.

Designer: **Joe Colombo** (Italian, 1930–1971)
Materials: acrylonitrile-butadiene-styrene (ABS), steel,
polypropylene (PP)
Manufacturer: Bieffeplast, Padua, Italy (from 1970–c.1999) and
B–Line, Grisignano di Zocco, Italy (from 1999 to present)
Measurements: 42 cm wide, 43 cm deep, 52.5 cm high (two tiers),
73.5 cm high (three tiers), 94.5 cm high (four tiers)

Videosphere
portable television, 1970

The Victor Talking Machine Company of Japan was founded in 1927, since when JVC (as it later became known) has continually been at the forefront of developments in the electronics industry. During the late 1960s and early 1970s, JVC (along with other Japanese manufacturers such as Panasonic) began to produce progressive designs within the Pop idiom, intended for a more youth-based audience. Inspired by the Space Race these designs were highly futuristic. In fact, with their unusual forms, their incorporation of innovative functional devices and their brightly coloured plastic casings, they must initially have seemed like products from another planet. Undoubtedly, JVC's *Videosphere* portable television was the best example of this Japan-goes-Pop design phenomenon. Looking like a spaceman's helmet, with its spherical housing made of glossy ABS and its visor-like screen made of smoky-grey PMMA, this product made a literal reference to the Space Age, whilst also capturing the forward-looking spirit of the time through its miniaturisation of technology and its inventive use of synthetic polymers. Extremely popular in both Europe and America, it helped establish Japan's reputation for design innovation within the consumer electronics market. The *Videosphere* could either hang from the ceiling using a chain or sit on a base with a scooped indentation that enabled easy positioning. As a contemporary advertisement noted, 'The JVC *Videosphere* TV is a fascinating new and innovative concept in entertainment design. It's a mobile, a hanging sculpture, a show-piece, a conversation piece, and a most convenient way to watch TV anytime... anywhere!' It could be plugged into a car or camper van's power supply using a special lighter cable, and the optional rechargeable battery pack made it a truly portable design. In some models, the base also incorporated an alarm clock. Above all, the *Videosphere*, perhaps more than any other television, demonstrated the transformative power of plastics to mould previously undreamt of forms – making futuristic design visions into stylish realities.

Designer: **Japan Victor Company** (Japan)
Materials: acrylonitrile-butadiene-styrene (ABS), polymethyl
methacrylate (PMMA), other materials
Manufacturer: Japan Victor Company, Yokohama, Japan
Measurements: 36 cm high (with stand), 28 cm diameter

Model No. 290
chair, 1970

Designer: **Steen Østergaard** (Danish, 1926–1990)
Materials: glass-reinforced polyamide (PA-GF)
Manufacturer: France & Son for Cado, Aarhus, Denmark
Measurements: 78 cm high, 52 cm wide, 51 cm deep

Contemporary photograph
showing stacked *Model No. 290*
chairs on specially designed
'dolly', c.1970

After the success of the *Panton* chair, many other
designers were inspired to create similar single-form,
single-material chairs made in a variety of different
plastic compounds. One of the most successful of
these was Steen Østergaard's seminal range of seating
for Cado, the progressive Danish furniture manufacturing company established by Poul Cadovius in
the late 1950s. In fact, Østergaard's *Model No. 290*
chair of 1970 can be considered a far more resolved
design than Verner Panton's, because it used less
material, stacked more efficiently and, perhaps most
importantly, was infinitely more comfortable to sit in.
Available with or without a seat cushion, the *Model
No. 290* was the first chair to be injection-moulded
entirely in glass-filled nylon (glass-reinforced polyamide) – a composite material developed around 1970
that exponentially increased the polymer's resistance
to wear, while enhancing its structural strength. The
material was coloured all the way through, antistatic
and weather-resistant. Together with Østergaard's
matching *Model No. 265* lounge chair and M*odel No.
291* armchair, this elegant cantilevered plastic chair
provided, according to the journal *Design from
Scandinavia*, 'comfortable seating in a timeless design
appropriate to any setting'. Lightweight yet strong, the
Model No. 290 could be stacked in up to twenty-four
units on a purpose-designed stand on castors – an
eloquent example of how plastics can be used to create
efficient and functional designs with the minimum
of means.

Cado publicity photograph
showing *Model No. 290* chairs,
c.1970

Fish
bath toy, 1970

After the huge commercial success of his best-selling *Playplax* constructional toy in the mid-1960s – designed while he was still a student at the Royal College of Art in London – Patrick Rylands decided to continue designing child-centred toys after his graduation as a ceramicist. Over a thirty-year career, most of his work was distinguished by simple forms and primary colours, exemplified by two of his earliest designs: the sculptural *Fish* and *Bird* bath toys. These comprised two-part mouldings, made of hard and shiny ABS plastic, that were then glued together. ABS was, in fact, the perfect choice of material for toy-making. Virtually indestructible, ABS can also be moulded with ease into glossy, smooth-edged surfaces that are easy to clean and safe for children. The *Fish* and *Bird* self-righting floating toys were radically different from earlier toy designs, not simply in their use of plastic, but in the tactile abstraction of their forms, decorated only with simple eye motifs. Crucial to their success was their sensitivity to the limited cognitive and physical abilities of a small child. Patrick Rylands puts it slightly differently, insisting that they were, 'designed for the child in me'. His ability to create such beautiful yet rational designs in plastic also owed much to his training in ceramics, and to his early design work for pottery manufacturers. An ability to manipulate clay into sculptural forms gave Rylands an insight into the newly available synthetic materials, and the skill to mould them in ways that elegantly expressed their inherent plasticity. In addition, the biomorphic shapes of these toys closely reflected the influence of contemporary fine art, lending them an aesthetic sophistication that was then, and remains now, a rarity in the design of plastic toys. Between 1970 and 2002, Rylands went on to design well over one hundred children's toys for the Dutch manufacturer, Ambi. The majority were produced in ABS, and they collectively demonstrate that an intelligent approach to the design process, allied to state-of-the-art plastics manufacturing techniques, can beget designs for children that are physically durable, visually delightful and, above all, playful.

Patrick Rylands, *Bird* toy for Trendon, 1970

Designer: **Patrick Rylands** (British 1942–)
Materials: acrylonitrile-butadiene-styrene (ABS)
Manufacturer: Trendon, Malton, Yorkshire, UK
Measurements: 6.5 cm high, 12.5 cm wide, 5 cm deep

Designer: **Alexander Begge** (German, 1941–)
Materials: glass-reinforced polyamide (PA-GF)
Manufacturer: Casala Werke, Lauenaur, Germany (reissued by
Casala Meubelen Nederland, Culemborg, Netherlands)
Measurements: 77 cm high, 49 cm wide, 50 cm deep

Since the dawn of industrialisation, designers have striven to create objects with fewer components and materials, knowing that greater unity and simplicity in design facilitate high-volume manufacture, production efficiency and enhanced profitability. For furniture designers, this has meant the dogged pursuit of the one-piece, one-material chair, preferably made of plastics. In 1968, Verner Panton was the first designer to realise a single-material, single-piece chair in injection-moulded thermoplastic. Other designers, though, attempted to achieve this seating nirvana with their own structurally and materially unified designs. One of the most successful of these was the *Casalino* chair, created by a German designer, Alexander Begge, between 1970 and 1971. Before this, Begge had trained as a carpenter and a potter, and had also studied interior architecture at the Werkkunst-schule (School of Arts and Crafts) in Düsseldorf from 1962 to 1967. He then began working as a designer at the Casala furniture factory, and it was there that one day he had a vision of 'a wisp of fog' that became the inspiration for his influential seating collection. With its cantilevered base, the *Casalino 2004* also had a gracefully flowing profile, while the distinguishing cutout in its

base enhanced the design's overall visual and physical lightness. Awarded the Die Gute Industrieform Prize at the Hanover Fair in 1971, the *Casalino* stacking chair – elegant and robust with its sculpturally rounded edges – was produced using glass-reinforced nylon, which meant that it was easy to clean, anti-static, colourfast, scratch-proof and, most importantly, weather-resistant. Two smaller, child-sized versions of the chair, the *Casalino 2000/00* and the *Casalino 2000/01*, were also produced for toddlers and school-aged children respectively, but unlike the adult-sized chair these models had solid bases. In addition, the range included the matching *Casalino 2007* armchair and the *Casalino 2012* stool. The *Casalino* range has recently been reissued employing the original moulds that were rediscovered by chance at a depot in Antalya, Turkey. A strengthened polyamide, known as PA-GF 30, is being used for the adult chairs, while the *Casalino 2000* children's versions are made from BASF's Luran S, an acrylonitrile styrene acrylate compound. Sadly, the *Casalino* range was Begge's first and only foray into the world of furniture design. He subsequently founded a firm manufacturing furnaces, and thus abandoned a promising career in design.

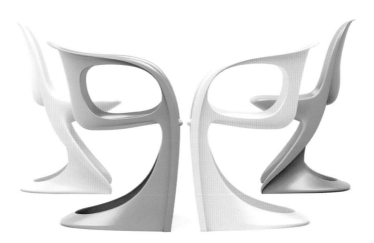

Alexander Begge, *Casalino 2007*
armchair, 1970–1971

Multiset
trays, 1970

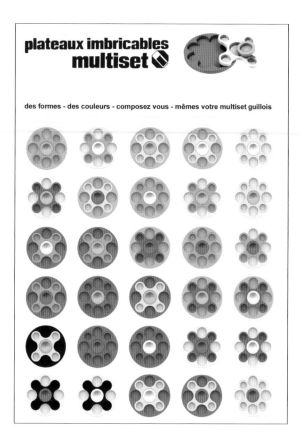

plateaux imbricables
multiset ◈

des formes - des couleurs - composez vous - mêmes votre multiset guillois

Edition Guillois advertisement
showing different *Multiset* tray
combinations, 1970

Throughout his prolific career, Jean-Pierre Vitrac has
consistently created functionally and aesthetically
innovative products that exemplify his belief that
design should involve the 'conception of radically new
products'. One of his earliest designs was a trio of
interlocking trays, known as the *Multiset*, made in
a variety of colours in shiny and rigid, injection-
moulded ABS. As Vitrac explains, 'The goal of this
design was a set of trays that played with the idea of
geometric shapes. Each element was produced in
several colours, and all the trays were composed by
mixing these different coloured pieces, which allowed
a great number of variants.' The largest tray had a
recessed, eight-petal form into which the medium-
sized, quatrefoil-shaped tray could be fitted. This, in
turn, was designed to accommodate the smallest
component: a circular, bowl-like element. Drinking
glasses could be slotted into the tray's smaller, circular
recesses so that they would not move about when
carried; the larger recesses could be used for bottles,
and the central section functioned as a bowl for olives,
crisps or nuts. Like other radical designs from this
period, the *Multiset* tray system invited a degree of
interaction from its users, promoted through its
advertising with the line: 'Forms – colour – you
compose your own *Multiset*.' During this period, and
especially in France, art multiples became extremely
popular, and although this progressive design clearly
has functional utility, it also makes a striking aesthetic
statement. In fact, when the tray is not in use, it looks
just like an Op Art multiple wall sculpture. In 1980,
Vitrac returned to the concept of interlocking plastic
elements with the design of his *Set 9* drinking set, in
which beakers slotted into the handle of a pitcher.
With these attractive and functionally innovative
designs he demonstrated that, if skillfully handled,
plastics could provide their own sophisticated and
unique aesthetic sensibility, and powerfully set
themselves apart from any other medium.

Designer: **Jean-Pierre Vitrac** (French, 1944–)
Materials: acrylonitrile-butadiene-styrene (ABS)
Manufacturer: Edition Guillois, Jura, France
Measurements: 13.3 cm, 37 cm, 40.3 cm diameters

Export 2000
kitchen scales, 1970

Between 1958 and 1977, Marco Zanuso and Richard Sapper collaborated on the design of numerous award-winning products, many of which were notable for their innovative use of plastics. In the late 1960s, the French weighing-scale manufacturer, Terraillon, commissioned this talented duo to design a new set of bathroom scales. Launched in 1968, the resulting product was known as the *T111*, and had a soft-edged design that used ABS in a variety of colours. A few years later, Zanuso and Sapper designed an even more commercially successful set of kitchen scales for Terraillon – the *Export 2000*. Produced from 1971, this product incorporated a housing made of colourful, injection-moulded ABS in which the bowl, suitable for measuring dry ingredients or liquids, could be inverted to form a flat-topped lid for easy storage. Sleek and compact, the *Export 2000* was, according to the plastics historian Sylvia Katz, 'a fitting weighing machine for the land of gourmets'. Certainly it was appreciated as much for its stylish good looks, which epitomised early 1970s geometric Pop Modernism,

as for its functionality. The design went on to become a bestseller in France, and within three years of its launch a staggering 378,000 units had been sold. Among the reasons for its great success was the fact that it was an elegant yet logical design that looked good on a counter-top, but which could also be neatly and efficiently stored away when not in use. Its inverted bowl-cum-lid also gave the design a playful, puzzle-like quality, and it sometimes took people a little while to figure out how to use it. In addition, the scales had an angled magnifying lens made of PMMA, which meant that the weight measurement indicator was easy to read from a counter-top position. The phenomenal sales success of the *Export 2000* illustrated that thermoplastics could be used to create completely new interpretations of a product, giving a manufacturer a real competitive advantage in the process. Zanuso and Sapper designed other products for Terraillon in subsequent years, including the innovative *Minitimer* (1971) that shared a similar, pared-down aesthetic.

Richard Sapper, *Minitimer*
kitchen timer for Terraillon, 1971

Designers: **Marco Zanuso** (Italian, 1916–2001) and
Richard Sapper (German, 1932–)
Materials: acrylonitrile-butadiene-styrene (ABS), polymethyl
methacrylate (PMMA)
Manufacturer: Terraillon, Chatou, France
Measurements: 11.7 cm high, 16.7 cm wide, 11 cm deep

HL 70
desk fan, 1970

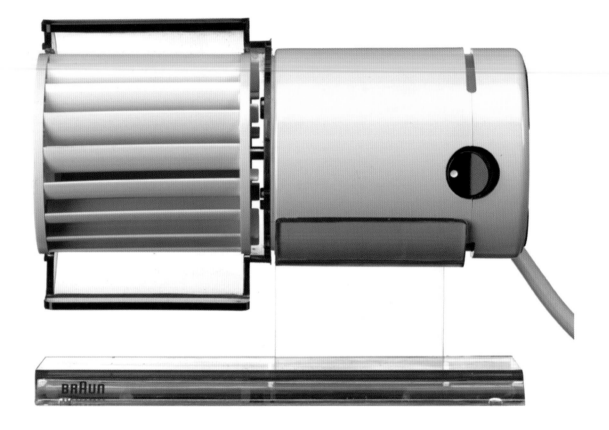

Designers: **Reinhold Weiss** (German, 1934–) and
Jürgen Greubel (German, 1938–)
Materials: acrylonitrile-butadiene-styrene (ABS), polymethyl
methacrylate (PMMA)
Manufacturer: Braun, Frankfurt, Germany
Measurements: 10.7 cm high, 15.1 cm wide, 8 cm deep

Reinhold Weiss, *HL 1/11* table fan
for Braun, 1961

From 1955 to 1995, Dieter Rams instigated a rational
system of product development at Braun, initially in
his capacity as a designer, and later as the firm's design
director. During his tenure, the company's products
came to symbolise the design purity and manufacturing excellence of German industry. Their international
reputation owed to their clear demonstration of what
constituted good design – innovation, usefulness,
durability, honesty, intuitiveness and logic – in addition to which they possessed a quietly unobtrusive
essentialist aesthetic. During the 1950s and 1960s,
most Braun products comprised some plastic elements
alongside metal parts, and employed a muted palette
of white, grey and black, as exemplified by Reinhold
Weiss's *HL 1/11* desk fan of 1961. In the 1970s, however,
Braun's design department adopted a brighter and
more varied colour palette, and ABS increasingly
became the team's material of choice. This change of
emphasis can be seen in the *HL 70* desk fan designed
by Reinhold Weiss and Jürgen Greubel in 1970, with its
sleek and shiny, injection-moulded ABS casing, and its
elegant transparent acrylic hood and stand. Although
this design revealed rather more of a Pop sensibility
than the earlier model, it still possessed the elegant
and seemingly effortless simplicity that had become
synonymous with the Braun name. Interestingly,
it could also be removed from its stand and placed
on its end, if required. The *HL 70* unambiguously
demonstrated that plastic objects could have an
aesthetic and functional integrity, as well as a superlative functional durability – the very antithesis of the
throwaway mentality generally associated with plastic
objects.

Vicario
armchair, 1971

Designer: **Vico Magistretti** (Italian, 1920–2006)
Materials: glass-reinforced polyester (GRP), rubber
Manufacturer: Artemide, Pregnana Milanese, Italy
Measurements: 68 cm high, 72 cm wide, 67 cm deep

In 1969, Vico Magistretti designed the *Selene* stacking chair, a remarkable single-piece composition made of compression-moulded Reglar (glass-reinforced polyester). As Magistretti later explained, 'I didn't want a chair to be composed of several different parts, I wanted a single unit; nor did I want to create a chair like Joe Colombo's, that, with its thick, heavy legs looked like an elephant... the key that helped me find the solution for the *Selene* was the leg's 'S' section.' Following on from the development of the *Selene* side chair, Magistretti then turned his attention to the creation of two armchairs. He employed a similar configuration for their legs, but this time chose a W-shaped profile that ensured extra strength and stability while also conferring lightness. The resulting designs were the *Gaudì* (1970), and the larger and lower *Vicario* (1971), both manufactured by Artemide. For these more technically complex designs, Magis-

tretti perforated the seats so that they would 'flow' into the rear legs, permitting a unified construction that could be efficiently moulded in polymer resin as a single unit. In Magistretti's words: 'the curves, long and connected... the general sinuous aspect... though well suited functionally for the chair, all stem from a need that addressed a specific constraint of the project' – namely the choice of materials and manufacturing process. Although the *Selene* constituted a technical breakthrough in terms of its manufacture, it was thus the later, and amply proportioned *Vicario* that is perhaps the more impressive accomplishment, as the first large-scale, single-piece plastic armchair to be moulded in a single material. Rationally conceived through a process-driven approach to design, these elegant chairs by the master form-giver, Vico Magistretti, contributed greatly to the elevation of the broader perception of plastics.

Vico Magistretti, *Selene* chairs for
Artemide, 1969

Vico Magsitretti, *Gaudì* armchair
for Artemide, 1970

HLD 6/61

hair drier, 1971

Designer: **Jürgen Greubel** (German, 1938–)
Materials: acrylonitrile-butadiene-styrene (ABS)
Manufacturer: Braun, Frankfurt, Germany
Measurements: 20 cm high, 19.5 cm wide, 6.2 cm deep

Packaging showing *HLD 1000*
hairdryer designed by Jürgen
Greubel for Braun, 1975

After studying industrial design at Wiesbaden Senior
Technical College, Jürgen Greubel joined the renowned
in-house design team at Braun, then under the
legendary direction of Dieter Rams. Between 1967 and
1973, and as part of this remarkable concentration of
design talent, Greubel created a number of appliances
that introduced both a softer line and a more colourful
palette into Braun's product line. Skilfully exploiting
the formal potential of ABS, with bold yet soft-edged
forms and glossy surfaces, his work expressed the
more casual and youthful aesthetic of product design
in the early 1970s. Although the inverted 'L' shape of
Greubel's *HLD 6/61* hair dryer derived from earlier and
more traditional models, it was nonetheless a radical
reworking of the concept, with its colourful ABS casing
partially covering the side air inlets, giving the design
a more unified and streamlined look. In 1975, Greubel
redesigned the hair dryer, resulting in his *HLD 1000*
model, which incorporated seven rings of ventilation
holes in the ABS casing, and had a similarly soft-edged
aesthetic. Although less restrained than other Braun
products, Greubel's designs, notably his hair dryers
and his Multipress *MP 50* juice extractor (1970), were
in total accord with Dieter Rams's 'Ten Command-
ments of Good Design', being not only innovative,
functional, aesthetically pleasing and durable, but
also being conceived to be used intuitively. Importantly, Greubel's product designs for Braun showed that
plastics could be used to make appliances that harmoniously synthesised superior utility with a modern and
essentialist aesthetic.

Capitello
chair, 1971

Between 1967 and 1976, Gufram introduced its iconic *I Multipli* series of furnishings, made of self-skinning polyurethane foam. These challenging and quirky objects were not intended to be functional design solutions but playful products of the imagination. Created by the Turinese design group, Studio 65, the *Capitello* was one of the most widely publicised designs in the collection, and certainly the most influential, to the extent that it predicted the work of Post-Modern classicists such as Robert Venturi, Michael Graves and Hans Hollein. Mocking the intellectual pretensions of classical architecture and the reverence paid to the classical orders, the *Capitello* was radical in its intellectual provocativeness and also visually arresting, thanks to its out-sized and out-of-context Pop sensibility. Taking the form of a gigantic Ionic capital, the *Capitello* also tore up another tenet of good design – truth to materials – with its use of soft yet structural polyurethane foam, which mimicked the appearance of carved stone. Originally developed for military use, flexible polyurethane foam began to be produced commercially in 1954. By the mid-1960s, it was widely used in the automotive sector as a component of dampening systems, as well as finding applications in the furniture industry as spring-less upholstery. Around 1970, a system of cold moulding was developed which produced polyurethane foams possessing even greater elasticity. It was this type of self-skinning, squishy, cold-foamed polyurethane that was used in varying densities by Gufram to produce the self-cushioning *Capitello*, which weighed in at twenty-five kilogrammes. In fact, the *Capitello* – always more functional art object than serious seating solution – could be used in conjunction with two other pieces from Gufram's range, the *Attica* chair and table (1972), to turn even the most modern of apartments into a surreal archaeological site. Irreverent and monumental, the *Capitello* expresses the youthful and experimental *zeitgeist* of the 1960s Plastic Age that questioned long-held preconceptions about design and 'high art', and replaced them with playful, tongue-in-cheek Pop irony.

Studio 65, *Attica* table and (right) chair for Gufram, 1972

Design Group: **Studio 65** (Italian, est. 1968)
Materials: Guflac-coated, self-skinning, cold-foamed
polyurethane (PU)
Manufacturer: Gufram, Turin, Italy
Measurements: 110 cm high, 82 cm wide, 120 cm deep

Divisumma 18
electronic printing calculator
1971–1973

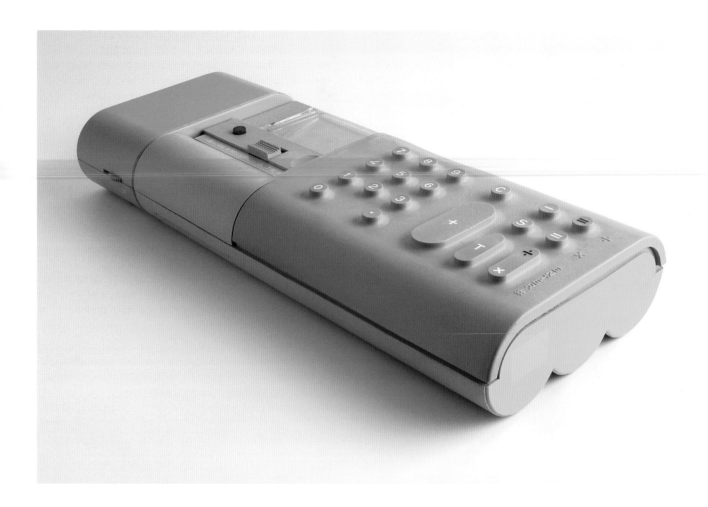

Designer: **Mario Bellini** (Italian, 1935–)
Materials: acrylonitrile-butadiene-styrene (ABS),
synthetic rubber (SR), melamine formaldehyde (MF)
Manufacturer: Ing. C. Olivetti & Company, Ivrea, Italy
Measurements: 4.8 cm high, 24.8 cm wide, 12.1 cm deep

Throughout his long and highly productive career, the Italian industrial design supremo, Mario Bellini, has created literally hundreds of innovative designs for a wide range of manufacturers. Between 1963 and 1991, he was also the chief design consultant for Olivetti – a company famous for its design-led office machines. In this capacity, Bellini was responsible for developing numerous groundbreaking products, including the *Divisumma 18* printing calculator. This either battery- or mains-operated design was highly influential for two principal reasons: the tactile, synthetic-rubber elastomer that coated its keyboard section, and the bright and playful yellow colouring that differentiated it from the drab, muted appearance of earlier office equipment. By using a combination of three different plastics – ABS, elastomer and melamine – Bellini was also able to make his calculator considerably lighter, smaller and more portable than earlier models. The elastomer-covered, nipple-like buttons that were one of the design's novel features have since been widely copied throughout the consumer electronics industry. Seizing on the tactile and expressive potentialities of the newly available synthetic materials, Bellini used them to relate the rapidly evolving technologies of the electronics industry to the playful visual aesthetic of 1960s Pop culture. In the December 1973 issue of *Domus* magazine, Bellini described the *Divisumma 18* as: 'A strange object which can be stood upright like a small, reassuring totem; a curious object with the capacity, perhaps, to create what might even be a flow of mutual understanding, seeing that by now everyone is capable of calculating.' By demonstrating that electronic products could be sensual, fun and empowering, Bellini blazed a fresh and more youth-oriented trail in industrial design, one that would increasingly rely on the use of plastics to forge emotional bonds between object and user. Sculptural form, physical tactility and a Pantone rainbow of colours would distinguish the new objects of desire.

Olivetti advertisement showing
Divisumma 18 calculator, 1974

Pluvium
umbrella stand, 1972

On completing his studies at the Istituto Statale d'Arte in Bologna in 1960, Giancarlo Piretti joined the progressive furniture company Anonima Castelli, where he became head designer and also the firm's head of development until 1972. In this capacity, he created not only the award-winning *Plia* folding chair (1967), but a variety of other furnishings notable for their innovative use of newly available plastics and their unusual yet functional forms, such as his *Pluvium* umbrella stand of 1972. A highly rational design especially in terms of its manufacturability, the *Pluvium* comprised a stable cylindrical base and six identical rotating circular elements – all made of injection-moulded ABS – to hold the umbrellas. When not in use, these swivelling elements could be stacked one on top of the other to save space. The *Pluvium* was a commercially successful design, which married utility with a stylish and contemporary look, ensuring that it could be used in both fashionable homes and modern offices. It was produced in a wide range of colours – white, blue, orange, grey, red, black and yellow – and, because it was injection-moulded in a hard and shiny thermoplastic, it was highly durable and easy to keep clean. Its name means 'rain' in Latin and, when all the elements are stacked together, the *Pluvium* certainly has a quasi-classical, columnar appearance. Piretti also designed a coat stand in 1972, known as the *Planta*, which had hooked elements that could be folded away when not in use, and that possessed a similar contextual flexibility, making it popular in both domestic settings and contract environments. Above all, Giancarlo Piretti's designs demonstrated that the introduction of injection-moulded ABS made it possible to develop new forms that not only delighted the eye, but also at the same time provided outstanding function and durability.

Pluvium umbrella stands in 'closed' position

Designer: **Giancarlo Piretti** (Italian, 1940–)
Materials: acrylonitrile-butadiene-styrene (ABS),
Manufacturer: Anonima Castelli, Bologna, Italy
Measurements: 49.5 cm high, 29 cm diameter

Ariante
electric fan, 1973

Designer: **Marco Zanuso** (Italian, 1916–2001)
Materials: acrylonitrile-butadiene-styrene (ABS), chromed metal
Manufacturer: Vortice Elettrosociali, Milan, Italy (produced
from 1974)
Measurements: 18.5 cm high, 18.3 cm wide, 10.9 cm deep

In 1954, the Vortice Elettrosociali manufacturing
company was founded in Milan, and went on to
produce numerous innovative electric fans and
ventilation systems. To this end, in the early 1970s the
company sought the design expertise of Marco Zanuso,
who had already earned a considerable reputation as
an industrial designer of innovative household
appliances, including a sewing machine for Borletti
(1956); and the *Doney* television for Brionvega (1962),
which was Europe's first portable model. Like his other
designs for industry, the resulting *Ariante* electric fan,
with its simple, box-like ABS casing, possessed a
refined elegance that seamlessly merged form with
function. The fan's distinctive diagonal elements
functioned as a barrier, protecting fingers from the
internal, propeller-like blades. Yet, at the same time,
this grill-like construction gave the *Ariante* an
interesting Op Art aesthetic. With this landmark
design, Zanuso fully exploited the new polymer's
structural rigidity and smooth high-gloss surface,
while the use of ABS also substantially determined the
ultimate form of the product, which was radically
different from earlier fan designs. Produced in red,
black or white, the *Ariante*, with its simple yet
dynamic form, was a veritable masterpiece of Italian
design, and as such received a prestigious Compasso
d'Oro award in 1979.

Prydan Model Nos. 4075 and **4077**
bowls, 1974

During the 1960s and 1970s, various Swedish companies began to produce high-quality plastic homewares that were not only extremely stylish, but also sensitively emphasised the form-giving qualities of newly available plastics, such as ABS. The *Prydan* bowls from the mid-1970s, designed by Hans Skillius, exemplify this particularly Scandinavian approach to synthetic materials, with their bold, sculptural forms injection moulded in high-gloss white, yellow, blue or red ABS. After studying at the Konstindustriskolan (School of Design and Crafts, University of Gothenburg) from 1964 to 1968, Skillius initially worked as an in-house designer for Hasselblad (from 1968 to 1970), and then for Hammarplast (between 1970 and 1976). For the latter company, he designed various kitchenwares, including a colander in ABS, as well as products for the garden and a children's sledge. His *Prydan* bowls, however, were quite different from Hammarplast's regular product line: they were more self-consciously about interior design, and they were infinitely more stylish. The name of the bowls stems from the Swedish word *pryden* which means 'adorn'. Their unusual form, though, was derived from the *Lampara* hanging light (1965) produced by the famous Italian company, Fontana Arte. In the words of Skillius himself: 'What inspired me to design the *Prydan* bowls was an Italian lamp that I bought at the time. I put the shape of the light upside down in my mind and found that it could make nice bowls.' Interestingly, the bowls (which came in three different sizes) were intended to be multi-functional, and Skillius suggested various possible uses: 'Fruit bowl. Flower vase. Outside ornament. Roses floating in water. On pillars outside the country cottage (with geraniums in). Sweets bowl. Chips bowl. Almonds. Snacks! Ice bucket. Christmas nuts. Easter eggs. Punch bowl. Pipe stand. Ashtray. All those leftover foreign coins. Money box. Candle holder. In the bathroom with all those bits and pieces! For mending, with needles, thread and balls of wool. Or just full of bills! But mostly on the window sill, the table or mantelpiece. *Prydan* is what you want it to be.' Hygienic, democratic and durable, the *Prydan* bowls were an affordable yet stylish design that exemplified the Swedish approach to mass-produced plastic homewares, and which powerfully expressed the noble qualities of these new wonder materials.

Hammerplast advertisement showing the multi-functional uses of the *Prydan* bowls, 1974

Designer: **Hans Skillius** (Swedish, 1941–)
Materials: acrylonitrile-butadiene-styrene (ABS)
Manufacturer: Hammarplast, Tingsryd, Sweden
Measurements: *Model No. 4075*: 17 cm high, 16 cm diameter |
Model No. 4077: 21 cm high, 25 cm diameter

Plack
disposable picnic set, 1977

Designer: **Jean-Pierre Vitrac** (French, 1944–)
Materials: polystyrene (PS)
Manufacturer: Diam, Les Mureaux, France
Measurements: 28 cm long

Jean-Pierre Vitrac's *Plack* disposable picnic set was an extremely rational design in terms of its overall concept and method of manufacture, with the plate, knife, fork, spoon and cup all made from a single thermoplastic moulding. As Vitrac explains, 'The objective was a compact shape, moulded in one piece, which allowed the individual pieces to be snapped apart and used for parties. Although it was intended to be a throwaway design, the pieces were actually very often reused, particularly by children.' The greatest technological hurdle that had to be overcome in bringing this design to large-scale mass production was finding the right plastic material. As Vitrac recalls, the design required a material that struck a 'balance between being easily breakable but also resistant when manipulated during transport and storage'. After experimenting with several options, polystyrene was finally deemed the most appropriate polymer for the job. From 1977 to 1980, this innovative and inexpensively manufactured picnic set was mass produced by Diam and distributed by another French company, Co&Co. The plastic, tray-like sets were stacked for easy transportation, and exemplified Vitrac's core belief that design should be about 'the conception of radically new products'. Symbolic, sadly, of our wasteful, consumerist culture, very few *Plack* sets have survived, and something designed to be momentary is now ironically valued for its rarity.

Jean-Pierre Vitrac, *Set 9* drinking set for Bourbon, 1980

Design 10
cutlery, 1978–1979

Don Wallance is best remembered for his ergonomically refined cutlery. However, he also designed furniture and, furthermore, chronicled the design process itself through his seminal book, *Shaping America's Products* (1956), which incorporated case studies of well-designed products. He trained at New York University and the Design Laboratory (both in New York City), and then designed products in wood and metal for the US Army Quartermaster Corps, between 1942 and 1948. In 1951, Wallance began designing sculptural tableware and accessories for the H.E. Lauffer Company in New York – a collaboration that lasted thirty years. He also designed other flatware ranges for European companies, most notably Hugo C. Pott in Germany, and Norsk Stålpress in Norway. Most of his flatware ranges were made of high-quality stainless steel, such as his elegant *Magnum* flatware range (1970); however, Wallance also explored the potential of thermoplastics as a suitable material for cutlery. His *Design 10* flatware range was manufactured in Lexan, a tough polycarbonate discovered in 1953 by Dr Daniel Fox, a

scientist in the chemical development division of General Electric who was trying to develop a new insulating material for wiring. Interestingly, one week later and working entirely independently, Dr Hermann Schnell of Bayer in Germany also discovered Lexan. Although the polymer looks similar to acrylic (polymethyl methacrylate), it is actually exponentially more resilient – in fact it is so tough that it is now used to make bulletproof glass. Given the incredible, hardwearing durability of Lexan, it is not surprising that Don Wallance decided to use this sturdy plastic for his *Design 10* flatware. Wallance's design, with its almost archetypical form, is surprisingly comfortable to handle and is a tribute to its creator's understanding of ergonomics. Mass produced by Jersey Plastic Molders for H.E. Lauffer from 1981, this simple four-piece range was inexpensive to produce and confirmed that, with the correct selection of synthetic materials, even those most disposable of objects – the humble plastic knife, fork and spoon – could be transformed into durable and useful products.

Designer: **Don Wallance** (American, 1909–1990)
Materials: Lexan / polycarbonate (PC)
Manufacturer: H.E. Lauffer Company, Somerset (NJ), USA
Measurements: knife: 18.8 cm long | fork: 17.8 cm long |
tablespoon: 17.6 long | teaspoon: 16.6 long

Dalila II
chair, 1980

Designer: **Gaetano Pesce** (Italian, 1939–)
Materials: epoxy-coated rigid polyurethane foam (PU)
Manufacturer: Cassina, Meda, Italy
Measurements: *Dalila II*: 85 cm high, 49 cm wide, 55 cm deep |
Dalila III: 71 cm high, 53 cm wide, 62 cm deep

Gaetano Pesce, *Sansone* table for
Cassina, 1980

Throughout his career, Gaetano Pesce has experimented with new plastic materials and has applied them within unusual design applications. By using plastics in an almost artisanal manner, he has frequently managed to imbue his designs with an element of handcrafted individuality. For Pesce, plastics are not about the exact replication of a design within the context of industrial mass production. Instead he aims to highlight the variations that can be achieved when a design is serially produced on a limited scale, so that each design is unique. In 1980, Pesce designed three chairs – *Dalila I*, *Dalila II* and *Dalila III* – to complement his *Sansone* table of the same year. This furniture group was inspired by the biblical story of Samson's love for the treacherous yet beautiful Delilah. The freeform table with its precariously angled legs evoked the duped Samson's furious shattering of columns at the temple of the Philistines, while the chairs, in contrast, echoed the soft forms of Delilah's curvaceous body. Although the *Dalila I* chair existed only as a prototype, the *Dalila II* side chair and the *Dalila III* armchair were both put into production by Cassina, using rigid polyurethane foam coated in either grey, black or terracotta red epoxy resin. These sensuously anthropomorphic chairs with their undulating profiles countered the hard-edged aesthetic of most mass-produced furniture, and expressed the wonderful plasticity of synthetic polymers. Although the rigid plastic was hard to the touch, it looked soft and tactile – a flair for the paradoxical that runs through Pesce's work, as does the use of innovative forms, figurative abstraction and references to femininity and religion. Pesce has always embraced a wide range of polymers, from soft polyurethane foam to cast liquid resins, in order to create functional objects that possess a strong artistic sensibility and often an overt symbolism, features not usually associated with designs in plastic.

Radio-in-a-Bag

1981

In 1981, for his postgraduate degree project at the Royal College of Art in London, Daniel Weil designed a series of bag-enclosed radios and inflatable radios made of silkscreen printed PVC that were intended to break new ground in 'the thinking of design'. The traditional values associated with radios were playfully subverted in these landmark objects that introduced a new Post-Modern language into the world of consumer products. The most celebrated of these designs, *Radio-in-a-Bag*, was subsequently put into production by Weil's own manufacturing company, Parenthesis, and was also produced under licence in Japan by Apex International Company. The working parts of the radio were embedded in a heat-sealed PVC envelope and, unlike previous designs where the mechanism was hidden within a solid housing, here it was plain to see through the transparent plastic. In so doing, Weil made these frequently overlooked components an essential part of the object's aesthetic. The dual function of this provocative design was also highly influential and contradicted the notion of the radio as a static object. By using PVC, a material that was generally seen as eminently disposable, Weil also attempted to show that the role of plastics in product design could be elevated both aesthetically and

culturally. Moreover, the silkscreen printing that adorned the *Radio-in-a-Bag* powerfully captured the anarchic *zeitgeist* of early 1980s Punk. As such, Weil also blazed the trail for new directions in the perception of products, with his shift towards aesthetic individualism and symbolic value, rather than mass-produced commercialism. Between 1982 and 1983, he evolved these anti-commercial ideas through a series of clocks and radios for Memphis – the latter provocatively combining flexible PVC, a material perceived as almost valueless, with silk, a material associated for centuries with luxury. Like his earlier designs, these mixed-media hybrids heralded a new way of thinking about product design. A subsequent generation of designers has absorbed this approach, and its insistence that a connective, poetic or symbolic quality can accompany or transcend a product's function and styling. As a revolutionary exercise in product deconstruction, *Radio-in-a-Bag* was a highly influential Post-Modern design that spawned numerous imitations. Even more importantly, perhaps, it was a design that countered the lowly status of synthetic materials and celebrated their expressive and formal potential.

Daniel Weil, *Radio*, 1982 – made from heat-welded envelopes of PVC encasing silk and cotton printed textiles

Designer: **Daniel Weil** (Argentine/British, 1953–)
Materials: silkscreen-printed polyvinyl chloride (PVC)
Manufacturer: Parenthesis, London, UK/Apex International
Company, Tokyo, Japan (from 1983)
Measurements: 20.5 cm wide, 29 cm high

Carlton

bookcase/room divider
1981

Designer: **Ettore Sottsass** (Austrian/Italian, 1917–2007)
Materials: high-pressure laminate (HPL), wood
Manufacturer: Memphis, Milan, Italy
Measurements: 195 cm high, 190 cm wide, 40 cm deep

Another type of plastic material that has been used widely within the design sector is HPL (high-pressure laminate), perhaps known better by its trade name: Formica. Two American engineers, Herbert A. Faber and Daniel J. O'Conor invented this versatile material in 1913, while they were looking for an insulating substance that could be used as a substitute for mica. Soaking layers of paper with a liquid plastic resin and then bonding it under high pressure and temperature, produced this durable plastic laminate. In 1927, Formica Ltd. began lithographing decorative motifs onto the surfaces of its laminates, and by the 1930s the design potential of this new wonder material was being explored by various American designers. After the Second World War, high-pressure laminates became popular with baby-boomers in America as modern, cost-effective materials that were perfect for the contemporary family home. These hardwearing laminates were also extremely popular in Europe during its period of reconstruction. Established in 1957, the Italian manufacturer Abet Laminati tirelessly promoted these new materials to the Italian design community, and spearheaded their development over the next few decades. And rather than producing white or imitation wood laminates, the firm manufactured plastic laminates with bold, silkscreened patterns in bright colours. During the mid-1960s, Ettore Sottsass used Abet laminates for a number of totemic furniture pieces designed for Poltronova, and in so doing managed to elevate plastic laminates into materials of symbolic value. It was, however, the persisting kitsch associations of plastic laminates that explain their status as the materials of choice for designers working within the Post-Modern idiom during the early 1980s. For instance, the majority of furniture produced by Memphis, the radical Italian design group, incorporated laminates produced by Abet. This included the *Carlton* bookcase designed by Sottsass in 1981. Fully exploiting the decorative surface qualities of plastic laminates, this iconic design had a forceful presence that countered perceived notions of good design, and thereby 'good taste', and instead projected the concept of design as metaphor. As Sottsass was later to write, 'It is important to realise that whatever we do or design has iconographic references, it comes from somewhere; any form is always metaphorical, never totally metaphysical; it is never a "destiny" but always a fact with some kind of historical reference. To put an object on a base means to monumentalise it, to make everyone aware it exists.'

Ettore Sottsass, *Teodora* chair for Vitra, 1986–1987 – combining Abet high pressure laminate (HPL) with polymethyl methacrylate (PMMA)

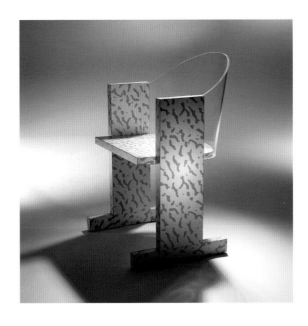

Designers: **Jacques Müller** (Swiss, 1947–) and
Elmar Mock (Swiss, 1954–)
Materials: acrylonitrile styrene acrylate (ASA), styrene acrylo-
nitrile copolymer (SAN), acrylonitrile-butadiene-styrene (ABS),
polymethyl methacrylate (PMMA), metal
Manufacturer: SMH (Société Suisse de Microélectronique et
d'Horlogerie), Bienne, Switzerland (from 1998: Swatch Group
Ltd., Biel, Switzerland)
Measurements: 23.2 cm long, 3.5 cm wide, 0.6 cm deep

Although the story of the *Swatch* being the saviour of the Swiss watch industry is legendary, the origins of this groundbreaking design are less well known. The concept of the *Swatch* can be traced to an earlier watch design, known as the *Delirium Tremens*, developed in 1979 under the guidance of Ernst Thomke, the president of ETA – a leading Swiss watch movement manufacturer. Throughout the 1970s, watchmakers had vied with each other to develop the world's thinnest watch, a goal decisively achieved by the *Delirium Tremens*, with its one-millimetre-thick case that contained far fewer working parts than traditional wristwatches. The only problem was its price tag of $5,000, which meant that only 5,000 units were sold. In the meantime, the Swiss watch industry was fighting for its very survival, with more and more consumers buying cheap yet fashionable digital watches from Japanese manufacturers such as Casio, Citizen and Seiko. Ernst Thomke at ETA came up with a novel idea to save the firm as well as its sister and parent companies, ASUAG and SSHI, from complete financial meltdown – an ultra-slim watch based on technology developed for the *Delirium Tremens*, but manufactured using an entirely automated production system. This proposal was later taken up by Nicolas G. Hayek, who had been brought in as a business consultant to oversee the liquidation of these companies. He decided, though, that they could be rescued by employing Thomke's design concept, and by focusing on a completely new area of business – inexpensive plastic watches in different styles and colours that could be marketed to fashion-conscious consumers. To this end, ETA filed a patent in August 1982 for a 'plastic watch casing with plastic crystal and process for joining the crystal to the casing', developed by its in-house engineers Jacques Müller and Elmar Mock. Launched in 1983, the first *Swatch* range of twelve watches employed this newly patented process for bonding plastics – a form of ultrasonic welding – as well as introducing technologies for automated assembly. These high-tech designs had cases and straps made from a range of different polymers including ASA, ABS and SAN, as well as synthetic crystals made of PMMA. Also enhancing their manufacturing viability was the fact that the *Swatch* consisted of only fifty-one components rather than the normal ninety-one or so, making it easier and thus cheaper to assemble. As an affordable piece of high fashion, the *Swatch* immediately caught the public's attention. It was radically different from anything seen before and, equally importantly, it communicated fun and youthfulness – a watch for an informal and democratic age. Boldly styled, high quality and containing a precise quartz mechanism, the nonetheless affordable *Swatch* was marketed as a fashion accessory through colourful and flashy advertisements that were the very antithesis of the staid world of traditional Swiss watchmaking. This, in turn, not only advanced the wider acceptance of plastic as a material for wristwatches, but also built a powerful brand identity. As Hayek was later to remark, 'If you combine powerful technology with fantasy, you create something very distinct.' The phenomenal and continuing global success of the plastic-cased *Swatch* is irrefutable evidence of the potentialities of synthetic polymers. Since its launch in 1983, over 200 million units have been sold, making it the best-selling watch of all time and also one of the most ubiquitous plastic designs of the last twenty years.

First *Swatch* watch collection, 1983

Designer: **Alberto Meda** (Italian, 1945–)
Materials: polyaramid polymetaphenylene isophthalamide
(m-Aramid), carbon fibre-reinforced epoxy resin (CFRP)
Manufacturer: Alias, Bergami, Italy
Measurements: 74.3 cm high, 55.2 cm wide, 49.5 cm deep

Alberto Meda's *Light-Light* chair was one of the first
furniture designs to use carbon fibre composites.
Although it was only produced in small quantities, this
light yet strong chair demonstrated the extraordinary
structural potential of advanced composites, which
had originally been developed for the aerospace,
motorsports and sporting equipment industries.
As a skilled design engineer, Meda understood the
tolerances of these new materials, and decided on a
construction incorporating a honeycomb core of
polyaramid polymetaphenylene isophthalamide
(better known as Nomex: a synthetic fibre launched by
DuPont in 1967), sandwiched between strengthening
layers of woven carbon fibre set in an epoxy resin
matrix. In order to optimise strength where the design
needed it most, the weave direction of the carbon fibre
was oriented to the areas of greatest stress. The
resulting chair weighed about one kilogram (two
pounds), making it the lightest 'traditional' four-
legged chair ever produced – a high-tech and super-
light offspring of Gio Ponti's classic *Superleggera* chair
of 1952. Although test users found the *Light-Light*
sturdy enough to sit on, its physical lightness was
somewhat disturbing and its overtly engineered Matt
Black aesthetic appeared a little too forbidding for
general taste. Another problem was that because the
chair was laid up by hand it was time consuming to
manufacture and, therefore, quite costly to produce.
All the same, as an experimental exercise in finding
applications for carbon fibre composites within the
furnishing sector, the pioneering *Light-Light* was a
hugely influential design. As Meda notes, 'Lightness
makes us dream, its secret cannot be revealed.
Lightness leads to unpredictable solutions.' The same
could be said for all pioneering uses of advanced
synthetic composites that attempt to bring plastic
dreams into reality.

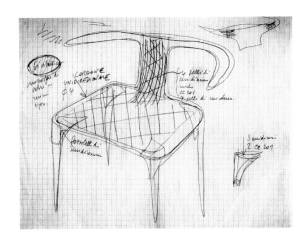

Alberto Meda, sketch for *Light-
Light* chair, c. 1987

Miss Blanche
chair, 1988

Shiro Kuramata was unquestionably one of the most influential Japanese designers of the twentieth century, whose work suffused a Minimalist aesthetic with poetic emotion to create objects of rare and ethereal beauty. Within his extraordinary body of work, the *Miss Blanche* chair from 1988 best exemplifies Kuramata's alchemical way of using synthetic polymers to create magical and otherworldly designs that bridged the age-old cultural traditions of the East with the Modernist design credo of the West. To understand Kuramata's work, one needs to appreciate the spatial tension he created between object and environment, with often his 'dematerialised' designs appearing to float lightly within a space. The *Miss Blanche* chair was named after the refined yet neurotic Blanche DuBois in Tennessee Williams's *A Streetcar Named Desire*, whose grip of reality was gradually surrendered to her fantasies. Kuramata's choice of falling red roses was directly inspired by a corsage worn by Vivien Leigh in the play's 1951 film adaptation. This remarkable chair was originally created for the Kagu Tokyo Designers' Week in 1988, and then produced in a limited edition of 56. Its

painstaking development involved the construction of numerous prototypes with different kinds of artificial blooms, in order to achieve a convincing impression of flowers suspended in space. The method of casting used to create this illusion involved pouring liquid acrylic resin into moulds and then carefully positioning the roses with tweezers. *Miss Blanche* was Kuramata's first design in cast acrylic, a material that captivated his imagination with its extraordinary sensory and spatial qualities, and to which he returned repeatedly in the three remaining years of his all too short life. Kuramata's cast acrylic designs artistically revealed the jewel-like qualities of synthetic polymers demonstrating that, with sensitive handling and delicate balancing of form and space, these materials could resonate with symbolism and poetry, and transcend function altogether. The press release for the travelling 'Shiro Kuramata 1934–1991' exhibition observed of the *Miss Blanche* chair that it 'represents the height of Kuramata's evocative powers: there is nothing soft or frilly about the chair itself, yet it stirs dreams and memories of languid afternoons and lilting Southern belles'.

Shiro Kuramata, *Feather Stool*
produced by Ishimaru Co., 1990

Designer: **Shiro Kuramata** (Japanese, 1934–1991)
Materials: polymethyl methacrylate (PMMA), anodized tubular aluminium, artificial roses
Manufacturer: Ishimaru Company, Tokyo, Japan
Measurements: 93.5 cm high, 63 cm wide, 58 cm deep

Basic

thermal carafe, 1988–1990

With its see-through polycarbonate body, the *Basic* thermal carafe heralded a new aesthetic of transparency that was to become a defining feature of product design in the late 1990s and early 2000s. Its co-designer, Ross Lovegrove, observed that it was, 'the first successful commercial icon to demonstrate the beauty of transparency in everyday affordable products. Composed of a crystal-clear polycarbonate skin and a vacuum metalised inner glass flask, its design carried with it something of a new value system.' Available in an array of colours – including cobalt blue, white, anthracite grey and lava red – the *Basic* flask was visually seductive and technologically persuasive, with its transparent scratch-proof casing forming a protective bubble around its silvered, double-walled glass liner. When launched, the design was named Product of the Year by the Fachverband Kunststoff Konsumwaren (Plastics Consumer Goods Association) and also won the Sonderschau Form Prize at Tendence lifestyle trade fair in Frankfurt. Like other products designed by Lovegrove, the *Basic* flask offered a tantalising glimpse of the future thanks to its pioneering use of new materials and technologies, while at the same time emphasising the form-giving potential and dazzling properties of plastics. Incredibly popular, especially among German consumers, the *Basic* flask was a highly functional design that brought a touch of polymeric magic into the home, and profoundly influenced subsequent generations of products.

Designers: **Ross Lovegrove** (British, 1958–) and
Julian Brown (British, 1955–)
Materials: polycarbonate (PC), mirrored glass
Manufacturer: Alfi, Wertheim, Germany
Measurements: 22.8 cm high, 17.8 cm diameter

Model No. 2 and Model No. 3
vases, 1989

Designer: **Shiro Kuramata** (Japanese, 1934–1991)
Materials: polymethyl methacrylate (PMMA), glass test tubes
Manufacturer: Ishimaru Company, Tokyo, Japan
Measurements: *No. 2*: 21.5 cm high, 11 cm wide, 11 cm deep |
No. 3: 30.5 cm high, 27 cm wide, 8 cm deep

Although Shiro Kuramata's designs did not evolve straightforwardly from either a Western or Eastern design tradition, they did possess a clearly identifiable Japanese poetic quality. Crucially, his work demonstrated with great skill that design could not only exist independently of large-scale industrial production, but that it could be a highly creative activity revealing a deeply personal vision of the world. His astonishing body of work, which is perhaps best exemplified by these two exquisite vases, was the result of a deep understanding of spatial concepts and an equal sensitivity to the materials being used. Like many of his designs, the *Model No. 2* and *Model No. 3* vases have an ethereal quality that appears to take them beyond the realms of our everyday material world. The vases are made from rectangular, column-like blocks of cast acrylic, which have inner cores of magenta dye that appear magically suspended within the clear polymer. As Kuramata once noted, 'The ideal is to have things float in the air without any support... from there design begins to evolve... I feel attracted by transparent materials, because transparency belongs to no one place in particular, and yet exists.' The painstaking process developed by Kuramata to create these vases echoed the meticulous attention to detail

of Japan's age-old craft traditions; yet, for these designs, he was using a fundamentally modern medium rather than materials such as wood, bamboo, steel or lacquer. One of the reasons why acrylic became his material of choice during the late 1980s was its amazing range of optical qualities – properties that he fully explored in creating objects that, like these vases, seem to transcend time and space. Kuramata also appreciated the inherent contradictions of acrylic (more often known as Perspex or Lucite): its ice-like appearance, for instance, conceals its tactile warmth; and this 'lowly' plastic can be used to make sparkling, jewel-like objects. Kuramata's vases are suffused with an amazing sense of visual lightness that gives them a surreal quality, especially when flowers are placed within their standard glass test tubes in a symbolic juxtaposition of natural and synthetic worlds. Through these landmark designs, Kuramata thoroughly exploited the visual and optical potential of cast acrylic resin. At the same time, he powerfully demonstrated that plastics can be used to make beautiful, precious objects with a Zen-like aesthetic, countering in the process the long-held myth that synthetic materials have less intrinsic value than natural ones.

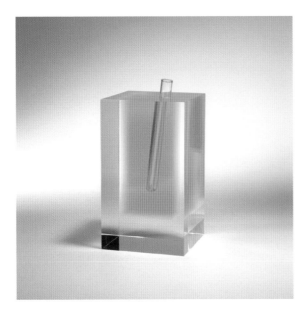

Bubu 1er
stool, 1991

Designer: **Philippe Starck** (French, 1949–)
Materials: polypropylene (PP)
Manufacturer: XO, Servon, France
Measurements: 43 cm high, 32.5 cm diameter

Philippe Starck, *Prince AHA* stool
for Kartell, 1996

One of the best-selling designs of the 1990s, Philippe Starck's playful *Bubu 1er* stool has a characteristically whimsical humour that epitomises the designer's mischievous, tongue-in-cheek approach to design. Its structural simplicity – just two injection-moulded elements made of colourful and robust polypropylene – makes it very efficient to produce and relatively cheap to buy. Yet at the same time, this tooth-shaped 'container stool' gives the impression of contemporary luxury, with its almost neo-baroque flair bestowing a strong sculptural presence that expressively exploits the thermoplastic's form-giving potential. The *Bubu 1er* is not a worthy-but-boring product intended to sit quietly in the background providing mundane utility. Instead, it is a theatrical design extrovert that claims centre stage in a room, and offers a host of functional possibilities to be playfully explored. Its manufacturer, XO, puts its ubiquitousness down to its adaptability, describing it as, 'The most versatile of stools, that does not take itself seriously, is now part of everyday's vocabulary. A vase, a universal container, a laundry basket, an ice bucket, a small pedestal table, a stool even, a tooth crown... It's up to you to invent the rest. One thing is certain. *Bubu 1er* is at the same time a monolithic sculpture and the royal emblem of modernity.' Like so many of Starck's designs for the home, the *Bubu 1er* stool has a distinctive personality that helps forge an emotional bond with the user – a feature that has ensured its resounding sales success. Today, the *Bubu 1er* is manufactured in polypropylene in nine solid and five translucent colours, and also in ABS with a gold or silver lacquer finish. With this design, Starck demonstrates that plastics can be used to create functional yet playful objects that add a touch of inexpensive glamour and cutting-edge style to the everyday domestic environment.

Euclid
thermal jug, 1992

Designer: **Michael Graves** (American, 1934–)
Materials: acrylonitrile-butadiene-styrene (ABS), vacuum glass
Manufacturer: Alessi, Crusinallo, Italy
Measurements: 23 cm high, 25 cm wide, 17.5 cm deep

One of America's leading architects, and an influential Post-Modern classicist, Michael Graves has succeeded throughout his long and prolific career in instilling emotional and intellectual meaning in his designs for buildings and objects. As he puts it himself: 'As an architect I've always believed that what can make a domestic setting truly home is the infusion of a cultural dimension.' This idea of bringing cultural and artistic value into the realm of everyday objects gained increasing currency during the early 1980s, as Post-Modernism blossomed into a truly global phenomenon. As part of this growing international movement, Graves became the first American designer to develop a household product for the progressive Italian manufacturer, Alessi – his famous *Model No. 9093* tea-kettle, launched in 1985. This best-selling design led to a mutually fruitful collaboration spanning more than a quarter of a century, and leading to the creation of over 150 products, including the *Euclid* thermal jug. An enduring plastic icon of Post-Modernism, the spherical body and cube feet of this insulated flask were inspired by Euclidean geometry, and the design was produced in a number of striking colour combinations – green and blue, yellow and orange, red and blue, pale blue and white and, finally, black – which emphasised its bold, neo-classical form. The thermal jug was part of an extensive *Euclid* range devised by Graves for Alessi, which included a kitchen roll holder, a kitchen storage container, a square tray, a napkin holder, a salad bowl, salad servers and a wine cooler. Produced from 1994, the jug was made of matt-surfaced ABS, and captured Graves's playful approach to the design of housewares, which combined a Neo-Pop aesthetic with Post-Modern classicism and resulted in quirky, architectonic objects that were intended for, in his words, 'your own realm of cultured domesticity'.

Model No. 2530–4802 salad servers produced by Copco (USA), c.1985 – showing influence of Post-Modernism within the design of mainstream plastic homewares

Kazumi Shigeto, *Conique* thermal flask manufactured by Zojirushi and Guzzini, c.1983 – a similar Post-Modern design

RCP2
chair, 1992

Jane Atfield initially studied architecture at the Polytechnic of Central London (now the University of Westminster), before training as a furniture designer at the Royal College of Art in London, from where she graduated in 1992. For her final project at the RCA, she designed a chair made of imported recycled plastic – one of the first ever furniture designs made entirely of consumer waste. Around this time, Atfield also acquired an old plywood press, which she used to develop her own recycled plastic material made from discarded detergent containers, shampoo bottles and yoghurt pots. She then used the resulting mottled sheets of sturdy recycled plastic to create her first *RCP2* chair in 1992. The sheets were cut using band saws, and then either screwed or slotted together to create this simple and influential seating solution. The following year, Atfield established her own company, Made of Waste, to develop various other recycled plastics and also to produce her own designs. These included a number of site-specific commissions, the majority of which incorporated multi-coloured plastic sheets made of recycled, shredded and heat-compressed polyethylene bottles. She also designed a version of the *RCP2* with arms, and a smaller child-sized variant, as well as tables, shelving, stools,

cupboards, bowls, rubbish bins and children's alphabet letters. Despite its critical success, the *RCP2* chair was only ever made in batch production – six chairs at a time – because Atfield could never find a company prepared to take it into full-scale production. As she notes, 'The *RCP2* might be considered to be of significance due to the environmental issues it was addressing before they became mainstream with design. It hinted at a future for design that seemed unfashionable or alternative at the time, linking it with social and political factors and rejecting the prevailing status and slick furniture of the 1990s. Ironically, despite its pioneering character, it proved very difficult to get backing for the production of the chair or for that matter with producing the recycled plastic sheets from waste.' Significantly, the *RCP2* chair, with its straightforward archetypal form, focused attention on the role of recycled materials within design, and showed that what was once regarded as waste could be transformed into something of lasting aesthetic and functional value. Produced from 1993 to 2000, the design also celebrated the intrinsic qualities of recycled materials, and helped to promote them among designers, manufacturers and consumers alike.

↑ Contemporary photograph of *RCP2* chairs, 1992

← Jane Atfield, *RCP2* armchair for Made of Waste, 1992

Designer: **Jane Atfield** (British, 1964–)
Materials: recycled high-density polyethylene (HDPE)
Manufacturer: Made of Waste, London, UK
Measurements: 81 cm high, 37 cm wide, 43.5 cm deep

DC01
vacuum cleaner, 1993

Designer: **James Dyson** (British, 1947–)
Materials: acrylonitrile-butadiene-styrene (ABS), polycarbonate (PC), other materials
Manufacturer: Dyson Appliances, Malmesbury, UK
Measurements: 107 cm high, 30 cm wide, 35 cm deep

In 1978, the British designer and inventor James Dyson devised a new type of vacuum cleaning technology. It was based on the idea of a cyclone, and dispensed with the bags required by traditional models which quickly became clogged with dust, decreasing suction and ultimately performance. After five painstaking years of research and development, as well as 5,127 prototypes, Dyson's concept was turned into a working model. No established manufacturer, however, would consider this bag-less vacuum cleaner, let alone produce and market it when they were making substantial profits from selling bags. Eventually, in 1986, his first production model began to be made and sold under licence in Japan. Known as the *G Force*, this early design was made in the rather sickly colour combination of lilac and pastel pink ABS, presumably in an attempt to appeal to female consumers. Dyson ultimately determined that the only way to penetrate the UK market was to manufacture the design himself. So, after numerous refinements, in 1993 he launched the *DC01*: a paradigm shift in vacuum cleaner technology, with its constant-suction, dual-cyclone technology, telescopic hose, and a transparent bin that allowed the user to see when it needed emptying. Made of a combination of ABS and polycarbonate, the *DC01* also looked completely different, with its purposeful, no-nonsense aesthetic. Furthermore, Dyson chose the more masculine colour scheme of silver grey and bright yellow – the former looking like machined aluminium, and the latter used to highlight key features of the machine. As Dyson noted, 'We wanted it to look like a piece of NASA technology. Its superior performance had to be visible. It had to look the business.' The use of robust ABS and the macho colouring helped to communicate these associations and powerfully differentiated the Dyson cleaner from other models on the market. The clear polycarbonate bin also visually distinguished the design, and enabled sales staff to visibly demonstrate the *DC01*'s superior efficiency by revealing the impressive amount of dirt it collected. By choosing

ABS and polycarbonate – some of the strongest plastics on the market – and by allowing form to follow function, Dyson gave the *DC01* a characterful toughness that expressively conveyed the design's robust efficiency. As the world's first bag-less vacuum cleaner, the *DC01* was an important and influential design that demonstrated that plastics could be used to create durable, hard-working products with an engaging, high-tech engineering aesthetic. Unsurprisingly, less than two years after its launch, the *DC01* had become the best-selling vacuum cleaner in Britain despite being considerably more expensive than its competitors.

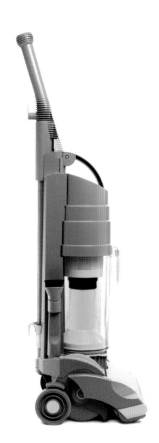

Mobil
container system, 1993–1994

Receiving a Premio Compasso d'Oro award in 1995, the *Mobil* storage system epitomises the dematerialistic style of the 1990s with its emphatic, pared-down Neo-Industrial aesthetic. This landmark product series also introduced semi-transparent PMMA to furniture design, giving the drawer units an attractive, frosted appearance that was a completely new look in the world of home furnishings. Conceived as a multi-functional container system, the *Mobil* is made up of drawers that function as basic modular elements, held in place by an exoskeleton-like frame made of chromed steel. The elements can be stacked to make a simple chest of drawers (with or without handles), or they can be placed side by side to create low cabinets, which function well as stands for televisions or hi-fi systems. The drawers are supported on a fixed frame or on castors, which provide the additional function of mobility. This inherent flexibility allows the *Mobil* system to be used in numerous configurations and in different settings, such as bedrooms, bathrooms, living rooms, kitchens and offices. Its commercial success is also owed to the wide range of colour options available, including icy translucent white, cobalt blue, citron yellow and orange. The *Mobil* is a creative response to the popularity of flexible living and working environments, but its enormous impact is inseparable from its stunning exploitation of the jewel-like qualities of semi-transparent acrylic – indeed a precious material.

Designer: **Antonio Citterio** (Italian, 1950–) and **Glen Oliver Löw** (German, 1959–)
Materials: polymethyl methacrylate (PMMA), acrylonitrile-butadiene-styrene (ABS), chromed steel
Manufacturer: Kartell, Noviglio, Italy
Measurements: *2 drawers*: 48 cm high, 49 cm wide, 47.5 cm deep | *3 drawers*: 63 cm high, 49 cm wide, 47.5 cm deep | *6 drawers*: 109 cm high, 49 cm wide, 47.5 cm deep

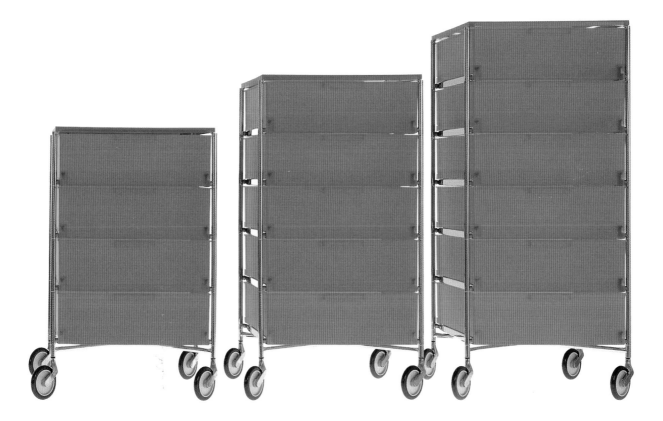

Bookworm
shelving, 1994

Since the early 1980s, Ron Arad has forged a formidable international reputation for his iconoclastic limited edition and one-off designs made from *objets trouvés*, rough-and-ready welded metal or highly polished, mirror-surfaced stainless steel. Because of their painstaking and time-consuming execution, these sculptural yet functional 'design art' pieces have been the preserve of wealthy collectors. However, in the mid-1990s Arad began translating some of his metalwork designs into thermoplastics, so they could be mass-manufactured and thereby enjoyed more widely. One of his earliest ventures into the world of high-volume plastics manufacturing was the squirming *Bookworm* shelf: a typically innovative and artistic solution made from strips of extruded polyvinyl chloride. These tough, load-bearing elements can be joined together to whatever length required, and are flexible enough to allow the wall-mounted shelving to be bent into different shapes. Importantly, this ability to freely configure the sinuous design allows the user a degree of personal creativity. This is unusual for a plastic object – the nature of plastics moulding and the high costs associated with making tools normally dictate that such products conform to a one-size-fits-all philosophy. Available in six different colours, and made of fire-retardant, batch-dyed PVC, the *Bookworm* can accommodate up to ten kilograms of books per section and comes with sturdy bookend supports. It can be mounted in snail-like spirals or undulating wave-shaped patterns, and as such is the sculptural antithesis of the traditional wooden or metal bookshelf. Like so many of Arad's designs, the *Bookworm* is the result of his instinctive understanding of materials and broad knowledge of manufacturing processes, coupled with an imaginative brilliance that allows him to think outside the box – in this case quite literally.

Designer: **Ron Arad** (Israeli/British, 1951–)
Materials: polyvinyl chloride (PVC)
Manufacturer: Kartell, Noviglio, Italy
Measurements: 19 cm high, 32 cm wide, 20 cm deep (per section)

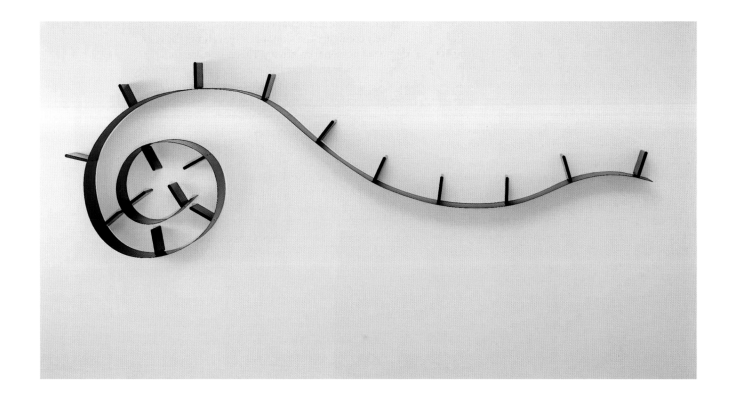

Mary Biscuit
container, 1995

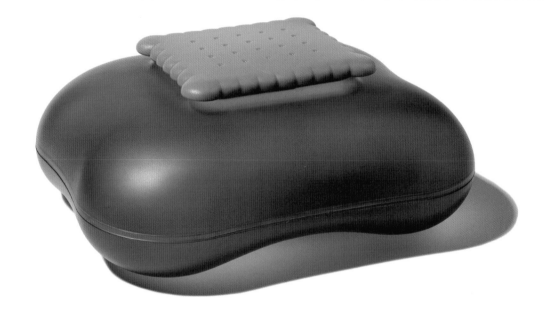

Designer: **Stefano Giovannoni** (Italian, 1954–)
Materials: ethylene vinyl acetate (EVA), polymethyl methacrylate
(PMMA)
Manufacturer: Alessi, Milan, Italy
Measurements: 11.5 cm high, 28 cm wide, 22 cm deep

During the 1990s, Stefano Giovannoni designed
innumerable household products for Alessi, which
were distinguished by characterful, cartoonised forms
and brightly coloured, state-of-the-art tecnopolymers.
A rhetorical use of metaphor is often central to
Giovannoni's playful approach to design. In his *Mary
Biscuit* container, for example, the cookie-shaped lid
symbolises the overall concept, while the actual
container stands for the content. As Alessi's catalogue
from 2000 noted, the design's playful, toy-like aspect
'helps create a surprise effect… it raises a smile and
brings a bit of happiness every time it is picked up.'
This, of course, helps to forge emotional bonds
between object and user that rapidly translate into
commercial success. The colour and tactility of the
thermoplastics used also lent this design qualities far
removed from the Modern Movement's utilitarian
'form follows function' aesthetic. Giovannoni used
bold, cartoon-like shapes for many other Post-Modern
homeware designs, including his *Merdolino* toilet
brush (1993) that took the form of a shooting plant
emerging from a flowerpot, and was produced in a
tough thermoplastic resin. As Alberto Alessi has
observed of Giovannoni, 'He has a true genius for
designing small objects. He works in direct contact
with our emotions and instincts, particularly with the
"motherly instinct" and the "childish instinct". I'm
convinced that all his items smile at us, just as the
Mona Lisa smiles at us with a mysterious, warm smile.'
And without his knowledge and mastery of thermoplastics, it would have been absolutely impossible for
Giovannoni to create these seductive objects of
child-like delight.

Stefano Giovannoni, *Merdolino*
toilet brush for Alessi, 1993

Garbo
multi-purpose container,
1995

Since the mid-1990s, Karim Rashid has been on a one-man mission to convert American companies to the merits of contemporary design. Like the first generation of American superstar design consultants from the 1930s, Rashid has given all kinds of products a touch of 'designer' glamour, while at the same time often enhancing their functional performance. Unlike some European practitioners, Rashid is not elitist regarding either the types of products he designs or the companies he designs them for. In fact, for him, the more universal the product and the more mainstream the company, the better. The first product to bring him widespread recognition was his *Garbo* container for Umbra – an elegantly curvaceous waste-bin made of translucent and recyclable polypropylene. Inexpensive to manufacture and cheap to buy, the *Garbo* and its smaller sister, the *Garbino* (1996), brought high-style design into Joe Average's American home, often for the very first time. According to Rashid, somewhere between four and six million of these award-winning waste-bins were sold. The flowing lines of the one-piece *Garbo*, with its integral handles, marked a new sculptural confidence in American design and, as the curator of MOMA's architecture and design department, Paola Antonelli, later noted of the container, 'It is good design. It is inexpensive, it is for everybody, it's durable, it's made with processes that, at that time, were among the most up-to-date.' Marrying sensual form with practical function, the *Garbo* container was, thanks to its use of high-volume plastics manufacturing technology, a highly democratic design. More recently, Umbra has begun producing this ubiquitous design in polylactic acid resin (PLA) – or, as it is more commonly known, 'corn plastic' – a sustainable and renewable alternative to conventional oil-based plastics, which can be composted at the end of its useful life.

Designer: **Karim Rashid** (Canadian, 1960–)
Materials: polypropylene (PP)
Manufacturer: Umbra, Buffalo (NY), USA
Measurements: 33 cm high, 24.5 cm diameter

Jack
light, 1996

Tom Dixon, *Octo* light for
Eurolounge, 1998

Throughout his career, Tom Dixon has created innovative products that are functionally inspiring and visually delightful. As a hands-on designer, Dixon's furniture and lighting concepts are often process-led and notable for their use of unusual materials applications. His designs are also frequently unconventional and sculptural in form, with a strong elemental quality. In 1994 he established his own manufacturing company, Eurolounge, to produce his lighting designs using rotational moulding technology, which had previously been used to make industrial objects with large, mostly hollow forms such as trash containers, water tanks and plastic pallets. The *Jack* light, the firm's first product, was intended to be a multifunctional object, and was described at its launch as a 'sitting, stacking, lighting thing'. With its stack-able form, which meant that several lights could be placed one on top of the other to create a tower, and its pioneering use of rotational-moulded polyethylene, the *Jack* light epitomised Dixon's experimental and playful approach to design and manufacturing. The *Jack* light was also sufficiently strong structurally to be used as an illuminated stool, and came in a number of colours. Eurolounge also produced several other rotational-moulded plastic lights, including the *Stick Light* designed in 2001 by Michael Young. The company's designs were hugely influential, and within a few years this technique for moulding polyethylene became widely used within the lighting and furniture industries, due to the relatively low tooling and production costs, and the structural resilience and impressive durability of the material.

Designer: **Tom Dixon** (British, 1959–)
Materials: polyethylene (PE)
Manufacturer: Eurolounge, London, United Kingdom
Measurements: 60 cm high, 60 cm wide, 60 cm deep

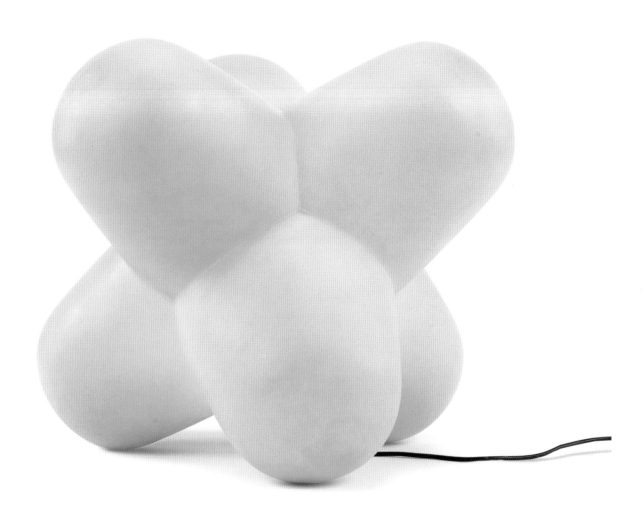

FPE
chair, 1997

Like other chairs manufactured by Kartell, the *FPE* is made without a single human hand touching it, as it is transformed from plastic pellets to a ready-to-ship boxed product. It also has an impressively quick cycle time of around two minutes, which means that it can be produced in very high volumes for a relatively low cost. Its title is an abbreviation of Fantastic Plastic Elastic, which eloquently describes the attributes of this lightweight and flexible stacking chair. Its seating section is made from a flat strip of smooth, batch-dyed polypropylene. This is automatically slotted into an extruded tubular aluminium profile, and is then bent in a special curved machine to form a resilient supporting frame. The polypropylene section is held in place within the frame without the use of any additional screws or fittings, so the entire chair is constructed of only three elements. The *FPE* scores the maximum five out of five in official resistance, impact, fatigue and scratch tests – meaning that it is strong and durable enough for heavy contract use. Yet it still weighs just 3.75 kilograms. Available in opalescent white, as well as translucent blue and red, the *FPE chair* is suitable for both domestic and commercial applications, and its use of tough materials also makes it relatively resistant to weather, allowing it to be placed outdoors. Polypropylene, however, is not particularly stable when exposed to ultraviolet radiation, so it is not a good idea to position the chair in direct sunlight for prolonged periods of time. As Kartell notes of this sinuously beautiful and highly practical chair, 'it is fantastic due to its exclusive technology which allows the creation of a robust but elastic structure.' As with other designs by Arad for this renowned Italian company, the *FPE* exploits the formal potential of polymers by using innovative and fully automated production techniques.

Designer: **Ron Arad** (British, 1951–)
Materials: polypropylene (PP), painted extruded aluminium
Manufacturer: Kartell, Noviglio, Italy
Measurements: 78 cm high, 43 cm wide, 59 cm deep

iMac
computer, 1998

Designer: **Jonathan Ive** (British, 1967–) and the
Apple Design Team (American)
Materials: polycarbonate (PC), other materials
Manufacturer: Apple, Inc., Cupertino (CA), USA
Measurements: 38.1 cm high, 38.1 cm wide, 43.2 cm deep

At the launch of the first *iMac* in 1998, Steve Jobs, the co-founder of Apple, enthusiastically introduced this revolutionary computer as follows: 'the whole thing is translucent, you can see into it, it is so cool, we've got stereo speakers on the front, we've infrared right up here... we've got the coolest mouse on the planet... around the back we've got a really great handle here, the back of this thing looks better than the fronts of the other guys... this is incredible compared to anything else out there, it looks like it's from another planet, a good planet, a planet with better designers.' For once, it was a product that lived up to and beyond the marketing hype, and Jobs was correct that the *iMac* marked an absolute paradigm shift in computer design, with its seductive, unified gumdrop form. Before the *iMac*, computer housings were box-like in form, and were made of ABS in either matt beige or pale grey, both of which were visually boring and often became grubby after only just a few months of use. In contrast, the sleek yet friendly *iMac*, with its bright, two-tone colour combination of gleaming opaque and translucent polycarbonate, had a visual freshness that massively differentiated itself from the stale aesthetic of virtually all other personal computers. The success of the *iMac* not only dramatically rescued the declining fortunes of Apple, but heralded the departure of the computer industry as a whole from the prevailing aesthetic of the dull, lifeless box. The design's impact was such that it also influenced a host of other products. For instance, Artemide even manufactured *iMac*-inspired task lights, produced in brightly-coloured translucent polycarbonate – a thermoplastic material that also offered excellent durability along with its vibrantly glossy surface. Above all, the *iMac* showed that if manufacturers spent a little more on design and development, and maybe a fraction more on materials and manufacturing, then they could create a premium product with an emotive quality that not only captured people's imaginations, but also the money in their pockets. By using plastics in an intelligent and thoughtful way, Jonathan Ive and the Apple Design Team eloquently illustrated that office equipment made of synthetic materials could be beautiful as well as logical. Crucially for Apple, once the emotional connection had been forged between an *iMac* and its user, the latter was far more likely to buy other Apple products too, thereby demonstrating that pioneering design and carefully selected materials have the power to transform a company's fortunes.

Apple Inc. publicity photograph for the first *iMac* computer, 1998 – showing the various colour options available

La Marie
chair, 1998

Designer: **Philippe Starck** (French, 1949–)
Materials: polycarbonate (PC)
Manufacturer: Kartell, Noviglio, Italy
Measurements: 87.5 cm high, 38.7 cm wide, 52.5 cm deep

Philippe Starck, *Louis Ghost*
armchair for Kartell, 2002

Launched in 1998, Philippe Starck's *La Marie* chair marked a huge technical breakthrough in plastic chair manufacturing, being the world's first completely transparent chair formed from a single moulding of polycarbonate. Although its form is based on an archetypal four-legged chair, it is a truly advanced design created in a completely automated factory. The crystal-clear transparency of the polycarbonate also gives the design a visual lightness and delicacy that belies the robustness of its structure. *La Marie* is a wholly unified design, both in terms of construction and materials, and was the first of several 'invisible' chairs that Starck created for Kartell as part of his highly successful *Ghost Series*. Since the era of the Bauhaus, it had been a Modernist fantasy to create a completely dematerialised chair – in effect, a column of air that could be used as a seat. *La Marie* was a knowing, Post-Modern attempt to capture this vision with a state-of-the-art polymer and cutting-edge

moulding technology. Shockproof, weather-resistant, scratchproof, easy to clean and available in four attractive, batch-dyed colours, *La Marie* is an elegant and versatile stackable chair that can be used indoors or outdoors. Importantly, because it is made from a single shot of one polymer it is not only relatively cheap to make on an industrial scale (and therefore affordable to buy), but it can also be easily recycled at the end of its practical life. Like so many of Starck's products, *La Marie* has an engaging identity that derives from his masterful blending of historic forms and advanced materials to produce designs that are innovative, essential and emotionally resonant. With a strong sense of character and an undeniable sculptural presence, *La Marie* and its successors *Louis Ghost* (2002) and *Victoria Ghost* (2005) are seating solutions that succeed, through the inspired use of transparent polycarbonate, to communicate an almost magically ethereal lightness.

Philippe Starck, *Victoria Ghost*
chair for Kartell, 2005

Air One
chair, 1999

Made of expanded polypropylene beaded foam, the *Air One* chair shows how a material that is mainly used for the disposable packaging of electronics and white goods can, with a little bit of imagination, be creatively reapplied to the construction of stylish furniture. Throughout his career, Ross Lovegrove has been captivated by the formal and functional potential of new polymers and advanced composites, alongside those of everyday plastics and age-old natural materials. He often uses materials in surprising and innovative ways, allowing a medium's intrinsic qualities to directly inform his designs, whether it is bamboo or bulletproof Kevlar fibre. Durable and attractive, the stackable *Air One* chair was designed for Edra, an Italian furniture manufacturer well known for its progressive and experimental work. Importantly, the choice of expanded polypropylene means that the chair has excellent impact resistance and durability making it ideal for use at public events such as trade fairs. Like other products by Lovegrove, the *Air One* derives from an organic, essentialist approach to design – the marrying of sculptural forms inspired by ergonomics and elements from the natural world to the logical arrangement of only those elements that are absolutely necessary for the accomplishment of a particular purpose. Harmonious and intelligent, the structure of the *Air One* is extremely lightweight yet strong, whilst also being impermeable to water and fully recyclable. Perfect for indoor and outdoor lounging, this low-slung seating solution is a three-dimensional manifestation of Lovegrove's desire to highlight the impact of industrial production on our shared environment, and to reveal the dignity of polymeric materials. Easy to carry, the technologically inspired *Air One* and the matching *Air Two* stool (1999) can also be seen as commentaries on the increasingly nomadic nature of contemporary life.

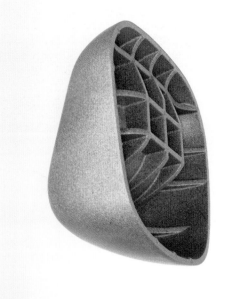

Designer: **Ross Lovegrove** (British, 1958–)
Materials: expanded polypropylene (EPP)
Manufacturer: Edra, Perignano, Italy
Measurements: 50 cm high, 115 cm wide, 115 cm deep

Air-Chair

1999

Designer: **Jasper Morrison** (British, 1959–)
Materials: glass fibre reinforced polypropylene (PP)
Manufacturer: Magis, Motta di Livenza, Italy
Measurements: 77.5 cm high, 49 cm wide, 51 cm deep

The groundbreaking *Air-Chair* is an elegant and highly rational design made entirely of polypropylene strengthened with glass fibres. Using state-of-the-art gas moulding technology, nitrogen is injected at high pressure during the moulding process, which reduces the length of the production cycle and introduces an internal air cavity, so that less material is required. In fact, the cycle time for the *Air-Chair* is just three minutes, which demonstrates the impressive manufacturing efficiency of gas-assisted injection moulding. Obviously, this complex processing technology requires absolutely perfect moulds that can withstand high-stress, and these are very expensive to produce – costing literally millions of Euros. Initially, Jasper Morrison designed the chair using CAD software, and then the design was carefully translated into a wooden prototype in 1999. As the manufacturer, Magis, explains, 'The mould was designed to be as simple as possible in order to prevent the formation of defects in the form of scratches produced by the movement of the chair within the mould. Much care was taken in the positioning of the impression and the injection and removal points to guarantee a perfect result and to simplify use.' After a year of intensive development, Magis began mass-producing the *Air-Chair*, which became an instant critical and commercial success. Inexpensive and apparently indestructible, the *Air-Chair* is a coherent and structurally unified design, which stacks very efficiently and is totally recyclable. It is available in a range of colours – orange, fuchsia pink, sky blue, bright green, olive green, yellow and white – and features a cut out in the middle of the seat that functions as a hand hold, which makes moving the chair easier while also providing drainage for rainwater when it is being used outdoors. Achieving a total design unity through its adoption of a single material and a single form, Morrison's *Air-Chair* is a truly beautiful, universal design solution – quite simply, it is a masterpiece of process-led, essentialist design. Since the launch of the *Air-Chair* in 2000, Morrison has extended the *Air Family* with a folding chair, an armchair and a table, all of which possess a similar formal purity. With this furniture group, Morrison fluently demonstrates that, when used rationally and sensitively, synthetic materials can be used to create high-quality yet affordable objects possessing outstanding utility and durability.

Ty Nant
water bottle, 1999–2001

Ross Lovegrove is a leading industrial designer whose work often pushes the boundaries of materials and technologies. He has described his role as, 'a 21st-century translator of technology into products that we use every day and relate beautifully and naturally with.' Lovegrove's observational skills, honed as a beach-combing child in his native Wales, together with a deep love of the forms and processes found in the natural world also directly inform his work. His water bottle for Ty Nant was inspired by his analysis of how water flows, and represents his attempt at capturing its essence: purity, fluidity and grace. From a few quick sketches in his notebook, the bottle was then digitally modelled on computer, and the resulting data was used to make a solid model milled from a block of acrylic. Initially, it was felt that the design was impossible to produce because of its unusual asymmetrical form. However, after months of development it was finally put into mass production.

Lovegrove recalls that when the first bottle was received from the manufacturer it, 'felt like nothing... [but] when I put water into it, I realised I'd put a skin on water itself.' Although the *Ty Nant* bottle is made of blow-moulded PET, which is exactly the same material that is used for other drinks bottles, Lovegrove's design exploits the material's plasticity when heated to create an intelligent form that expresses the preciousness of water and emphasises its remarkable optical qualities. The *Ty Nant* bottle fits comfortably in the hand thanks to Lovegrove's understanding of ergonomics, and possesses a sculptural elegance that sets it apart from similar products. If, as Lovegrove claims, 'industrial design is the art form of the twenty-first century', then this groundbreaking water bottle is one of its early masterpieces, revealing how everyday plastic can be transformed into objects of rare beauty, without sacrificing functional practicality.

Ross Lovegrove, Preliminary sketch of the *Ty Nant* bottle showing the flow of water, 1999

Milled steel moulds used to mass-produce the *Ty Nant* bottle

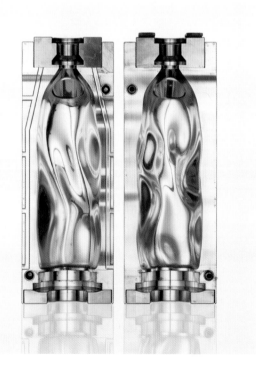

Designer: **Ross Lovegrove** (British, 1958–)
Materials: polyethylene terephthalate (PET)
Manufacturer: Ty Nant Spring Water, Llanon, Ceredigion, Wales, UK
Measurements: *500 ml*: 23 cm high | *1 litre*: 28.3 cm high |
1.5 litre: 32 cm high

Vas-one
planters, 2000

President of Italy's famous Industrial Design Association (ADI), Luisa Bocchietto is a highly influential figure within the contemporary Italian design scene. She studied architecture under Marco Zanuso at the Politecnico di Milano, graduating in 1985, while simultaneously obtaining a certificate from the European Design Institute of Milan. Since then, she has worked on numerous projects, from urban regeneration plans and residential architectural schemes to exhibition displays and furniture designs. It is, however, her gigantic *Vas-one* planters for Serralunga that have brought her some of the greatest recognition. Originally, these impressive, over-scale flowerpots were created specifically for the trade fair stands of the Milan-based plastics company Sarge. In 2002, however, they were put into series production by Serralunga, and have since made a striking impression in numerous environments, from hotel lobbies and retail spaces to public gardens. The company's owner, Marco Serralunga, was the first Italian plastics manufacturer to recognise the potential of rotational-moulding in the production of design-led products, and imported the necessary machinery from America. Until then, this moulding technology had been used predominantly for the manufacture of 'non-designer' products such as industrial mouldings, municipal refuse bins and water tanks. First developed in the mid-nineteenth century for the manufacture of metal armaments, the rotational moulding process was being used to make hollow chocolate Easter eggs by the early twentieth century. It was not until the 1950s, however, that plastics began to be rotationally moulded, most notably for the mass production of dolls' heads. Even then, it was only in the 1980s that this technology became fully viable, with the introduction of new polymers such as low-density polyethylene and polycarbonate. Employing this relatively low-tech and inexpensive process, Luisa Bocchietto's *Vas-one* planter draws on the archetypal form of the traditional flowerpot and, through the use of immense size and recyclable polyethylene, transforms it into a dramatic design statement. The *Vas-one* is resistant to weather and ultraviolet light and is virtually indestructible, while also being light enough to place on balconies with load restrictions.

Vas-one planters in situ.

Designer: **Luisa Bocchietto** (Italian, 1960–)
Materials: polyethylene (PE)
Manufacturer: Serralunga, Biella, Italy
Measurements: 120 cm, 150 cm or 180 cm high; 130 cm, 160 cm
or 200 cm diameter

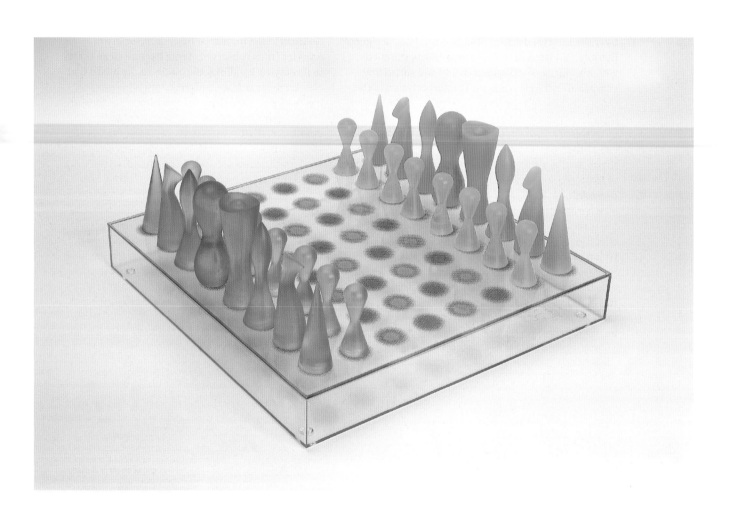

Designer: **Karim Rashid** (Canadian, 1960–)
Materials: polymethyl methacrylate (PMMA), polypropylene (PP)
Manufacturer: Bozart Toys, Philadelphia (PA), USA
Measurements: 12.7 cm high, 38.1 cm wide

Over the last two decades, Karim Rashid has designed literally hundreds of innovative products stamped with his quirky post-Pop sensibility and surprising compositional freshness. His reinterpretation of the classic chess set for Bozart's *Toys by Artists* collection incorporates an acrylic storage box that also doubles up as the board, with silkscreened, Op Art-like circles rather than the traditional squared grid. In addition, the chess pieces have abstract, 'blobular' forms made of frosted translucent polypropylene in contrasting, eye-catching fluorescent orange and lime green (or, alternatively, in ice-white and smoky grey plastic). Like other designs by Rashid, the *Model No. 10046* chess set is highly futuristic, and has a playful Jetsons-meets-Sottsass aesthetic. With its ultra-modern look, this product typifies Rashid's output, which consistently captures the extraordinary properties of today's polymers – from their engagingly soft tactility to their almost magical optical qualities, including translucency and luminescence. As Jordan Nollman of the Industrial Designers Society of America (IDSA) observes, 'From its pure clean forms to its easy-to-handle tactile pieces to the board that also serves as storage and packaging, this product has reinvented the chess set as we know it. The use of materials makes it not only inexpensive, but innovative. It's fun, attractive, enjoyable and, best of all, affordable.' Furthermore, the two types of plastic used for the chess set are also one hundred per cent recyclable. A landmark design, using state-of-the-art synthetic materials to re-conceptualise a traditional board game as a stylish but still democratic object, the *Model No. 10046* chess set won a gold award from the IDSA in 2002. Rashid's *Model No. 10050* backgammon set, also designed for Bozart, similarly incorporates 'fun to touch' pieces moulded in colourful translucent polypropylene. His imaginative use of contemporary materials has renewed the appeal of some extremely ancient pastimes.

Karim Rashid, *Karim Rashid High* shoes for Melissa, 2006 – another design by Rashid that reveals his form-giving mastery of plastic materials

Take

table light, 2003

Ferruccio Laviani studied architecture at the famous Politecnico di Milano, graduating in 1986. That same year he took part in the *12 Nuovi Memphis* collection, and also became a partner in the Michele De Lucchi design office based in Milan. There, he worked on numerous projects for a plethora of well-known, design-led manufacturers from Mandarina Duck and Olivetti to Pelikan and Swatch, honing his understanding of different materials and especially of plastics along the way. In 1991 he left Studio De Lucchi and began working as a consultant to Kartell, where he was responsible for designing its eye-catching presentations and exhibits, as well as its colourful stands at the annual Milan Furniture Fair. He was eventually appointed the company's art director, and in 1998 he created the *Max* table – his first design to be produced by the Milanese firm. Since then, he has designed another table and seven innovative lights for

Kartell, including the quirky *Take* light, which is made from two mirror-image, injection-moulded, polycarbonate elements that refract and diffuse the emitted light almost like a crystal chandelier. As a humorous reinterpretation of the traditional pleat-shaded table lamp, the *Take* light is a late Post-Modern design that fuses an archetypal form with an advanced transparent polymer to create a vivid, compelling and inexpensive design. As its name suggests, the *Take* light was designed to be bought easily off the shelf, and even its packaging was kept to a minimum to avoid bulk and unnecessary weight. Cheap to produce because of its rational two-part construction, its use of polycarbonate and its fully automated manufacturing process, the innovative *Take* light democratised high-style design for the fashion-conscious consumer. It made the act of purchasing a lamp as easy and affordable as buying a pair of shoes.

Pietro Ferruccio Laviani, *Bourgie*
table light for Kartell, 2004

Designer: **Pietro Ferruccio Laviani** (Italian, 1960–)
Materials: polycarbonate (PC)
Manufacturer: Kartell, Noviglio, Italy
Measurements: 30 cm high

Fresh Fat
bowl, 2003

Tom Dixon, *Fresh Fat* chair, 2003

Since the mid-1980s, Tom Dixon has created numerous innovative designs that have explored the formal parameters and emphasised the intrinsic qualities of the materials and technologies he employs – from welded metal rods to rotational-moulded polyethylene. In 2001, he developed a mobile machine that extruded spaghetti-like strands of plastic, and subsequently used it to produce his *Fresh Fat Plastic* range of objects, including lights, chairs and bowls. The following year – as part of the Perrier-Jouet Selfridges Design Award for the 'most significant contribution to the shape of design today' – the machine was set up as an installation in the window of Selfridges department store in London's Oxford Street. Although Dixon did not actually win the award, his *Fresh Fat Plastic* machine stole the show as it spewed out hot strands of polymer that could be manipulated and woven into objects that were made to order while the customer waited, and could then be taken home while still warm. Today, most plastic objects are produced on a mass industrial scale. Not least, this situation reflects the fact that, because tooling costs are so high, profits can only be achieved by enormous economies of scale. Dixon's machine demonstrated, however, that the creation of plastic objects does not always have to be about exact replication or lowest production cost. Instead, his designs insisted that unique and beautiful plastic objects could be created, in effect, by hand, and in so doing he showcased the remarkable qualities of plastics in a wholly innovative way. Glistening as though made of liquid glass, Dixon's subsequent *Fresh Fat* bowl was, like his earlier extruded designs, made of polyethylene terephthalate glycol – a polymeric resin developed specifically for profile extrusion where high clarity, high gloss and good resilience are crucial. Significantly, Dixon's pioneering designs created from this recyclable and food-safe polymer shatter the widespread preconception that plastics are cheap, throwaway materials, and instead highlight a range of new associations for synthetic materials: preciousness, uniqueness and sophistication.

Designer: **Tom Dixon** (British, 1959–)
Materials: polyethylene terephthalate glycol (PETG)
Manufacturer: Tom Dixon, London, UK
Measurements: 15 cm high, 55 cm diameter

Supernatural
chair, 2005

Often the beauty of Ross Lovegrove's work belies the design logic that underpins it. More than any other designer working today, Lovegrove understands the ecological necessity of an essentialist approach to design, and he strives to achieve this by means of advanced materials and cutting-edge manufacturing processes. His goal is 'fat-free' design that intelligently employs materials in a thoughtful and appropriate way. His stackable indoor/outdoor *Supernatural* chair was the result of his desire to lighten the mass of a chair's structure to produce a model weighing less than 2.5 kilograms. The form originated from the flow patterns of the polymer when it cools in the mould, resulting in a hard and rigid structure. As Lovegrove explains, 'Using gas-injection assist technology all internal cavities within the frame of the chair are hollow like a bone.' Because any extraneous material is removed, the *Supernatural* is, he continues, 'half the weight of other competitors, which means two chairs are made for the material of one'. Apart from embodying an efficient use of resources, this also means that the chair is easy to lift and transport, as well as being aesthetically elegant. In Lovegrove's words again,

'It represents a new vision of form, generated by digital data, resulting in a chair to be used every day, slender, lively and healthy. The liquid, organic nature of its form combines the beauty of the human anatomy with the most advanced industrial processes and 21st-century polymers. These extremely sophisticated technologies enable the use of two layers of polypropylene with glass fibres to achieve a harmony between the internal structural characteristics and the external aesthetic qualities.' Although appearing to be a decorative motif, the perforations on the chair's back section are actually another way in which Lovegrove has reduced the amount of material used. While wholly synthetic, the *Supernatural* chair's form paradoxically possesses a strong organic presence, which is heightened by the design's perforations, which cast leaf-like shadows. It is ironic that the materials best able to capture the abstract essence of nature are themselves frequently inorganic. Then again, we should not forget the origins of these synthetic polymers – prehistoric plant and animal matter in the form of the oil reserves that have proved such a troubled legacy.

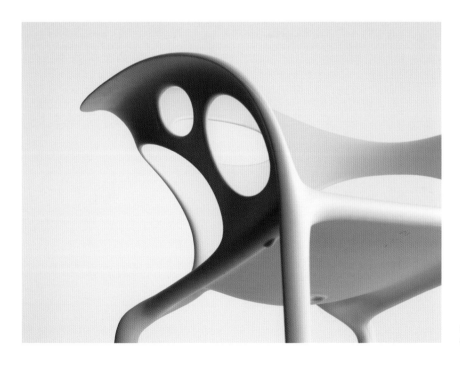

Ross Lovegrove, *Supernatural* armchair for Moroso, 2006

Designer: **Ross Lovegrove** (British, 1958–)
Materials: glass-reinforced polypropylene (PP)
Manufacturer: Moroso, Cavalicco, Italy
Measurements: 81 cm high, 53 cm wide, 51 cm deep

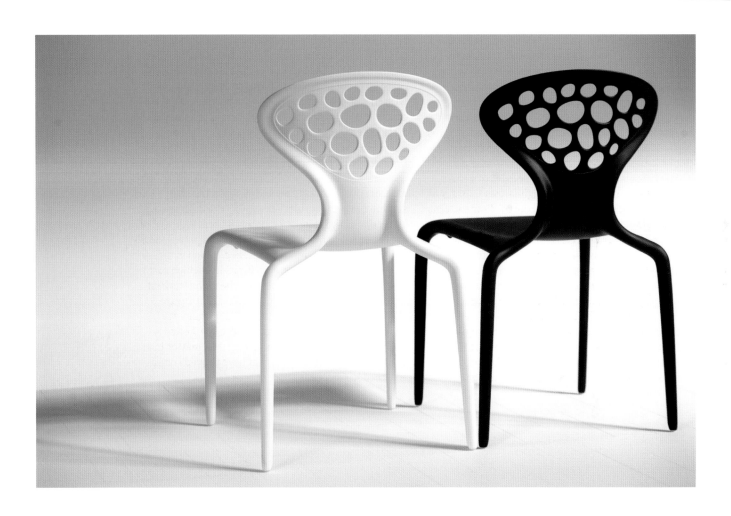

Amazonia

vase, 2006

Since the mid-1960s, Gaetano Pesce has explored the seemingly unlimited creative potential of synthetic materials in order to construct challenging designs that both surprise and delight – from his moulded polyurethane foam *Up Series* of 1969 (a seating collection that was compressed and vacuum-packed into PVC envelopes which, when opened, allowed the chairs to literally bounce into life) to his sculptural *Dalila* chairs (1980) made of rigid polyurethane foam. In the early 1980s, he also began exploring the formal, aesthetic and structural possibilities of coloured polyurethane resins, initially in his designs for the *Sansone* table (1980) and later for his *Pratt* series of chairs (1983), both of which explored the concept of serially producing 'unique' designs. Between 1995 and 1999, Pesce's own New York-based manufacturing company, Fish Design, serially produced one-off objects such as vases, trays and mirrors in translucent and coloured polyurethane resins. In 2003, the company was re-established in Milan to manufacture various designs, including the *Amazonia* vase, which is individually made by hand using flexible poly-urethane resins that are poured over a mould with each one being allowed to set before the next one is applied. This means of fabrication ensures each piece is necessarily unique, with the bubbles, imperfections and slight variations in size being an inherent part of the manufacturing process. As Pesce has noted, 'Fish Design is a polyhedric collection of artefacts... each one different from the next. The creativity of the craftsman, the unpredictability of the fluids and the opportunity to insert variables from the choice of colour to the distribution of the materials, are some of the paths to obtaining... diversity and uniqueness.' This craft-design approach to making objects in plastics runs counter to the notion of exact replication that has for so long been associated with the use of synthetic polymers. Instead Pesce creates 'design art' objects that possess emotional warmth and an engaging individuality, and in so doing celebrates the astonishing beauty and artistic latency of plastic materials.

Gaetano Pesce, *Ogiva Special XXL* vase manufactured by Fish Design, 2006 – launched at the Now! Design à Vivre exhibition in Paris in 2006

Designer: **Gaetano Pesce** (Italian 1939–)
Materials: flexible polyurethane resin (PU)
Manufacturer: Fish Design, Milan, Italy
Measurements: 37 cm high, 28 cm diameter

Flow
planter, 2007

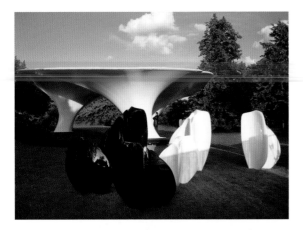

Launch of *Flow* planters in the ancient cloisters of the Università degli Studi, Milan, 2007

Zaha Hadid's radical architecture and progressive design work are characterised by the use of dynamic, flowing lines that seamlessly meld one geometric plane into another. Using sophisticated CAD software and advanced manufacturing technologies, Hadid is able to create furniture, lighting and other products with extremely fluid forms that exquisitely balance sculptural beauty with practical function. Her *Flow* planter designed for Serralunga, for example, could only have been realised by resolving its complex geometry with three-dimensional digital modelling. The nature of the material itself inspired the design, with the oozing liquid state of heated plastic reflected in the pot's asymmetry. As Hadid herself comments on the role of polymers in design, 'Plastic started a new generation of ideas and possibilities; it could be moulded into myriad shapes and was easy to mass produce. I especially admire the Verner Panton chair for its fluid form and use of this material.' Her own handling of polymers in the production of the *Flow* planter is a similar *tour de force* of plastics design and manufacturing. This impressively large object is available in two sizes, and is made of rotational-moulded polyethylene that is then coated with either black or white lacquer. Its sinuous form is the very antithesis of the traditional planter, and gives the design a strong sculptural presence whether it is used on a patio or in a garden. Indeed, its shape is so elegant that it is difficult to believe that it shares its moulding process with industrially manufactured municipal refuse bins. In common with other designs produced by Serralunga, Zaha Hadid's *Flow* planter embodies the innovation and creativity that Italian manufacturers continue to perpetuate through their commitment to progressive design and the innovative use of plastics manufacturing technologies.

Designers: **Zaha Hadid** (Iraqi/British, 1950–) and
Patrik Schumacher (German, 1961–)
Materials: polyethylene (PE)
Manufacturer: Serralunga, Biella, Italy
Measurements: *Medium*: 120 cm high, 117 cm wide |
Large: 200 cm high, 146 cm wide

MYTO
chair, 2007

Designer: **Konstantin Grcic** (German, 1965–)
Materials: polybutylene terephthalate (PBT)
Manufacturer: Plank, Ora, Italy
Measurements: 82 cm high, 51 cm wide, 55 cm deep

BASF's Ultradur High Speed polymer is a special polybutylene-terephthalate resin, specifically developed for the exterior lighting bezels used on cars, as well as other high-stress engineering parts employed in the automotive, construction and electronics industries. One of its main benefits, in addition to the fact that it can be coated in metal without the need for a base coat, is its very high flow rate, which enables faster cycle times and makes it an excellent material for moulding complex forms and fine details. In late 2006, BASF commissioned the celebrated German industrial designer, Konstantin Grcic, to come up with a new application or product using this recently invented and highly durable polymer. Grcic had previously designed the award-winning *Miura* stackable stool (2005) in reinforced polypropylene for the Italian furniture manufacturer Plank. As a designer he therefore already had a good understanding of the formal and structural potential of advanced polymers and available moulding techniques. Working closely with the engineers and technicians at BASF and Plank, Grcic spent several months refining a design for a new stacking chair – research and development time that

proved wholly justified with the resulting product constituting a significant benchmark in both plastics moulding technology and furniture design. When the fully recyclable *MYTO* cantilevered monobloc chair was eventually presented for the first time in October 2007 at the plastics industry's largest trade exhibition, the K Fair in Düsseldorf, it caused a complete sensation. This reaction was an acknowledgement both of its materials innovation and its striking, faceted form that gives the design a strongly masculine and high-tech look, almost reminiscent of an *F-117 Nighthawk* stealth fighter. The main concept behind the chair is a supporting frame that seamlessly dissolves into a mesh-like, perforated seat section. With its high flow rate and excellent strength, the Ultradur thermoplastic also permits an elegant transition from the thickest parts of the chair to its thinnest cross-sections. Virtually indestructible, the *MYTO* has excellent impact resistance, and can be mass-produced in high volumes thanks to its logical, process-driven design and the remarkable 'flowability' of its polymeric material.

Designer: **Humberto Campana** (Brazilian, 1953–) and
Fernando Campana (Brazilian, 1961–)
Materials: polyvinyl chloride (PVC)
Manufacturer: Melissa, Farroupilha, Brazil
Measurements: 41 cm high, 28 cm wide

Humberto & Fernando Campana,
Melissa Campana shoes for
Melissa, 2008

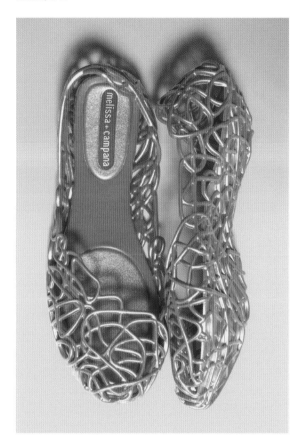

Founded in 1971, the Brazilian company Grendene is one of the largest producers of plastic shoes in the world. It invented the now ubiquitous 'jelly shoe' in 1979 – a modern interpretation of the traditional leather sandals used by fishermen that innovatively used flexible PVC. That same year, Grendene also created the brand known as Melissa to manufacture high style, design-led plastic shoes for more fashion-conscious consumers. Since then, Melissa has forged a powerful identity within the shoemaking and fashion worlds, while also developing innovative designs that push the physical and formal boundaries of plastic moulding technologies. Melissa's highly talented creative director, Edson Matsuo, has not only developed impressive products himself, such as his best-selling *Ultragirl* footwear range, but has also commissioned some of the world's leading designers to create shoes and other accessories for the company. As Matsuo observes, 'I'm fascinated by plastic, a simple material with many possibilities of being. It gives freedom for the creative process and has a great affinity with Brazil. I believe plastic is only limited by the designer's creativeness.' The upshot has been an extraordinary product line that includes designs by, among others, Karim Rashid, Zaha Hadid and Vivienne Westwood. Not surprisingly, as a prominent Brazilian company, Melissa has also collaborated with the São Paulo-based Campana brothers – Humberto and Fernando – who have risen over the last decade to become true international design superstars. Altogether, the Campanas have designed seven different shoe ranges for Melissa, drawing inspiration from their playful, *arte povera* furniture assemblages. Looking as though they have been made from overlapping slivers of discarded wood, randomly placed string or scrunched up wire, these wearable 'design art' pieces are comfortable thanks to Melflex™, the high-quality PVC specially developed by Melissa to provide the optimum balance between flexibility and stability. The PVC pellets are heated to 160° Celsius before being mixed with a special 'tutti-frutti' scent and then injection-moulded into extremely complex

forms, such as the *Melissa Campana* bag – the shape of which was derived by the Campana brothers from a prototype made of twisted and bent aluminium wires. Like the design duo's matching shoes, the bag looks as though it has been made from colourful looped spaghetti. This remarkable design reflects how beauty can be found in chaotic disorder – a theme that is central to their idiosyncratic and poetic work. Intended for use as a summer bag or on the beach, the *Melissa Campana* is made of thirty percent recycled material demonstrating that, when used imaginatively and responsibly, plastics can be transformed into durable and functional products with high aesthetic value.

Melissa + Zaha Hadid
shoes, 2008

Zaha Hadid's shoes, designed for the Brazilian company Melissa, powerfully demonstrate the extraordinary ability of polymeric compounds to generate abstract organic forms. In fact, the term plastic derives from the Greek word *plastikos,* which means to mould or shape, and certainly these materials are unrivalled for the moulding of complex forms. An internationally renowned architect known for her use of multifaceted and flowing shapes, Hadid's extraordinary shoes, with their soft, rounded forms and strategically placed cutouts, were inspired by the fluid movements of the human body. As she explains, 'The fluidity of our design combined perfectly with the plastic technology used by Melissa, injecting pieces without closures or seals', while the use of asymmetry gave, 'an inherent sense of movement to the design, evoking continuous transformations.' A technically challenging project for both designer and manufacturer, the resulting products are perfect expressions of Hadid's dynamic and daring approach to design and architecture. This project for Melissa allowed Hadid to move into a completely new area of design, and she clearly relished the opportunity to work on a different scale, within different functional parameters and with different materials. The latter, in this case, involved injection-moulded Melflex™ – a patented non-toxic, hypoallergenic and recyclable PVC specially developed by Melissa – which is soft enough to be comfortably supple, yet sufficiently rigid to provide the necessary support. The resulting limited-edition shoes, with their generous openings and sloping straps, are highly sculptural as well as versatile, practical and comfortable. Beyond this, though, the shoes are true objects of desire – spectacular designs in plastic that fully exploit the form-giving potential of the medium and which, to all intents and purposes, can be seen as wearable pieces of avant-garde architecture.

Designers: **Zaha Hadid** (Iraqi/British, 1950–) and
Patrik Schumacher (German, 1961–)
Materials: polyvinyl chloride (PVC)
Manufacturer: Melissa, Farroupilha, Brazil
Measurements: various sizes

Cosmic Leaf
suspension light, 2009

The use of sophisticated three-dimensional modelling software, such as Rhino and Autodesk's Maya, has dramatically extended the formal and functional possibilities of product design, allowing designers to create extraordinarily complex and highly fluid forms. Ross Lovegrove's work marries this type of complex digital technology with a deep understanding of materials and their intrinsic properties. His designs are frequently an astonishing marriage of advanced materials and cutting-edge technologies with visually seductive forms inspired by the natural world. Lovegrove's work often looks as though it has been plucked from some weird sci-fi landscape, and certainly his *Cosmic Leaf* lighting range for Artemide appears almost supernaturally hyper-modern with its glimmering, scale-like surfaces. An external, low-energy LED source throws light onto a leaf-shaped diffusing element made of thermo-formed PMMA. The otherworldly quality of the design is further enhanced by the fact that this textured diffuser is covered with dichroic filters – applied as a thin, semi-reflective film coating – which absorb certain wavebands of coloured light and reflect others. The overall effect is an emitted light that has warmth, intensity and unusual optical qualities. The development of this light initially involved the careful modelling of the diffuser's form on computers at Lovegrove's studio in London. The algorithmic data from the final virtual model was then exported to a milling machine at Artemide, where it was used to make a precise steel mould that would shape the heated sheets of transparent PMMA during the thermo-forming process. The finished design, as Lovegrove observes, 'appears as a digital leaf from another world, embedded with scales like a reptile or an insect which gather light and shadow on its body to seduce a mate.' This haunting design has a rare, exquisite quality that derives from Lovegrove's skilled handling of the plastic material. By using advanced technopolymers, state-of-the-art modelling software and cutting-edge manufacturing processes, today's designers, like Lovegrove, can turn their future visions into present day realities — plastic dreams gloriously transfigured into actual products.

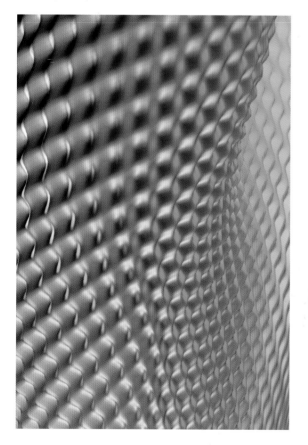

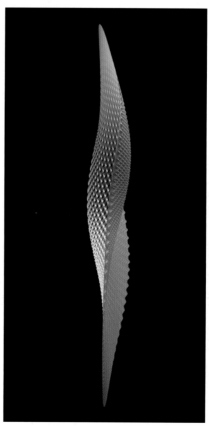

Computer renderings of *Cosmic Leaf*

Designer: **Ross Lovegrove** (British, 1958–)
Materials: polymethyl methacrylate (PMMA), chromed steel
Manufacturer: Artemide, Pregnana Milanese, Italy
Measurements: 192 cm high, 38 cm diameter

MATERIALS

Plastics can be grouped into three different types:

Thermoplastics: polymers that can be repeatedly reheated and then remoulded.
Thermosets: polymers that undergo chemical changes when heated that result in them becoming permanently rigid, i.e. they cannot be reheated and then remoulded.
Elastomers: thermoplastic or thermosetting polymers that have an inherent elasticity that allows them to retain their original shape after having been distorted through pressure.

Selected Modern Plastics – Technical Information

Acrylonitrile Styrene Acrylate (ASA) (thermoplastic)

Acrylonitrile Styrene Acrylate is an ABS-like material but with enhanced weather resistance. It is mainly used for outdoor applications and is also extensively used in the production of automotive parts.

Properties: Good weather resistance, high heat resistance, high impact resistance, good UV resistance and good chemical resistance.
Trade Names: Luran S (BASF)

Acrylonitrile Butadiene Styrene (ABS)
(thermoplastic)

Acrylonitrile Butadiene Styrene is a versatile thermoplastic that is widely used thanks to its excellent strength-to-weight ratio and its good load-bearing tolerances. Although it is more expensive than polystyrene to produce, ABS is generally regarded as a superior material because of its enhanced hardness, colourfastness and attractive surface lustre. Its natural colour is ivory, however, it is easily coloured with the addition of pigments and dyes. ABS is used extensively in the manufacture of automotive parts, electrical goods, electronic equipment and office equipment.

Properties: Lightweight yet strong, good rigidity, glossy surfaced, good heat resistance, excellent scratch and wear resistance.
Trade Names: Cycolac (Sabic Innovative Plastics), Magnum (Dow Chemicals), Lustran (Lanxess GmbH), Novodur (Lanxess), Terluran (BASF), Ronfalin (Perrite)

Aramids: p-Aramid fibres

Aromatic polyamides, usually referred to as Aramids, are a group of heat-resistant and super-strong synthetic fibres which are used for body armour and also in Formula 1 racing cars because of their extraordinarily high strength-to-weight ratio, for example Kevlar (poly-para-phenylene terephthalamide) is weight-for-weight five times stronger than steel. These advanced materials are also utilised in aerospace components, arc-welding torches and as high-temperature resistance foams and reinforcing fibres.

Properties: Rigid, opaque, high strength-to-weight ratio, exceptional thermal and electrical resistance (up to 480° C), resistant to ionising radiation and expensive.
Trade Names: Kevlar (DuPont), Nomex (DuPont), Twaron (Akzo)

**Carbon fibre-reinforced polymer (CFRP)/
Carbon fibre-reinforced plastic (CRP)**

One of the best known composite materials, carbon fibre should more correctly be called a carbon fibre-reinforced polymer. Essentially a reinforced plastic, this lightweight material gets its strength from extremely thin filaments of carbon fibre (sometimes called graphite fibre) that are woven together to form a supporting structural matrix. Usually carbon fibre is used in conjunction with epoxy resin to create high-performance products, which need to be incredibly light yet extremely strong. The 'pre-impregnated' method used to produce such products involves the soaking of the carbon fibre matrix in a liquid epoxy prior to it being moulded into the required form and then cured using heat and pressure.

Properties: High strength-to-weight ratio, corrosion-resistant, not suitable for high-volume mass-production, expensive.

Cellulosics: Cellulose Acetate (CA), Cellulose Acetate Butyrate (CAB), Cellulose Nitrate (CN), Cellulose Acetate Propionate (CAP), Ethyl Cellulose (EC) (thermoplastics)

This family of plastics is made from a naturally occurring polymer, cellulose, which is derived from cotton linters or wood pulp. Because of their different molecular constituencies, cellulosic plastics have a wide range of properties and are sold in transparent, translucent or opaque form. Some are even pearlescent or mottled. They are used for among other things, eyewear frames, toothbrushes, pen barrels, tool handles, transparent wrapping and metallised components (such as reflectors.)

Properties: Rigid, transparent, good toughness, low electrostatic pick-up, easy to mould and low cost.
Trade Names: Tenite (Eastman), Dexel (Courtaulds), Cellidor (Albis)

Epoxy Resins (EP) (thermoset)

Epoxy (or polyepoxide) is formed through a chemical reaction between epoxide and polyamide. Often epoxies are used as paints or adhesives as well as being used to encapsulate carbon fibre and other reinforcing materials. They are also extremely tough, which makes them ideal for the manufacture of composite structural materials, such as those used for aerospace panels.

Properties: Higher strength and higher chemical resistance than unsaturated polyesters, and with low shrinkage during curing.
Trade Names: Hysol (Dexter), Epon (Shell), DER (Dow)

Ethylene Vinyl Acetate (EVA) (thermoplastic)

A copolymer of ethylene and vinyl acetate, ethylene vinyl acetate is a flexible and rubbery elastomer. It is mainly used for soft-grip handles, teats, flexible tubing, cabling and hosing. It is, however, also used as a coating material and for various healthcare items and packaging.

Properties: Good flexibility, transparent, low-temperature flexibility (-70° C), good chemical

resistance and high frictional coefficiency.
Trade Names: Evatane (Arkema), Taisox (Formosa)

Glass-reinforced Plastic (GRP) (thermoset)

Frequently referred to as fibreglass, glass-reinforced plastic is the most commonly used plastic composite material. Polyester is normally used to make fibreglass, however, other plastics such as epoxy are also used to a lesser extent. The fibres, which are made of finely spun glass, strengthen the polymer, thereby acting almost like a substructure. Glass-reinforced plastic is also sometimes referred to as FRP (fibreglass-reinforced plastic or fibreglass-reinforced polymer). An incredibly useful material, GRP can be used for a wide range of applications, from car bodies and furniture to piping and liquid storage containers.

Properties: Excellent weather resistance, variety of surface finishes, very strong yet relatively lightweight.

High-Pressure Laminates (HPL)

High-pressure laminates are composed of layers of different materials (such as melamine and chipboard) that are then sandwiched together with an adhesive using heat and considerable pressure, usually around 1200-2000 pounds per square inch (8–14 × 106 pascals). Their hardwearing surfaces are perfect for countertops as well as many other diverse high-wear applications.

Properties: Surfaces can be patterned, durable and with good heat resistance.
Manufacturers: Formica, Pionite, ABET.

Melamine-Formaldehyde (MF) (thermoset)

Melamine-formaldehyde, which is usually just known as 'melamine', is a highly durable thermosetting plastic resin that was used extensively during the 1950s, 1960s and 1970s for dinnerware and picnic wares. It can also be used to make decorative laminates, surface coatings, lighting fixtures, heavy-duty electrical equipment, bottle caps and toilet seats.

Properties: Hard, opaque, tough, scratch-resistant, self-extinguishing, free from taint and odour, wide colour range, resistant to detergents.
Trade Names: Melochem (Chemiplastica), Melcam (Elchi)

Phenolics (PF) (thermosets)

Very popular in the 1920s and 1930s, phenolics are a broad group of thermosetting phenol-formaldehyde resins that have different properties according to what fillers they are mixed with. Perhaps better known under the commercial trade name Bakelite, phenol-formaldehydes are still used today for the production of ashtrays, lamp holders, bottle caps, saucepan handles, domestic plugs and switches, welding tongs and electrical iron parts.

Properties: Hard, brittle, opaque, good electrical and heat resistance, resistant to deformation under load, low cost, resistant to most acids.
Trade Names: Bakelite (Bakelite), Durez (Occidental), Genal (GE)

Polyamide (PA)/Nylon (thermoplastic)

Polyamide, more commonly known as nylon, was discovered in the early 1930s. In 1938 commercial production of Nylon 6,6 began and the following year nylon stockings were showcased for the first time at the New York World's Fair. In 1941 nylon moulding powders were introduced, however, they were not widely used until the 1950s and 1960s. Today nylon is used for automotive parts, carpets, ropes, curtain hooks, gears and clothing.

Properties: Stronger than ABS or PVC, excellent toughness, good abrasion resistance, slightly water absorbent and low coefficient of friction.
Trade Names: Celanese (Hoechst), Ultraform (BASF), Durathan (Bayer), Ultramid (BASF), Zytel (DuPont)

Polybutylene Terephthalate (PBT) (thermoplastic)

Closely related to other polyesters (such as PET), Polybutylene Terephthalate is used almost exclusively in the electrical and electronics industries as an insulator. Like PET, it is a crystalline thermoplastic, however, it is not as strong, although it does have better impact resistance and can be processed at lower temperatures. PBT is also used for plastic door and window hardware, as well as for automotive body panels and headlight reflectors.

Properties: Excellent optical clarity, excellent electrical resistance and good toughness.
Trade Names: Valox (Sabic Innovative Plastics), Celanex (Ticona), Ultradur (BASF)

Polycarbonate (PC) (thermoplastic)

A jewel-like synthetic polymer, polycarbonate is so tough that it is used for protective shields, as well as safety glasses, safety helmets and vandal-proof street-lighting covers. It is also used for furniture, household appliances (such as hairdryers), high-impact windows and automotive parts.

Properties: Optical clarity, tougher than nylon but not as strong or stiff, good chemical resistance and expensive.
Trade Names: Lexan (GE), Merlon (Bayer)

Polyethylene Terphthalate (PET) (thermoplastic)

Polyethylene Terphthalate (PET) is the plastic used to make blow-moulded soft drinks bottles, water bottles, cooking oil bottles and peanut butter jars. PET can also be used to make synthetic clothing such as fleeces, film for audio cassettes and videotapes, carpet fibres and automotive trims.

Properties: excellent optical clarity, strength and stiffness slightly less than nylon, moderate chemical resistance
Trade Names: Kodar (Eastman), Rynite (DuPont), Hytrel (DuPont), Mylar (DuPont), Dacron (DuPont)

Polyethylene (PE) (thermoplastic)

There are two types of polyethylene: flexible HDPE (High Density Polyethylene) which is used for soft drinks bottles, water bottles, cooking oil bottles, peanut butter jars, toys and jerry cans; semi-rigid LDPE (low-density polyethylene) is commonly used for carrier bags, trash can liners, food storage containers and toys, as well as gas and water pipes.

Properties: Flexible or semi-rigid, good chemical resistance, translucent, weather-proof and inexpensive.
Trade Names: HDPE: Hostalen (LyondellBasell), Lacqtene (Total Petrochemicals), Lupolen (LyondellBasell), Rigidex (INEOS), Stamylan (DSM); LDPE: BP Polyethylene (BP), Dowlex (Dow Chemical), Eltex (INEOS)

Polylactic Acid (PLA) (thermoplastic)

This renewable and biodegradable thermoplastic polyactide is derived from carbohydrate-rich plants, such as maize, sugar cane and wheat. Although it was discovered over a century ago, it is only in recent years with the rise of ecological concerns that PLA has become commercially available. The cornstarch, wheat starch or cane sugar is fermented to produce lactic acid that is then oligomerised and then catalytically dimerised to produce a usable biopolymer, which is often referred to as 'corn plastic'. It is mainly used for biodegradable food packaging, compostable bags and other disposable products, but also has biomedical applications.

Properties: Biodegradable, renewable resource content, compostable, food safe, good impact resistance and high rigidity.
Trade Names: Ingeo (Natureworks LLC), Purasorb (Purac)

Polymethyl Methacrylate (PMMA) (thermoplastic)

Polymethyl Methacrylate (PMMA) is better known as acrylic and is a commonly used transparent plastic that has excellent optical qualities. It is used for signage, lighting diffusers, automotive taillight lenses, leaflet dispensers and inspection windows. It can also be easily thermoformed from sheets and can be cast in moulds.

Properties: Glass-clear, hard, rigid, glossy, weather-resistant
Trade Names: Perspex (Lucite International), Diakon (Lucite International Inc.), Oroglas (Arkema Group), Plexiglas (Arkema Group), Lucite (Lucite International Inc.)

Polypropylene (PP) (thermoplastic)

Polypropylene is a widely used thermoplastic that is suitable for a variety of applications. It is most commonly used in the injection-moulding of low-cost high-volume items such as bottle tops and food containers. It is also often used for plastic containers with integral hinges and microwavable containers. Lightweight yet strong, it is additionally utilised in the manufacture of various types of medical equipment and for utility fibres in carpets and rope.

Properties: Food safe, lightweight, good impact resistance even at low temperatures, good chemical and water resistance, and low cost.
Trade Names: Marles (Phillips), Polyfort (Schulman), Pro-Fax (Montell), Vistalon (Exxon), Vrestolen (Huls)

Expanded polypropylene (EPP) (thermoplastic)

An engineering plastic foam material, expanded polypropylene is formed from small plastic beads and is 100 percent recyclable. It is mainly used for industrial packaging, such as in the transportation of automotive parts and white goods.

Properties: Very lightweight yet strong, relatively impact-resistant with good durability, resistant to water and chemicals and can endure extremes of temperature (-35° C to 130° C).
Trade Names: Arpro (JSP)

Polystyrene (PS) (thermoplastic)

General-purpose polystyrene (PS) is one of the most widely used thermoplastics and is frequently employed in the manufacture of toys, rigid packaging, cosmetics containers and CD cases. It is also the polymer most commonly used for disposable cups, plates and containers. Unfortunately, it yellows with age and can become very brittle.

Properties: Inexpensive, brittle, transparent, odour-free and taste-free.
Trade Names: Polystyrol (BASF), Palstyrol (Pal Plast), PolyRex (Chi Mei Corporation), Sicostirolo (MP Compounds), Dylene (Nova Chemicals)

High-Impact Polystyrene (HIPS) (thermoplastic)

High-impact polystyrene (HIPS) is used to make among other things, vending cups, instrument control knobs and toilet seats. This lightweight yet stiff thermoplastic is also widely used to make refrigerator linings.

Properties: Hard and rigid with good chemical resistance and excellent impact strength.
Trade Names: Lacqrene (Total Petrochemicals), Dafnestil (Nord Color), Denistyr (Vamptech)

Expanded Polystyrene (EPS) (thermoplastic)

Expanded polystyrene is widely used as a packaging material. It is the beaded polymer that is used to make packing 'peanuts', for example, and the moulded packing used to cushion fragile items when transported in boxes. It can also be manufactured as a lightweight sheet, which is commonly known as bead-board. EPS has low thermal conductivity, which makes it an ideal insulating material.

Properties: Low thermal conductivity, low density and non-biodegradable.
Trade Names: Styrofoam (Dow Chemical Co), Styrodur (BASF)

Polyurethane (PU) (thermoplastic or thermoset)

Polyurethanes are polymers with chains of organic molecules that are joined with urethane (carbamate) links. There are many different polyurethane formulations, which provide a wide range of flexibilities and densities: from low-density flexible foam (used for upholstery) and low-density rigid foam (thermal insulation), to semi-solid elastomers (gel-pads) and solid plastics (hard-wearing structural components). The most common applications include sports shoe soles, car fenders, skateboard wheels and printing rollers.

Properties: Tough, abrasion-resistant, wide range of flexibilities and densities.
Trade Names: Baydur (Bayer), Hypol (WR Grace), Pellethane (Dow), Elastollan (BASF), Estane (BF Goodrich)

Polyvinyl Chloride (PVC) (thermoplastic)

Polyvinyl chloride is an extremely versatile material that can be either a very rigid plastic with the addition of fillers, or alternatively, a very flexible plastic if plasticised. It is widely used in the manufacture of piping, guttering, toys, bottles, packaging film, window frames, car mats and foamed pads. It is also used to make inflatable furniture.

Properties: Good chemical resistance, good weathering resistance, moderately strong, lightweight, low cost, flame-retardant and can be easily coloured.
Trade Names: Armodur (Rhone-Poulenc), Ensolite (Uniroyal), Fiberloc (Uniroyal), Vynide (ICI), Vygen (General Tire), Palvinyl (Pal Plast), Vinuran (BASF)

Silicones (SI) (thermoset)

Silicones are a group of semi-organic polymeric resins that are thermoset polycondensates. They are used as high-performance elastomers and are also employed as the materials used to make moulds. Additionally, they can be utilised in the manufacture of gaskets and joint or seam caulking products.

Properties: Good thermal and environmental resistance, excellent flexural recovery and dimensional

stability, low water absorption, good flame resistance and high release capability.
Trade Names: Baysilone (Bayer), Blu-Sil (Perma-Flex Mold Co.), Silastic (Dow Corning)

Styrene-Acrylonitrile (SAN) (thermoplastic)

Styrene-acrylonitrile (SAN) has been available since the 1940s but initially was relatively expensive so was rarely used. During the 1970s, however, it was widely employed for the production of household goods, especially kitchenware, and today it is used to manufacture among other things, automotive parts, electrical and electronic equipment, cosmetic packaging and healthcare products.

Properties: good chemical resistance, high heat resistance, high degree of rigidity and glossy surfaced.
Trade Names: Sangel (Bayer), Sanfor (So.F.Ter), Sanrex (Techno Polymer), Santron (Bhansali Engineering Polymers)

Synthetic Rubbers (SR) (thermoplastic or thermoset)

Synthetic rubbers (SR), also known as thermoplastic elastomers (TPE/TPV), are polymeric man-made materials that have such a good degree of elasticity that after being stretched they will return to their original form without any permanent deformation. They include among others, Silicone rubbers (SI), Polybutadiene rubber (BR), Butadiene Acrylonitrile (NBR), Ethylene Vinyl Acetate (EVA), Styrene-Butadiene Rubber (GR-S) and Polychloroprene (CR). The primary use of synthetic rubbers is in the manufacture of car tyres, but they are also used in the manufacture of wetsuits and soft-grip handles, or they can be used as effective substitutes for natural rubber.

Properties: Excellent elongation, high flexibility and good impact resistance.
Trade Names: Sanoprene (ExxonMobil Chemical), Neoprene (DuPont)

Urea Formaldehyde (UF) (thermoset)

This transparent thermosetting plastic material was predominantly used in the 1930s and 1940s, when it was commonly dyed to make colourful plastic casings. Today, it is still used in the manufacture of electronic fittings and also in the production of adhesives.

Properties: Good electrical insulator, high tensile strength, heat-resistant and brittle.
Trade Names: Beetle, Scarab, Mouldrite U

PROCESSES

Either **moulding processes** or **forming processes** are used to manufacture products in plastics.

Moulding Processes:

Blow moulding
Used to manufacture products with hollow internal cavities, such as drinks bottles and containers. The process involves first creating a tubular shape of molten plastic (either injection-moulded or extruded), which is called a Parison. It is then rotated into a blow-moulding tool. The halved moulds hold the upper end of the Parison, which is then injected with hot air to produce an internal cavity resulting in a bubble-like moulding. The moulding is then allowed to cool and the mould halves are opened so that the product can be extracted.

Calendering
Calendering is used to manufacture films, sheets and coating materials from plastics. It essentially involves the rolling out of an unset plastic material to a desired thickness through a system of rollers that feed the plastic into the machine, using tension to pull it into the required dimensions and then allowing it to cool.

Casting
The cheapest and easiest way to mould plastics, casting involves pouring an unset polymer into a female mould, made from either soft or rigid materials. Rarely used within the realms of mass-production, casting can be used to create simple plastic mouldings with often the resin used being cured with a catalyst to make it set.

Compression moulding
The most widely used process to manufacture products made of thermoset plastics, compression moulding involves placing a preformed slug of compressed plastic powder between two mould halves. The mould is then heated sufficiently for the 'preform' to become malleable and then the mould halves are squeezed together using pressure, thereby tightly sandwiching the plastic. Once the plastic is cured (i.e. the cross-links have been formed), the moulding is then ejected from the mould and allowed to cool.

Extrusion
A low-cost process used to make simple mouldings that have a continuous cross-section, extrusion involves putting thermoplastic powder into a hopper which then allows it to fall onto a rotating Archimedean screw that subsequently drives the plastic powder into the heated section of the extruder. Once softened by the heat, the plastic is then forced into a die by the rotating screw. On exiting the die the plastic moulding is cooled using a jet of water and then cut to the required length.

Gas-assist injection moulding
A relatively new process, gas-assist injection moulding reduces cycle times, wear on moulds and material requirements, while also producing better detailing than conventional injection moulding processes. Based on the same principles as traditional injection moulding, gas-assist injection moulding involves the injection of nitrogen gas at high pressure during the moulding cycle either directly into the mould or through a sprue. This process gives two benefits: the first is that it introduces an internal cavity of air into the plastic moulding (which means less material is required); and secondly it also reduces the occurrence of sink marks (localised depressions caused when pressure is too low or cooling time too short). The injection of gas also provides an additional cooling effect, which means the plastic solidifies quicker, thereby reducing cycle times.

Injection moulding
Used to mass-produce products made of thermoplastics, injection moulding allows synthetic polymers to be formed into complex three-dimensional shapes. Although the tooling costs associated with injection moulding are very high, the process allows high-volume mass production. This enables the manufacturer the opportunity to create low-cost products, which can earn back the original investment in a relatively short space of time. The process involves placing plastic granules into a hopper from which they fall onto a rotating Archimedean screw that moves the polymer into the heated section of the injection-moulding machine. The heat turns the granules into a softened state so that the material is malleable enough to be injected by force into the mould using a hydraulic ram. The high pressure exerted by the ram ensures that the cavity of the mould is completely filled with the polymer. The moulding is then allowed to cool enough so that it solidifies before being ejected from the mould.

Rotational moulding
Rotational moulding (also known as roto-moulding) is ideal for the manufacture of three-dimensional hollow objects, such as road cones and storage tanks. A roto-moulding machine has a number of arms onto which moulds are attached. The moulds are rotated around two perpendicular axes by the arms that are themselves attached to a fixed central point. This relatively inexpensive process involves placing the exact amount of material required into the mould halves, which are then clamped together. The moulds are then rotated towards a heated chamber so that the polymer reaches melting point and then begins to evenly coat the inside of the moulds. Once this stage of the process has been completed, the mould is then cooled and opened so that the product can be removed.

Forming Processes:

Line bending
A simple method of processing plastics, line bending involves the bending of a thermoplastic sheet using the warmth of an electric heater to soften the plastic so that it is malleable enough to be bent, usually using jigs.

Thermoforming
Thermoforming is very similar to the vacuum forming process, but uses two moulds instead of one. Once the plastic has reached its 'softening point' the two mould halves are closed and a vacuum is applied to the lower one. The use of two moulds rather than one helps to give better moulding definition and thereby a greater degree of detail.

Vacuum forming
Vacuum forming involves the heating of a plastic sheet to just above the temperature of its 'softening point' and placing it over a mould. A vacuum is then used to literally suck the softened plastic onto the mould, after which the moulding is allowed to cool and then trimmed of any excess material. This low-cost process is suitable for manufacturing simple products, but cannot be used for deep mouldings as the walls of the product can become stretched too thin.

Bibliography

Barthes, Roland, *Mythologies*, Hill and Wang, New York, 1972

Beil, Ralf and Buchholz, Kai (Eds.), *Plexiglas®, Material in Architecture and Design*, Wienand Verlag & Medien, Cologne, 2007

Brent Strong, A., *Plastics, Materials and Processing* (Third Edition), Pearson, Prentice Hall, Upper Saddle River (NJ)

Crawford, R.J., *Plastics Engineering*, Third Edition, Elsevier Butterworth-Heinemann, Oxford, 1998

Decelle, Philippe, Hennebert, Diane and Loze, Pierre, *L'Utopie du Tout Plastique 1960–1973*, Fondation Pour L'Architecture, Brussels, 1994

DiNoto, Andrea, *Art Plastic, Designed for Living*, Abbeville Press, New York, 1984

Dubois, J. Harry, *Plastics History U.S.A.*, Cahners Books, Boston (MA), 1972

Fielding, T.J., *History of Bakelite Limited*, Bakelite Limited, London, 1948

Fiell, Charlotte and Fiell, Peter, *1000 Chairs*, Taschen GmbH, Cologne, 1997

————, *1000 Lights, Vol.1: 1878–1959*, Taschen GmbH, Cologne, 2005

————, *1000 Lights, Vol. 2: 1960–Present*, Taschen GmbH, Cologne, 2005

————, *Design of the 20th Century*, Taschen GmbH, Cologne, 1999

————, *Domus (Volumes I–XII)*, Taschen GmbH, Cologne,

————, *Industrial Design A–Z*, Taschen GmbH, Cologne, 2000

Gloag, John, *Plastics and Industrial Design*, The Scientific Book Club, London, 1945

Hochheiser, Sheldon, *Rohm and Haas, History of a Chemical Company*, University of Pennsylvania Press, Philadelphia, 1986

Katz, Sylvia, *Plastics, Common Objects, Classic Designs*, Harry N. Abrams Inc., New York, 1984

Katz, Sylvia, *Plastics, Designs and Materials*, Studio Vista, London, 1978

Lefteri, Chris, *Materials for Inspiration*, RotoVision, Mies, 2006

————, *Making It, Manufacturing Techniques for Product Design*, Laurence King Publishing, London, 2007

————, *The Plastics Handbook*, RotoVision, Mies, 2008

Lindblad, Thomas, *Bruksföremal Av Plast*, Signum, Lund, 2008

Manzini, Ezio, *The Material of Invention: Materials and Design*, The MIT Press, Cambridge (MA), 1989

Maxwell, James, *Plastics, The Layman's Guide*, IOM Communications Ltd., London, 1999

Meikle, Jeffrey L., *American Plastic, A Cultural History*, Rutgers University Press, New Brunswick (NJ), 1995

Mossman, Susan, *Fantastic Plastic, Product Design + Consumer Culture*, Black Dog Publishing, London, 2008

Murphy, John (Ed.), *New Horizons in Plastics, A Handbook for Design Engineers*, Weka Publishing Group, 1991

Spark, Penny (Ed.), *The Plastics Age from Modernity to Post-Modernity*, Victoria & Albert Museum, London, 1990

Thomas, Islyn, *Injection Molding of Plastics*, Reinhold Publishing Corp., New York, 1947

Thompson, Rob, *Manufacturing Processes for Design Professionals*, Thames & Hudson, London, 2007

Westermann, Andrea, *Plastik und Politische Kultur in Westdeutschland*, Chronos, Zurich, 2007

Exhibition Catalogues & Periodicals

British Plastics (periodical), Iliffe & Sons Ltd., London

Classic Plastics: A Look at Design 1950–1974, Fischer Fine Art, London, 1989

Design Since 1945, Philadelphia Museum of Art, 1983

Italy: The New Domestic Landscape, The Museum of Modern Art, New York, 1972

La Donation Kartell, Un Environnement Plastique 1949–2000, Centre Pompidou, Paris, 2001

Modern Plastics, Breskin & Charlton Publishing Corp., New York

Modern Plastics, Catalog Directory October 1963, Breskin & Charlton Publishing Corp., New York

Modern Plastics, Encyclopedia Issue for 1961, Breskin & Charlton Publishing Corp., New York

Mutant Materials in Contemporary Design, The Museum of Modern Art, New York, 1995

Plastics + Design, Die Neue Sammlung, Staatliche Museum für angewandte Kunst, Munich, 1997

The ABC's of Modern Plastics, Bakelite Corporation, 1956

Picture Credits

Adelta, Dinslaken: 85, 134 (both images), 135
Alessi, Milan: 236, 237
Alfi GmbH, Wertheim: 221
Apple Inc., Cupertino: 244, 245
Artemide, Milan: 124, 125 (both images), 127, 159, 274 (both images), 275
Jane Atfield, London: 228 (both images)
Braun GmbH, Kronberg im Taunus: 188
Casala Meubelen Nederland, Culemborg: 183
Cassina, Meda: 208, 209 (bottom)
City-Furniture, Antwerp: 118 (bottom)
Danese, Milan: 130
Editoriale Domus, Milan: 86, 140, 170 (left & middle)
Dyson Ltd., Malmesbury: 230,231
Ergonomidesign, Stockholm: 172
Ericsson, Stockholm: 2 (frontispiece); 38 (both images), 79 (bottom)
Fiell Images/Fiell Publishing Limited, London: © Fiell Image Archive: 8, 10 (bottom), 14 (top), 19 (both images), 20 (both images), 21, 42 (top), 44 (bottom), 45, 47 (both images), 48, 54, 62 (left), 64 (top), 67 (top), 68, 70 (left), 89 (bottom), 92, 105 (right), 111 (all images), 112, 123 (top), 149, 179 (both images), 193, 197, 192, 193 (both images), 194, 199; © Fiell Images/Fiell Publishing Limited, London – photo: Paul Chave: 6, 10 (top), 13 (middle & bottom), 14 (bottom), 15, 16 (all images), 17 (top), 24, 35, 36, 37 (top), 41, 49, 57, 60 (both images), 61, 62 (right), 63, 64 (bottom), 65, 66, 67 (bottom), 69, 70 (right), 71, 72 (both images), 75, 78, 79 (top), 80, 83, 84, 89, 90, 91, 93, 97, 98, 99 (both images), 101, 104, 105 (left), 108 (both images), 109, 110, 113, 114, 115, 116 (bottom), 119, 121, 122, 123 (bottom), 126, 128, 129, 131, 132, 133, 138, 145, 147, 148, 160 (both images), 161, 168, 170 (right), 171, 173, 174, 175, 176, 177, 178, 182, 185, 186, 187 (both images), 189, 190, 191 (both images), 192, 196, 200, 201, 203, 206, 207, 211, 224, 226, 227 (both images), 240, 250, 251, 256, 257; © Fiell Images/Fiell Publishing Limited, London – photo: Anthony Oliver: 144; © Fiell Images/Fiell Publishing Limited, London – courtesy of David Tatham & Chris Reen /Origin Modernism – photo: Paul Chave: 198, 199; © Fiell Images/Fiell Publishing Limited, London – courtesy of Rick Gallagher – photo: Sarah Silver: 52 (top & bottom); © Fiell Images/Fiell Publishing Limited, London – courtesy of the collection of Roy Jones – photo: Paul Chave: 42 (bottom left & bottom right), 43; © Fiell Images/ Fiell Publishing Limited, London – courtesy of the collection of Daniel Ostroff – photo: Jerry Sarapochiello: 87; © Fiell Images/ Fiell Publishing Limited, London – courtesy of Plasticarium, Brussels– photo: Francis Jacoby: 146, 153, 155, 157, 169, 209 (top), 219, 225; © Fiell Images/Fiell Publishing Limited, London – courtesy of the collection of Patrick Rylands – photo: Paul Chave: 17 (bottom), 18, 55

Fish Design, Milan: 264, 265
Patrick Flottes, Île-de-France: 34
Ghyczy Selection BV, Swalmen: 152 (both images)
Gufram, Turin: 194 (both images)
Kartell, Milan: 29, 74, 76, 100, 118 (top), 120, 139 (both images), 232, 233, 234 (both images), 235, 242, 243, 246, 247 (both images), 258 (both images), 259
Lovegrove Studio, London: 25, 220 (photo: John Ross), 248 (photo: John Ross), 249 (photo: John Ross), 252 (left), 252 (right) (photo: John Ross), 253 (photo: John Ross), 262 (photo: John Ross)
Luka Stepan Industrial Design, London: 26
Alberto Meda, Milan: 217 (both images)
Melissa, Farroupilha: 30–31 (photo: Giovana Grigolin), 270 (photo: Giovana Grigolin), 271 (photo: Giovana Grigolin), 272 (photo: Giovana Grigolin), 273 (photo: Giovana Grigolin)
Moroso, Cavalicco: cover image, 263
© The Museum of Modern Art, New York/Scala, Florence: 77 (gift of Philip Johnson), 95 (gift of the manufacturer), 96 (gift of the manufacturer), 165 (gift of the manufacturer), 214 (gift of the manufacturer)
Olivetti, Ivrea: 163 (both images)
Pirelli, Milan: 94
Plank, Ora: 268, 269
Plasticarium, Brussels (photo: Serge Rovenne): 158
Quittenbaum Kunstauktionen, Munich: 50, 51, 143, 150, 164
Rosti, Ebeltoft: 82
Patrick Rylands, London: 117, 180, 181
Serralunga, Biella: 254 (both images), 255, 266 (both images), 267
Hans Skillius, Halmstad: 202
Swatch Group Ltd., Biel: 215
Tekniska museet (National Museum of Science & Technology), Stockholm (photo: Anna Gerdén): 39
Toledo Museum of Art, Toledo (OH) – Courtesy of The Mitchell Wolfson Jr. Collection, The Wolfsonian-Florida International University, Miami Beach (FL): 44
Tom Dixon, London: 260, 261
Vitra, Weil am Rhein: 27
Umbra, Buffalo (NY): 238, 239
Jean Pierre Vitrac/Design (Pool), Paris: 184, 204, 205 (both images)
Daniel Weil, London: 210
Wright, Chicago: 23, 46, 58, 73 (photo: Jerry Sarapochiello), 88, 102, 103, 106, 107, 141, 142, 151, 154, 162, 166 (both images), 167, 195, 212, 213, 216, 218, 222, 223, 229, 241
Zanotta, Milan: 22, 136, 137, 156 (both images)

Acknowledgements

As the first book to be published by FIELL, *Plastic Dreams* is a very special project for us and it would not have been possible without the assistance of a really great team. Special thanks must go to Judy Rasmussen for her production skills and invaluable guidance, Mark Thomson for his innovative graphic design and good natured suggestions, Paul Chave for his wonderful new photography, Quintin Colville for his excellent copy editing, Rosanna Negrotti for her insightful proofreading, and, of course, the team at DL Repro for their professional dedication. Special thanks must also go to the many designers and manufacturers who supplied images and the collectors, including Philippe Decelle, Patrick Rylands and Roy Jones, who kindly allowed us to photograph their beautiful objects. Thanks must also go to the various museums, picture libraries and auction houses for loaning images, with special thanks to Richard Wright and Arthur Floss. And lastly we would like to dedicate this book to our families for their endless support and to our two wonderful daughters, Emelia and Clementine who have been with us every step of the way as we have embarked on our new publishing adventure.

'More than a substance, plastic is the very idea of its infinite transformation; as its everyday name indicates, it is ubiquity made visible. And it is this, in fact, which makes it a miraculous substance: a miracle is always a sudden transformation of nature. Plastic remains impregnated throughout with this wonder: it is less a thing than the trace of a movement. And as the movement here is almost infinite, transforming the original crystals into a multitude of more and more startling objects, plastic is, all told, a spectacle to be deciphered: the very spectacle of its end-products.'

Roland Barthes,
Mythologies, 1972